## Quicken Icon

| To Do This: | Click This: |
| --- | --- |
| Balance your accounts | **Recon** in the iconbar or **Reconcile** in the HomeBase window |
| Close a window | **Close** in the active window |
| Create a graph | **Reports & Graphs** in the HomeBase window |
| Create a new something (account, category, etc.) | **New** in the active window |
| Create a report | **Reports** in the iconbar or **Reports & Graphs** in the HomeBase window |
| Create and edit a budget | **Budgeting** in the HomeBase window |
| Create and edit an investment account | **Investments** in the HomeBase window |
| Customize a graph or report | **Customize** in the graph or report window |
| Customize Quicken | **Options** in the window border |
| Delete a selected item | **Delete** in the active window |
| Edit a selected item | **Edit** in the active window |
| Exit Quicken | Exit Quicken in the HomeBase window |
| Hide and reshow the main iconbar | **Iconbar** in the window border |
| Open the Account List | **Accts** in the iconbar or **Account List** in the HomeBase window |
| Open an account register | **Registr** in the iconbar or **Register** in the HomeBase window |
| Open Feature Explorer | **Feature Explorer** in the HomeBase window |
| Open the Financial Address Book | **AddrBk** in the iconbar |
| Open the Financial Calendar | **Calendar** in the iconbar |
| Open an investment portfolio | **Port** in the iconbar |
| Open Investor Insight | **Investr** in the iconbar |
| Open Mutual Fund Finder | **MutualF** in the iconbar |
| Open online help | **Help** in the iconbar or **Help** in the window border |
| Open QuickBanking | **Online** in the iconbar or **Online Banking** in the HomeBase window |
| Open QuickBillPay | **Online** in the iconbar or **Online Bill Pay** in the HomeBase window |
| Open Quicken Home Inventory | **Inventry** in the iconbar |
| Print the current window, report, or graph | **Print** in the current window |
| Use the HomeBase window icons from another window | **GoTo** in the window border |
| Write checks | **Write Checks** in the HomeBase window |

## Idiot-Proof Guide to Setting Up a New Quicken Account

1. Click **Account List** in the HomeBase window.
2. Click **New**.
3. Click the type of account you want (checking, savings, credit card, cash, money market, investment, asset, or liability).
4. Follow the EasyStep instructions.

# Idiot-Proof Guide to the Checking Account Register

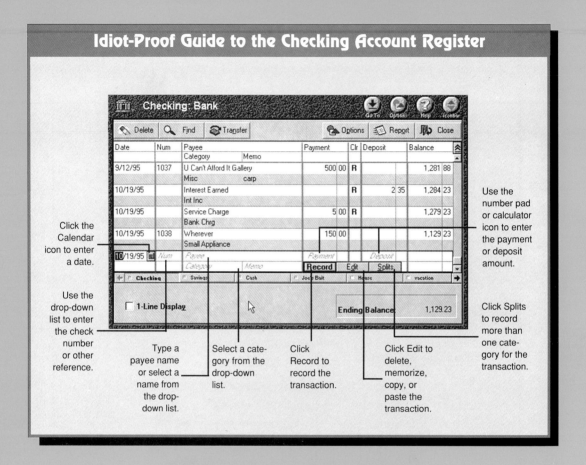

**Click the Calendar icon to enter a date.**

**Use the drop-down list to enter the check number or other reference.**

**Type a payee name or select a name from the drop-down list.**

**Select a category from the drop-down list.**

**Click Record to record the transaction.**

**Click Edit to delete, memorize, copy, or paste the transaction.**

**Click Splits to record more than one category for the transaction.**

**Use the number pad or calculator icon to enter the payment or deposit amount.**

## Ctrl-Key Combinations for Opening Quicken Lists

| To Do This: | Press: |
| --- | --- |
| Open the Account List | Ctrl+A |
| Open the Category & Transfer List | Ctrl+C |
| Open the Class List | Ctrl+L |
| Open the Memorized Transaction List | Ctrl+T |
| Open the Scheduled Transaction List | Ctrl+J |

# The COMPLETE IDIOT'S GUIDE TO

# Quicken® 5 for Windows

*by Beverly Roath*

A Division of Macmillan Publishing
201 W.103rd Street, Indianapolis, IN 46290 USA

International Standard Book Number: 0-7897-0630-X
Library of Congress Catalog Card Number: 95-71414

97  96  95      8  7  6  5  4  3  2  1

Interpretation of the printing code: the rightmost number of the first series of numbers is the year of the book's printing; the rightmost number of the second series of numbers is the number of the book's printing. For example, a printing code of 95-1 shows that the first printing of the book occurred in 1995.

Screen reproductions in this book were created by means of the program Collage Complete from Inner Media, Inc., Hollis, NH.

*Printed in the United States of America*

**Publisher**
*Roland Elgey*

**Vice President and Publisher**
*Marie Butler-Knight*

**Editorial Services Director**
*Elizabeth Keaffaber*

**Publishing Manager**
*Barry Pruett*

**Managing Editor**
*Michael Cunningham*

**Senior Development Editor**
*Seta Frantz*

**Technical Editor**
*Herb Feltner*

**Production Editor**
*Mark Enochs*

**Copy Editor**
*Paige Widder*

**Cover Designers**
*Dan Armstrong*
*Barbara Kordesh*

**Designer**
*Kim Scott*

**Illustrations**
*Judd Winick*

**Technical Specialist**
*Nadeem Muhammed*

**Production Team**
*Georgiana Briggs, Mona Brown, Charlotte Clapp, Mike Henry,*
*Louisa Klucznik, Paula Lowell, Donna Martin, SA Springer*

**Indexers**
*Gina Brown*
*Debra A. Myers*

# Contents at a Glance

# Contents

**Part 3: Quicken Makes House Calls** **235**

# Introduction

I remember it well: going to the bank to apply for my first checking account when I started college. It was so much fun playing grown-up. I practiced signing my name with a flourish until my signature was completely illegible, a sure sign of adulthood. I studied my bank statements with more care than I studied for exams. When I got my first box of checks, I felt like Steve Martin in *The Jerk* when he saw his name in the phone book: *I'm a real person!*

But after the novelty wore off, it annoyed me to no end that the bank insisted that I actually keep money in there all the time. I needed that balance of $10.64 for something really important, like pizza and beer. I closed the account before the first semester ended.

Now, an eon later, I really am an adult (or so they tell me), with bank accounts, credit cards, loans, a mortgage, and two daughters who will require orthodontia, car insurance, prom dresses, and college educations.

Although financial management is hardly my strong point, somehow the job of handling our family's finances has fallen to me (Dammit, Jim, I'm a writer, not an accountant!). I'm also self-employed, which means I have to handle all my own withholding and keep track of my income and business expenses.

Finding Quicken was like discovering the Holy Grail. It's so easy to use that, even if the thought of balancing your checkbook gives you hives, you'll feel like a member of the President's Council of Economic Advisors.

# Why Do You Need This Book?

So, if Quicken is so easy to use, why invest your hard-earned money in a book? Besides the fact that I need the royalties (and I thank you for contributing to my children's well-being), the combination of computers and finances can be intimidating if you're new to both. This book is written expressly for neophytes—it assumes you don't know anything about either one.

Even if you feel comfortable learning on your own, Quicken is a powerful software package with so many features that it would take years of poking around to find them all. I took the "I can do it all by myself" approach when I first encountered Quicken three years ago. In the process of writing this book, I've discovered capabilities I didn't even know existed. Had I done it right from the beginning and actually read a book, I would have saved myself a heckuva lot of work.

# Features of This Book

This book is divided into four parts, with the most commonly used features up front.

**Part 1: A Road Map Through Quicken** describes what everyone who uses Quicken needs to know. These chapters talk about the basics of Quicken and the most commonly used bells and whistles, such as printing checks and the Financial Calendar. You need to know how to use the features in Part 1 before you can move on to the more spectacular stuff in Parts 2-4.

**Part 2: Reports, Graphs, Planners, and Things That Make You Say "Ooh"** describes features that make Quicken more than a glorified checkbook. You can instantly create reports and graphs on every possible permutation of your finances; develop a budget; and use Quicken to help you plan for retirement, college, and other savings goals.

**Part 3: Quicken Makes House** Calls describes Quicken Home Inventory, with which you can record the value and location of your every possession, and the insurance policies that protect them.

**Part 4: Rolling Down Easy Street** takes Quicken into the world of high finance. These chapters talk about Mutual Fund Finder and Investor Insight, two Quicken features that help you manage your investments.

# How Do You Use This Book?

First of all, do not read this book cover-to-cover. The only people who read entire computer books are those who write, edit, and proofread them, and we get paid for it. You may find my pithy prose so entertaining that you yearn to read every word, but I doubt it.

This book is organized in a logical progression. While it's possible to jump around, later chapters build on information from earlier chapters. For example, before you can create reports (Chapter 12), you need to know how to use accounts, registers, and categories (Chapters 4, 5, and 6, respectively).

If you've never encountered Quicken before, I highly recommend you read Chapter 2 first, which will get you started and give you an overview of the basics of using Quicken.

How you use the book will depend on how you use Quicken. Read through the Contents at a Glance and see what you need to know most. You might just use Quicken to keep track of your accounts (Part 1) and never create a report or chart, in which case Part 2 won't do much for you. If you think stock is what you use to make soup, you can skip Part 3. Keep the book handy as you work and pull it out whenever you encounter a problem or want to learn something new.

## Conventions

This book does more than just provide rapturous descriptions of Quicken's power. It actually tells you how to do things. When I want you to do something, I'll use certain conventions so you know exactly what it is you're supposed to do.

If I want you to type something, I'll write:

> Type **this.**

with whatever I want you to type in bold. Dutifully, you type **this.**

There's going to be a lot of clicking going on around here. If I say "Click on the **File** menu," move your mouse pointer to the File menu and click on it. Whatever I want you to click on (menus, menu options, buttons) will be in bold and spelled exactly as they appear in Quicken (which means some strange abbreviations, such as MiscExp, pronounced MISK-exp). Double-clicking will also pop up occasionally, which means clicking your mouse button twice real fast.

To carry through the bolding motif, if I want you to press the Enter key on your keyboard, I'll write:

> Press **Enter.**

If you need to press two keys simultaneously, you'll see them printed like this:

Press **Ctrl+T.**

which means press the Ctrl key and the letter T at the same time.

Sprinkled throughout the book are helpful hints, tips, suggestions, warnings, and definitions that are not essential to using Quicken, but can smoothe the way.

### Technonerd Teaches

Here you will find definitions of technical terms. Because Quicken deals with finances, I've thrown in definitions of financial terms, too. Two for the price of one! You're really getting your money's worth here.

### Helpful Hints, Tips, and Shortcuts

In these useful little boxes, you'll find suggestions that make working with Quicken even, well, quicker.

# Acknowledgments

Thank you to the folks at Que Publishing for 1) not hanging up on me when I called, begging for work; 2) actually hiring me; and 3) putting up with my inane questions during the writing process. (Let's do it again real soon!) To Bulletin Board at the *St. Paul Pioneer Press* for the use of the Department of Duh. And especially, to Steve, *mon ami, mon amour, mon mari,* for tolerating two years of poverty as I started freelancing and for never once telling me I was nuts to try.

# Trademarks

Terms suspected of being trademarks or service marks have been appropriately capitalized. Que Corporation cannot attest to the accuracy of this information. Use of a term in this book should not be regarded as affecting the validity of any trademark or service mark.

EasyStep, Intuit, Quicken, QuickZoom, Qcard, and TurboTax are registered trademarks of Intuit Inc.

Billminder, Financial Calendar, Intuit Marketplace, Quicken Home Inventory, Quicken Deluxe for Windows, QuickFill, QuickPay, and QuickTour are trademarks of Intuit Inc.

Windows 95 is a registered trademark of Microsoft Corporation. Windows is a trademark of Microsoft Corporation.

# Part 1
# A Road Map Through Quicken

*Quicken combines two intimidating concepts: finances and computers. Eek! Fortunately, it makes them friendly, colorful, and downright cheery. If you can click a mouse button, you can organize all your financial information in a matter of hours.*

*The chapters in Part 1 cover what everyone who uses Quicken needs to know: how Quicken is organized; creating accounts; entering transactions; using categories; and balancing your accounts. It also covers other features that make working with the basics easier.*

*So gather up your checkbook and bank statements and get comfy. You're on your way to true financial responsibility.*

# Chapter 1

# The Top Ten Things You Need to Know

You heard somewhere that Quicken is *the* thing to have to organize your finances, but you're skeptical. You already have a checkbook and a calculator; what more can it do? Or maybe Quicken came with your computer, along with a bunch of idiotic games that would insult your eight-year-old, and you're wondering just what the heck it does.

Well, it does a lot. From the most basic bank accounts to high-rolling investment portfolios, Quicken organizes it all in one tidy package. Announcing the top ten things you can do with Quicken (drum-roll, please)...

## 1. Keep Track of Your Bank Accounts and Credit Cards

Quicken has accounts for every purpose. You can create accounts for checking, savings, and all your credit cards; cash accounts to keep track of real money; asset accounts for valuable possessions you own, such as your house or business equipment; liability accounts for valuable possessions the bank owns, such as mortgages and loans; and money market and investment accounts for the cash you stash.

Each account works like a checkbook register, where you can record deposits, withdrawals, payments, interest—whatever affects the account balance. You'll always know what you have in each account, and if you stay on top of it, you'll never be overdrawn again.

In my humble opinion, the simplest Quicken function is the best—you enter the amounts, and it calculates the balance for you. If you, like me, never made it past high school algebra (and couldn't remember anything about that if your life depended on it), it's manna from heaven.

## 2. Rent, Groceries, and Cuckoo Clocks: Categories and Classes

Besides entering amounts in your accounts, you can categorize each transaction so you know exactly where your money went and from whence it came. Quicken comes with a predefined list of common categories: rent, groceries, utilities, salary, and business expenses, among others. You can add categories to fit your own spending habits. If, for example, you collect cuckoo clocks, you can create a category for that so you know exactly how much you spend on little birds popping out of doors.

Classes group categories under a broader heading. Let's say you're renovating your house. You can set up a class for the renovation, then keep track of how much you spend on labor, materials, and miscellaneous expenses involved in the renovation.

## 3. You Spent How Much? Reports and Budgets

Quicken's reports gather the information from your accounts and put it all together. There are dozens of them so you can look at your financial picture from every possible angle. You can create a cash flow report that summarizes your income and expenses by category. Or you can see the total you spent on cuckoo clocks and home renovation with a category report.

You know the importance of having a budget for your household or business to prevent overspending, but poring over months of checkbook registers and bank statements to create one is a real pain in the tush. Quicken takes the transactions from your accounts and creates a budget for you. You can see where you're spending too much and adjust the budget accordingly.

## 4. If You Paid $400 for That Printer, You May As Well Use It

Got writer's cramp from writing out dozens of checks for your monthly bills? You can write (or more precisely, type) checks right in Quicken and print them on your printer, complete with the payee's address so you can mail the check in a window envelope. As an added bonus, Quicken automatically records the check in your account.

## 5. Or Pay Your Bills Electronically

You can eliminate checks altogether with QuickBillPay, Quicken's online service that lets you pay bills through your modem. When you pay a bill with QuickBillPay, Quicken sends the payment to your bank, who sends it on to the recipient, and records the payment in your account.

QuickBanking is another online service that lets you make deposits, withdrawals, and transfers to your accounts with your modem. You can also receive information about your accounts, such as balances and checks cleared.

## 6. Amaze Your Friends with Cool Charts and Graphs

One of Quicken's gee-whiz features is its ability to create 3-D color graphs and charts with a click. You can see bar and pie graphs of your monthly income and expenses, or a bar graph of your total net worth. Again, Quicken takes the transactions from your accounts to create the graphs.

## 7. Take the Pain out of Tax Time

It seems that the bureaucrats who write tax schedule instructions have only a passing acquaintance with English, not to mention reality. "If the amount in line 36a is less than or equal to your age times pi squared, you must complete Schedule 563728b, Allowances for Income Received During Months Ending in 'Y' in a Leap Year."

Quicken is designed to work with income tax software, such as Turbo Tax. With Quicken you can keep track of which transactions are tax-related (income, medical expenses, charitable contributions, business expenses, and so on). Come tax time, you can transfer that information directly to your income tax software, which inserts the amounts in the appropriate lines on the 1040 and other forms. Doing your taxes will be such a breeze you'll consider remembering the IRS in your will. Well, maybe not.

You can also use Quicken's Tax Planner to anticipate how much you'll have to pay on April 15 or how big a refund you'll get. If you're withholding too much or too little, Quicken will calculate how much to adjust your withholding.

## 8. Good Housekeeping with Quicken Home Inventory

With Quicken's Home Inventory, you can record every possession you own, where it is, what you paid for it, and how much it's worth now. You can also enter the serial number, make and model, and receipts and records for each item. That way, if you ever need proof for an insurance claim, you've got it.

## 9. Natural Disasters and Acts of God: Are You Covered?

You can also use Home Inventory to keep track of all your insurance policy information, and which possessions are covered by which policy. Quicken will help you determine if your insurance coverage is adequate. If a catastrophe occurs and you need to make a claim, Home Inventory will create a record of the claim, including when and how much your insurance company coughed up.

## 10. Where to Stash that Inheritance from Great Aunt Gertrude

When you reach that enviable point in your life when you can actually start investing money instead of just spending it, Quicken has features for that, too.

Mutual Fund Finder helps you choose a mutual fund that's right for you. Tell Mutual Fund Finder what you're looking for in a mutual fund and it creates a list of funds that meet your criteria.

With Investor Insight, you can create portfolios of your investments, or stocks and funds you just want to watch. Using your modem, Investor Insight sends you up-to-date mutual fund price information, stock quotes, and news stories about the companies you invest in. It automatically updates your portfolio to reflect the latest changes. Here, too, you can also create nifty charts and reports to see whether you're making a killing or losing your shirt.

So whether you're looking for something to balance your checkbook, create reports and graphs to knock your boss' socks off, or let you enter the exclusive world of Wall Street, Quicken's got it. And remember—Quicken was created for you, the financial and computer idiot. You're talking to a woman who once made a $1,400 error in her *employer's* checkbook. If I can use it, so can you.

# Chapter 2

# Start Your Engines: Get Quicken Up and Running

## In This Chapter

➤ Start Quicken

➤ Create your first account

➤ Files, accounts, and registers: How Quicken tracks your cash

➤ Follow the paths to Quicken's features

➤ What's in a window?

➤ Help is at hand

This chapter is going to give you an overview of how Quicken works and how to get started using it. I'll tell you how to open Quicken and go through New User Setup, a feature that takes you step-by-step through creating your first checking account on Quicken. I'll explain how Quicken is organized, and how to navigate your way through it. You'll see common features that you'll encounter as you make your way, and you'll also learn how to get help when you need it.

**First, You Have to Install Quicken** If you haven't installed Quicken yet, read the Installation section at the end of this book to learn how.

Don your Hawaiian shirt, black socks and sandals, hang a camera around your neck, and climb into the rental car. You're going to rubberneck at the basics of Quicken.

**Windows 3.1 Users** To start Quicken in Windows 3.1, double-click on the Quicken Program group and then on Quicken 5 for Windows icon.

# Turn the Key: Open Quicken

You open Quicken from your Windows 95 desktop. Here's how:

1. Click on the **Start** button in the taskbar.

2. Point to **Programs**.

3. In the menu list, point to **Quicken**. The Quicken folder contains all of the Quicken options you installed, as shown in the following figure.

*Opening Quicken.*

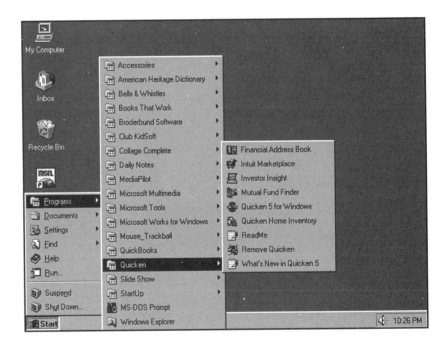

4. Click on **Quicken 5 for Windows** and Quicken starts right up.

# Open Your First Account with New User Setup

The first window you see is Quicken New User Setup, shown in the following figure. It will help you set up a checking account and give you the lowdown on categories (which we'll talk about in Chapter 6). I'll take you step-by-step through New User Setup.

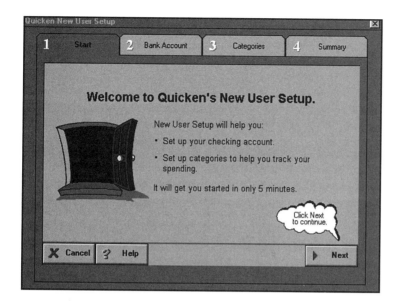

*New User Setup is an idiot-proof way to get started using Quicken.*

1. Click on the **Next** button at the bottom right corner of the dialog box.

2. First, you're going to set up a checking account on Quicken. In Account Name:, Quicken has already named the account "Checking." Leave it like that or type in a new name (if you have more than one checking account, you'll want to use a name that will differentiate between the two). Click **Next**.

3. Quicken asks if you have your last bank statement for the account. If you do, click **Yes** and you'll enter information from the statement in steps 4 and 5. If you don't, click **No** and **Next** twice. Skip to step 6.

4. In Ending Statement Date:, type the ending date on your bank statement. Type the date like this: **11/6/95**. Press **Tab**.

5. In Ending Statement Balance:, type the ending account balance on your bank statement. Quicken uses this as the opening balance for your new Quicken account. Click **Next**.

6. Quicken congratulates you on creating your first Quicken account. Click **Next**.

7. Quicken defines categories. *Categories* let you keep track of exactly what each transaction in your account is for: rent, utilities, salary, or whatever. I'll talk about categories in detail in Chapter 6. Click **Next**.

> **You May Want to Dig a Little Deeper for a Bank Statement** If you plan on creating a budget or using Quicken to help with your taxes, you may want to start with a statement from the beginning of the year or at least a couple of months back. You'll have to enter more information, but it will give a more accurate picture of your finances.

**9**

8. Quicken gives you information about home categories, which you use for your personal finances. Click **Next**.

9. Quicken talks about business categories—things like gross sales, freight, and office supplies. Quicken has predefined lists of both home and business categories for you to use, edit, and add to.

   Here Quicken asks if you want to use just home categories or both home and business categories. If you'll only use Quicken for your personal finances, click **I want home categories only**. If you'll also use Quicken for a small business, click **I want both home and business categories**. If you choose both, Quicken will combine its home and business categories in the same categories list. Click **Next**.

10. Another congratulatory message, showing the specifics of your checking account: name, statement date, ending balance, and whether you chose to include business categories. Click **Next**.

11. Quicken asks if you want to go through QuickTours, explained in the following section. To start QuickTours, click the **QuickTour** button. If you want to skip QuickTours and jump right into Quicken, click **Done**.

## Use QuickTours as Your Guide

QuickTours is like a museum brochure; it shows you where everything is so you don't have to trudge past 5,000 paintings to get to the Mona Lisa. The following figure shows the QuickTours window.

*Use QuickTours to get a feel for Quicken.*

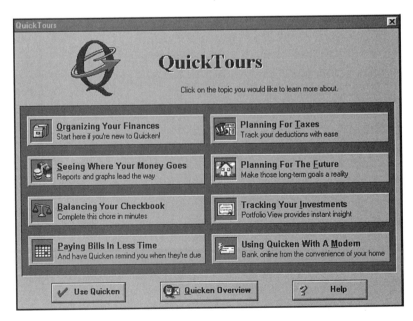

When you click on a topic, Quicken explains its features and how they help you solve your financial puzzles. I suggest starting with Organizing Your Finances, which describes the Quicken basics, or click **Quicken Overview** for a bird's-eye view. Click **Next** to go to the next QuickTours topic window. When you're ready to start using Quicken, click **Done**.

If you want to return to QuickTours later, click the **Help** menu and select **QuickTours**.

Before you get started using Quicken, you need to know how Quicken organizes your financial information and how to navigate through Quicken, issues addressed in the next few sections.

# From the Top Down: How Quicken Is Organized

Quicken uses *files*, *accounts*, and *registers* to organize all your financial information. Before you start using Quicken, you need to have a grasp of how they work, individually and together. All of Quicken's features use your files, accounts, and registers as the basis for what they do.

➤ A **file** is where Quicken stores everything you create with Quicken. A file holds all your accounts and the transactions for those accounts, plus related creations such as reports and graphs. Think of it as a humungous folder where you save everything that has to do with your finances. When you opened Quicken the first time, it automatically created a file for you. Chapter 3 describes how to create and work with files.

➤ **Accounts** are where you keep track of all the information for your bank accounts, credit cards, loans, assets, and investments. A file can hold dozens of accounts, and Quicken uses them to give you a complete picture of your finances. You already created a checking account when you went through New User Setup. Chapter 4 talks about the other types of Quicken accounts and how to use them.

➤ **Registers** are what you use to record *transactions* for an account. Each account has a register that's similar to a checkbook register where you can enter the date of a transaction, what it was for (a deposit or payment to someone), the amount, and its category. You'll learn how to use registers, categories, and special transactions in Chapters 5–7.

# Getting Around Quicken

Quicken offers several tour packages that all take you to the same place, but along different routes. Unlike airline specials, there's no fine print ("Must travel on the vernal equinox during a three-quarter moon. Those whose last names contain the letter T are ineligible for this offer."), so cruise around and decide what works best for you.

The following figure shows the five ways to get around Quicken: the HomeBase window, the Go To button, Feature Explorer, *menus*, and the main *iconbar*. To see the main iconbar, click the Iconbar button on the upper right corner of the HomeBase window. As an example, we'll use each of these features to get to the Account List, which lists all of the accounts you set up on Quicken and where you can create a new account.

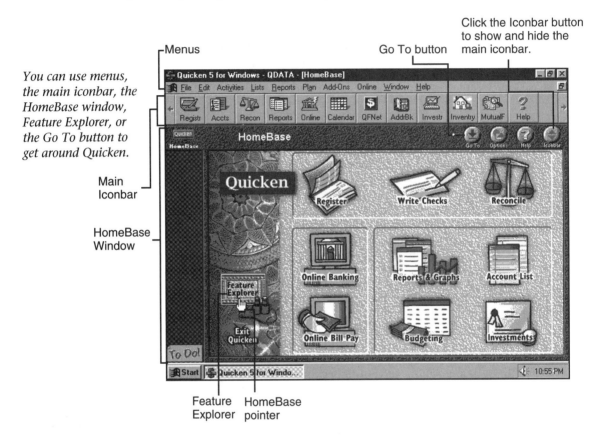

Click the Iconbar button to show and hide the main iconbar.

Menus

Go To button

*You can use menus, the main iconbar, the HomeBase window, Feature Explorer, or the Go To button to get around Quicken.*

Main Iconbar

HomeBase Window

Feature Explorer

HomeBase pointer

### Surf the 'Net

The **QFNet** icon gives you access to Quicken's home page on the World Wide Web, and from there, entry into the wild, wooly world of the Internet. If you didn't install the Internet access option when you installed Quicken, you may not see the **QFNet** icon on your iconbar. See Chapter 8 for more information on the this feature.

## The HomeBase Window

The first window you see when you finish New User Setup is the HomeBase window. This window gives you access to the most commonly used Quicken features. Think of the HomeBase window as the main square in a city from which you can walk to the cathedral, the statue of somebody nobody ever heard of, and the Museum of Potato Chips That Look Like Elvis.

When you move the mouse pointer over one of the icons in the HomeBase window, the pointer turns into a little hand and the title gets a black box around on it. To get to the Account List from here, click **Account List**.

## Feature Explorer

The Feature Explorer in the HomeBase window takes you deeper into Quicken. Click **Feature Explorer** and you'll see the window in the following figure.

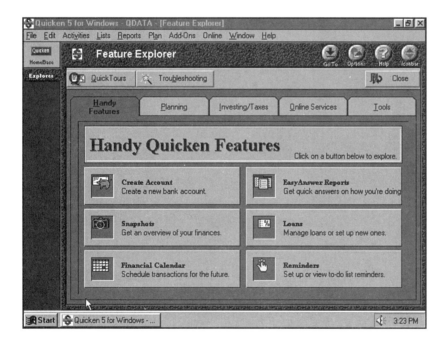

*Exploring Quicken's features.*

To use the Feature Explorer window:

1. Click a tab along the top of the window (Handy Features, Planning, Investing/Taxes, Online Services, and Tools) to see that topic's features.

2. Click the feature you want to use and you're instantly transported to that part of Quicken. For example, click **Create Account** to set up a new account.

13

You'll learn about each of these features as you progress through this lively and informative book. For now, click **Close** to return to the HomeBase window.

# Menus

All of Quicken's functions are listed in the menus along the top of your screen. To select a menu option, click the menu title, then click the option you want. To get to the Account List with the menus, click the **Lists** menu, then on **Account**.

# The Go To Button

You'll see the Go To button in every window in Quicken. Click on it, and it displays a menu with the same options as the HomeBase window, as shown in the following figure. It's like having HomeBase with you wherever you are in Quicken. Here, you'd click on **Account List** in the menu to get to the Account List.

*The Go To button menu.*

# The Main Iconbar

The main iconbar lets you perform the most common functions with just a click. With the main iconbar, you can click the **Accts** icon to bring up the Account List.

# Using Windows in Quicken

Each account and feature in Quicken, such as reports, has its own window. Each window will vary according to its function, but there are some common traits. As an example, let's look at the Checking Account window, shown in the following figure.

If the window seems crowded, click on the top arrow of the Iconbar button to hide the main iconbar. Click on the bottom arrow to show it again.

Each window also has an iconbar with functions and options that are specific to that window. For example, clicking the **Report** icon in the Checking Account window creates a report about the checking account. Every window (except HomeBase) has a Close icon that you use to close the window.

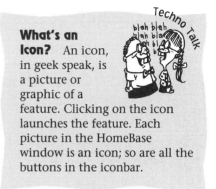

**What's an Icon?** An icon, in geek speak, is a picture or graphic of a feature. Clicking on the icon launches the feature. Each picture in the HomeBase window is an icon; so are all the buttons in the iconbar.

QuickTabs

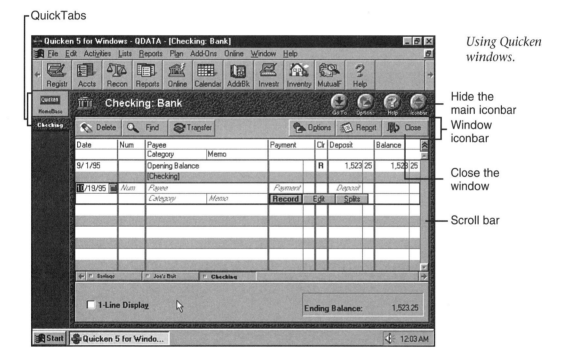

*Using Quicken windows.*

Hide the main iconbar
Window iconbar
Close the window
Scroll bar

If the window contains more information than can fit on the screen, it will have scroll bars. Click on the bottom arrow to scroll down; click on the top arrow to scroll up.

As you work with Quicken and move from one window to the next, the windows you're using are listed on tabs along the left. These are called QuickTabs. Jump around by clicking on the name of the screen you want. HomeBase is always there, so yes, Dorothy, you can go home again (heel-clicking optional).

## Dialog Boxes

Sometimes you need to give Quicken more specific information before it can do what you want it to do. For example, when you select **Open** from the File menu, you have to tell Quicken which file you want to open. When Quicken needs more information from you, it will open a *dialog box*. The following figure shows the Open Quicken File dialog box.

Like windows, dialog boxes will have different buttons and fields according to the information Quicken needs from you. But nearly all of them have three buttons in common: OK, Cancel, and Help.

➤ When you've entered all the information in the dialog box, click **OK** to carry out the function.

➤ Click **Cancel** if you change your mind and don't want to go through with it.

➤ Click **Help** to get help on using the dialog box.

*An example of a dialog box.*

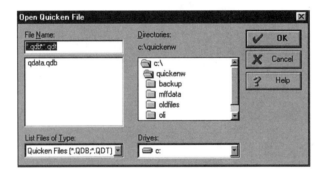

## Roadside Attractions

Just like a four-star hotel with mints on the pillow, 24-hour room service, and an honor bar, Quicken has funky little gizmos to help you enter information faster and keep it all organized: the calendar icon, the calculator icon, and drop-down lists.

You'll first encounter the calendar and calculator icons when you create new accounts (see Chapter 4). You'll also find them and the drop-down lists when you enter transactions in your account registers (see Chapter 5), and sprinkled throughout Quicken's features.

➤ Whenever you need to enter a date you'll see a *calendar icon*, as shown in the following figure. Click on the icon, and Quicken displays a calendar of the current month. Click on the arrows to move back or forward a month. Click on the day you want and poof! The date magically appears in the date field.

*Use the calendar to enter a date.*

➤ *Drop-down lists* (shown in the following figure) let you choose what to put in a field without typing it. The list drops down (get it?) when you click on the arrow in a field; then you click on the option you want and it's entered in the field. In the check register, when you type in a payee for the check, Quicken saves the name in the drop-down list. You never have to type the same name twice. Cool, huh?

Click on the arrow to see the ——— drop-down list.

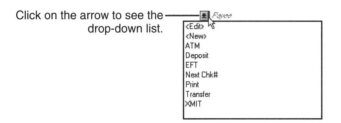

*Use the drop-down list instead of typing.*

➤ When you need to enter an amount, click on the *calculator icon* (shown in the following figure) and you won't have to count on your fingers and remove your shoes for numbers over ten. You can bring up the calculator any time by selecting **Use Calculator** from the Activities menu.

*The calculator's always there.*

## The Fastest Way to Calculate

You can use the calculator by clicking on each button with your mouse, a sure way to a case of the dreaded "mouse finger." A faster way is to use the number pad on your keypad.

# Help! I'm Lost!

I used to brag that I have been hopelessly lost in every major city in Europe. When you're 17, wandering in circles for hours is a kick. With Quicken, tour guides are always available, they always speak English, and they won't sneer at you if you try to ask where the bathroom is in Flemish.

There are three ways Quicken goes out of its way to help you out: *online help*, *Qcards*, and *flyover help*.

## Using Online Help

Quicken's online help defines terms, explains what the various features do and how to use them, and provides helpful hints. To get to it, click on the **Help** icon (the yellow question mark) in the main iconbar. Every window in Quicken also has a Help icon. Quicken is so eager to help you there's just no escaping it.

The Help window tells you about whatever window or feature you're using at the time. The following figure shows the Help window.

*Quicken Help is the friendliest tour guide in town.*

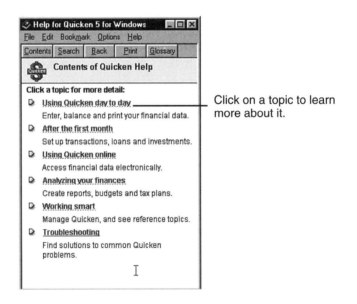

Click on a topic to learn more about it.

Some pointers for using online help:

➤ Every Help window will have some words underlined in neon green. Click on the word or phrase and Quicken goes into more detail on that topic.

➤ Click the **Contents** button to see general topics and frequently asked questions about Quicken.

➤ If you want to return to a topic, click the **Back** button to jump back to the previous Help window.

➤ When you're done, click the **X** icon in the upper right corner to close the Help window.

# Searching for a Help Topic

If the Help window you land on doesn't give you the answer you want, you can search for a specific topic.

1. In the Help window, click the **Search** button. The following figure shows the Search window.

2. Type the first few letters of the topic. The list of topics jumps down to the topics that start with those letters.

3. Click on the topic you want, and click **Display**. Quicken displays the Help window for that topic.

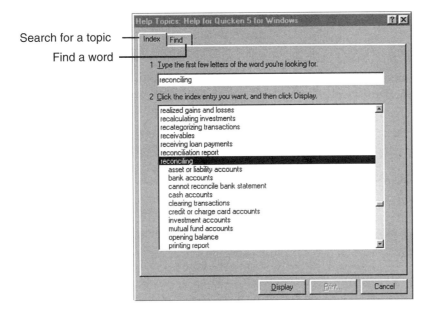

*Searching for a topic.*

Click the **Find** tab in the Search window and use the same procedure to find a specific word rather than a general topic. For example, you can find every instance when online help uses the word "amortization."

## Qcards

Whenever you open a window where you've never been before, you needn't fear sitting there with your mouth agape wondering what to do next. Quicken will display a little yellow window that tells you exactly what to do. These are called Qcards, and the following figure shows a Qcard for the checking account register.

When you complete the action on the Qcard, it changes to tell you the next step. On every Qcard you'll find the button with the ubiquitous yellow question mark to get to online help.

As you work with Quicken and become familiar with it, you may find the Qcards more annoying than helpful. You can turn them off and back on again by selecting **Show Qcards** from the Help menu.

*Qcards tell you what to do, politely, of course.*

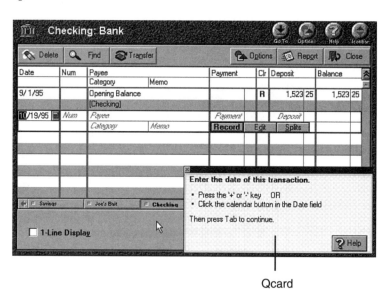

Qcard

## Flyover Help

Move your cursor along the iconbar and little yellow boxes tell you what you'll do if you click the icon. This is called *flyover help*. You'll find this helpful when you encounter an unfamiliar icon. You won't have to hold your breath waiting to see what happens if you click it.

If all those European cities had had such helpful signs, I could have spent less time figuring out where the heck I was and more time meeting men.

# Quick! Quit Quicken! (Say That Three Times Fast)

When you're done with Quicken for the day, you can quit Quicken by clicking **Exit Quicken** on the bottom left of the HomeBase window, choosing **Exit** from the File menu, or clicking on the close button in the upper right corner of your screen. When you quit, Quicken automatically saves your work for you.

This completes our tour of Quicken. I hope you enjoyed seeing it as much as I enjoyed showing it to you. Please make sure you remove all your personal belongings and watch your step on the way out.

# The Least You Need to Know

This chapter took you on an exotic, fast-paced tour of Quicken. Some of the highlights:

➤ Open Quicken from the Start menu in the Windows toolbar.

➤ New User Setup and QuickTours get you rolling in a flash.

➤ Quicken provides several different ways of doing the same thing, so you can decide what works best for you.

➤ Quicken uses windows and dialog boxes to perform its functions.

➤ Help is always only a mouse-click away.

# Chapter 3

# Rev 'Em Up: Using Quicken Files

## In This Chapter

➤ Creating a new Quicken file

➤ Opening files

➤ Operating on your files

➤ Backups and passwords

Somewhere in the back of a closet you probably have a box that contains a pile of cancelled checks, old checkbook registers, passbooks, bank statements, and a dead spider or two. A Quicken file is like that box, minus the dead spiders; it holds all your accounts, reports, graphs, and other information you enter in Quicken.

When you first opened Quicken, it automatically created a file for you. (Wow, that was easy.) Most people are going to have one Quicken file for all of their financial information. If you're also using Quicken to do accounting for a business, you'll probably want to have two files, one for your household finances and one for your business finances.

If you're satisfied with one file, you can skip the section on setting up a new file and jump to the sections on tinkering with your files, backing up and restoring files, and creating passwords.

### There Is a Method to My Madness

You may not need to know some of the things covered in this chapter, such as creating a new file or a year-end copy of your file, until you've worked with Quicken for a while and are comfortable with it. But I put this chapter here because you need to have a basic understanding of files before you can get into the details of working with Quicken. Skim the chapter, ignore what's over your head for the moment, and return to it when you need it. Do, however, read the sections on backing up files and creating passwords. These are important to know right from the start.

## Setting Up a New File

When you create a new file, you can use it to set up accounts, create charts and graphs, and use all of Quicken's myriad features. Both the file that was created automatically when you started Quicken and your new file are saved separately. Although you can transfer information from one to the other, Quicken doesn't exchange information between the two unless you tell it to. We'll talk about transferring information from one file to another in Chapter 18.

To create a new file:

1. Open Quicken and select **New** from the File menu.

2. There's that idiot-proof thing again: Quicken asks if you want to open a new file or a new account. You want a new file, so click **OK**. The following figure shows the Create Quicken File dialog box.

*Creating a new Quicken file.*

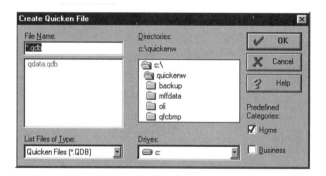

3. Now type a name for your file (no more than eight characters). Quicken automatically named your first file qdata.qdb, so you'll have to be more original than that. For example, you could name a file for your business **business.qdb**.

4. Quicken automatically saves all your files in the QUICKENW folder on your hard drive. If you want to save the new file in a different folder, double-click on the folder you want in the Directories: list. If you want to save the file to a different drive (for example, to a floppy disk in your disk drive), select the drive from the Drives: drop-down list.

5. Quicken has a predefined list of common categories for home and business use (Chapter 6 gives the details on categories). You can choose to include one or the other or both in your file. Under Predefined Categories:, click **Home** to include only home categories, **Business** to include only business categories, or click **Home** and **Business** to include both in your file. If you choose both, Quicken will combine its home and business categories in the same categories list.

6. Click **OK**. Quicken creates your new file and asks you to create your first account for the file (see Chapter 4). If you're not up to that yet, click **Cancel** and you'll see the HomeBase window. Now you can do everything with your new file that you can do with your old one. No, it won't walk the dog.

# Opening a File

When you start Quicken after creating a new file, Quicken opens the file you were working with the last time you quit. If you want to work with another file, you have to open it.

1. In the File menu, click **Open**. The following figure shows the Open Quicken File dialog box.

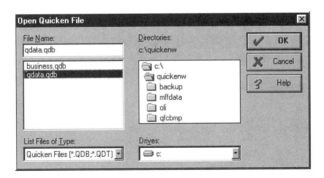

*Opening a Quicken file.*

2. In the File Name: list, click on the file you want to open.

### My File Isn't Listed

Quicken lists the files saved in the QUICKENW folder. If you saved your file in a different folder, double-click on it in the Directories: list, then click on the file name. If you saved your file to a different drive, select the drive from the **Drives:** drop-down list.

3. Click **OK**. Quicken closes the first file and opens the second. You can only have one Quicken file open at a time.

# Tinkering with Your Files (No Tools Required)

This section covers various operations you can perform on your files, without so much as a medical degree. They are: renaming, validating, and deleting a file; and creating a year-end copy, or *archive*, of your file.

## Renaming a File

As I told you earlier, Quicken automatically named the file it created for you qdata.qdb. It's a utilitarian sort of name, but boring. You can rename a file to give it your own personal flair.

1. In the File menu, point to **File Operations**. You'll see a *submenu* of things you can do to your file. Click **Rename**. The following figure shows the Rename Quicken File dialog box.

*Renaming a file.*

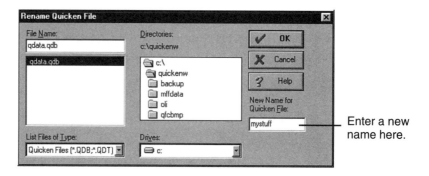

Enter a new name here.

2. Click on the file you want to rename in the File Name: list. If you need to, select a different drive from the Drives: drop-down list, or another folder from the Directories: list.

3. Click in the **New Name for Quicken File:** field.

4. Type the new name for the file, up to eight characters. Quicken will add the .qdb extension for you.

5. Click **OK** and Quicken renames the file.

# Validating a File

There may come a time when you're working merrily along in Quicken and something weird happens. Perhaps your cat pulls the power cord out from the socket and your computer shuts down. Or you get a scary-looking error message. *Validating* a file checks it for icky stuff and rebuilds it, hopefully getting rid of any bugs that might eat your data. It also makes a backup copy of the file so you won't lose everything.

1. In the File menu, select **File Operations**, then **Validate**.

2. In the File Name: list, click on the name of your file.

3. Click **OK**. Quicken checks your file and tells you that there are no errors in your file. Click **OK** to return to whatever you were doing.

# Deleting a File

I hesitate to even tell you this option exists because this is a case where a little knowledge is a dangerous thing. Delete trashes a Quicken file so its bytes and bits are nothing more than a pleasant memory. Everything in that file, and I do mean everything, is history. Do **not** delete a file unless you are absolutely, positively certain that you will never ever need that file again, or unless you're some kind of masochist.

Gulp. Working under the assumption that you know what you're doing, here's how to delete a file:

1. In the File menu, select **File Operations**, then **Delete**.

2. In the File Name: list, click on the file you want to delete.

3. Click **OK**.

4. It's not too late to back out. Quicken asks if you are absolutely, positively certain you want to delete the file. If you are, type **yes** and click **OK**. The file is vaporized. If you're not, click **Cancel** and the file is saved from extinction.

# Creating a Year-End Copy

When you reach the end of the year, you may want to "close out your accounts" by storing all the work you've done on Quicken for the year. You can create a copy of the year's work, called an *archive*. This is just another way of backing up your file, except it saves only the work done in the past year. If you make frequent backups of your file (see the next section in this chapter), this isn't really necessary, but you can do it anyway.

There are two ways of doing a year-end copy: you can copy all of the past year's transactions to a backup file, then continue adding transactions to your file as you have been. Or you can copy all of the past year's transactions to a backup file and start a new file for the new year. The new file will not have any of the old transactions in it, except investment transactions and transactions that have not yet been cleared. It will, however, retain your current account balances.

To archive your old transactions but retain them in your current file:

1. In the File menu, click **Year-End Copy**.

2. Click **Archive** and **OK**.

3. The Archive File dialog box shows you the name of the backup file where Quicken will save the past year's work. Click **OK**. Quicken will copy your file and tell you when it's done. Click **OK** again to return to your file.

To archive your old transactions and start over with a new file:

1. In the File menu, click **Year-End Copy**.

2. Click **Start New Year** and **OK**.

3. Type a name for the backup file where Quicken will save last year's file. Click **OK**. Quicken creates the backup file and deletes all of last year's transactions, except for investment transactions and uncleared transactions, from your file. It will tell you when it's done; click **OK** to use your new file.

# An Airbag for Your Files

I've made my living with computers for eight years, and I've seen some really ugly incidents. I once spent a week building a database of 400 addresses only to lose it because of a bad floppy. A lightning strike fried my modem. I worked on a computer that crashed if I looked at it funny. I have learned through painful experience that you can never assume your files are safe; you have to back them up.

Quicken does some of the work for you. Every seven days it automatically copies your files and puts them in a subdirectory called BACKUP in the QUICKENW folder. This way you always have a recent copy of your file and accounts.

However, because computers can be such touchy machines, I strongly recommend that you also back up your files onto a floppy disk at least once a month. Here's how to back up your file:

1. If you have more than one file, open the one you want to back up.

2. Select **Backup** from the File menu.

3. Put your floppy into the floppy disk drive. If necessary, select a different drive from the Backup Drive: drop-down list. Click **OK**. You may need several disks to save all your data. (Quicken will prompt you when you need to put in a new disk.)

If you haven't backed up your file in a while, Quicken will remind you when you quit Quicken. Put your floppy in the disk drive and click **Backup**.

Every time you back up your files, you should reuse the same floppy disks. Quicken will overwrite the previous backup copy. This way you'll always have the latest version of your data.

## Restoring Your Files

So your three-year-old stuck peanut butter in your disk drive and, after you got the repair technician to stop laughing long enough to fix it, you need to restore your files.

1. Put the floppy disk with your backup files in the disk drive.

2. Select **Restore** from the File menu. The following figure shows the Restore Quicken File dialog box.

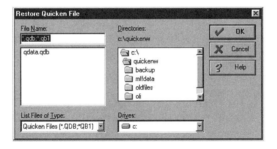

*Restoring a lost Quicken file.*

3. Choose the letter of your floppy disk drive (usually a:) from the Drives: drop-down list. Or, if you want to restore from Quicken's automatic backup, double-click on the **BACKUP** folder in the QUICKENW folder.

4. In the File Name: list, click on the name of your backup file (for example, qdata.qdb).

5. Click **OK**.

Your files will be restored, safe and sound. However, you'll have to redo any work you did between the time of your last backup and the demise of your files. Petition the peanut butter company to put a label on the jar: "Use only under adult supervision."

# Roadblock! Setting Up Passwords

If your computer is on a network, you probably don't want Joe from across the hall snooping through the company's finances. Or you may not want your teenage son to cleverly destroy your credit rating. Keep your files safe from hackers, lurkers, and other sneaky people by setting up passwords.

There are two types of passwords: file and transaction passwords. A *file password* controls who has access to your Quicken file. A *transaction password* controls who can change transactions in your accounts; anyone can open your file, they just can't enter or edit transactions. To set up a password:

1. In the File menu, point to **Passwords**. From the submenu, select either **File** or **Transaction**. The procedure for setting up a password is the same for both. The following figure shows the Set Up Password dialog box.

*Create a password for your files or transactions.*

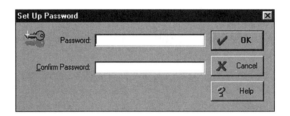

2. In the Password field, type your password. You'll see asterisks (*) in the field instead of the characters you type, so someone looking over your shoulder can't read it. Press **Tab** to move to the Confirm Password field.

3. Retype the password exactly as you did in step 2. This is to confirm the spelling and make sure you didn't type "fivl" when you meant to type "duck."

4. Click **OK**. If this is a file password, Quicken will make you type it every time you open Quicken. If it's a transaction password, Quicken will make you type it whenever you add or change transactions in your accounts.

### Do Not Use Your Name As Your Password

The trick to setting up passwords is to use a word that you'll remember but not one so obvious that any schmo can guess it. My husband, an art history major turned computer programmer, uses names of obscure artists for his passwords. Try to come up with something unique to you.

You should write your password down and store it someplace safe for the days when you can barely remember your own name. Don't write your password on a yellow sticky and paste it to the side of your computer. That kind of defeats the purpose.

# Changing Your Password

I know some companies require their employees to change their passwords regularly to make it harder for trespassers to guess the passwords. While this may not apply to you, you may just get tired of typing the same word every day, or you may decide you don't need a password at all.

1. Select **Passwords** from the File menu and click either **File** or **Transaction**.

2. In the Old Password: field, type your old password and press **Tab**.

3. In the New Password: field, type your new password and press **Tab**. If you want to delete the old password without replacing it, leave this field blank.

4. In the Confirm Password: field, retype your new password exactly as you did in the New Password field. If you're deleting the old password, leave this field blank.

5. Click **OK**. Quicken will only accept the new password.

# The Least You Need to Know

Quicken files keep your financial information in one place; they are the foundation on which everything you do with Quicken is built.

➤ If you have two separate sets of finances to keep track of, such as for home and for business, you can set up a file for each.

➤ You can rename your files to reflect your own unique personality.

➤ Validate your files to make sure there aren't any creepy crawly things eating away at your data.

➤ You can close out your accounts by creating a year-end copy.

➤ Protect your files from break-ins, power surges, and other disasters with passwords and backups.

# Chapter 4

# Take It All into Account: Setting Up Quicken Accounts

## In This Chapter

➤ Types of Quicken accounts

➤ Putting your accounts in place

➤ Fun things you can do with your accounts

Are you wondering how you could possibly be overdrawn when you still have checks left? When was the last time you actually opened your bank statement before tossing it in the shoe box behind your tennis racket in the closet? Does the thought of balancing your checkbook give you hives?

Well, dust off the shoe box, grab a cold one, and relax. Quicken makes it so easy to keep track of bank accounts, credit cards, loans, and other nasty little details of life that you no longer have an excuse for being a disorganized mess.

## Income and Outgo: Types of Quicken Accounts

The heart and soul of Quicken are its accounts. You use accounts to keep track of how your money comes in and where it goes. Quicken takes the information you enter in your accounts—dates, categories, amounts—and transforms it into budgets, reports, graphs, and planners. Master using accounts and you can use those shoe boxes to hold shoes. Just think, you can organize your finances and clean out your closet at the same time!

Quicken assumes you've got a lot of money to throw around and gives you the choice of eight different accounts:

➤ Checking accounts

➤ Savings accounts

➤ Credit Card accounts (MasterCard, Visa, Joe's Bait and Department Store)

➤ Cash accounts to keep track of how much you spend at the office candy and pop machines

➤ Money Market accounts

➤ Investment accounts for stocks, bonds, IRAs, and mutual funds

➤ Asset accounts for the things you own that are worth something, like your home or business equipment

➤ Liability accounts for those black holes of debt such as mortgages and loans

You can have one account or dozens of every type. As I explained in Chapter 2, Quicken saves them all together in one file. The accounts can then interact when you transfer money or create budgets.

## Setting Up Your Accounts

The process for setting up all the different accounts is the same, and so easy you could teach your toddler to do it. There are a few things you should have ready before you start.

➤ First, you need to crack open the shoe box so you can enter a starting balance for your account from your bank statement.

**Check This Out...**

**Put Your Modem to Work** With QuickBillPay, you can pay your bills electronically using your modem. QuickBanking lets you transfer funds and get information about your accounts, such as your balance and checks cleared, also with your modem. See Chapter 8 to learn about both services.

➤ Second, you need to decide from what date to start the account. You should use the closing date on your statement so the dates and balances match. If you plan on creating a budget or using Quicken to help with your taxes, you may want to start with a balance from the beginning of the year or at least a couple of months back. You'll have to enter more information, but it will give a more accurate picture of your finances.

➤ If you plan on using Quicken's online services, QuickBillPay and QuickBanking, you'll also need the welcome letter you received when you registered (see Chapter 8).

To set up a new account, select **Create New Account** from the Activities menu. Click on the type of account you want. The New Account Setup window leads you step by step through the process, telling you exactly what to enter when.

## New Account Setup Window Features

The New Account Setup windows are essentially the same for each account (see the following figure). The tabs on top tell you where you are in the process. A red check mark indicates you're done with that part.

When you're done entering information on one screen, click **Next**. If you want to return to a previous screen, click **Back**. **Cancel** stops the process without setting up the new account. The **Help** button gets you to online help.

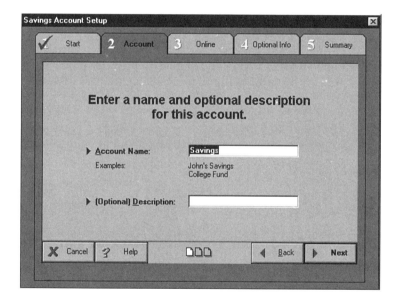

*Follow the leader: Quicken tells you exactly how to set up a new account.*

You already set up a checking account when you went through New User Setup (see Chapter 3). To give you more practice, I'll take you through setting up a savings account and a credit card account—two other accounts just about everyone will need.

## Set Up a Savings Account

Creating a savings account is very similar to creating a checking account. Here's how it goes:

1. Select **Create New Account** from the Activities menu.

2. Click **Savings**.

3. You'll see the Start tab in the Savings Account Setup window. Click **Next**.

4. Quicken suggests Savings as the name for the account. If you want, type in a new name. Click **Next**.

5. Quicken asks if you have your last bank statement for the account. If you do, click **Next** and go on to step 6. If you don't, click **No** and **Next**. Quicken tells you it will set up the account with a balance of $0.00 as of today's date. Click **Next** and jump to step 8.

6. In Statement Date, use the Calendar icon to enter the date of your bank statement. Press **Tab**.

7. In Ending Balance, type the ending balance on your bank statement. Quicken will use this as the opening balance of your Quicken savings account. Click **Next**.

8. Now Quicken wants to know if you have signed up to use QuickBillPay or QuickBanking with your savings account (see Chapter 8 on how to use Quicken's online services). If you haven't, click **Next** and skip to step 13. If you have, click **Online Banking** and/or **Online Bill Payment** and click **Next**.

9. From the Financial Institution drop-down list, select the name of the bank you're using for the online services. Press **Tab**.

10. Type the nine-digit routing number from your welcome letter and click **Next**.

11. Type your account number and click **Next**.

12. Type your Social Security number or Tax Identification Number. Enter the same number you used when you signed up for the online service. Click **Next**.

13. Quicken asks if you want to include optional information about your savings account, such as the name, address, and phone number of your bank. If you do, click **Yes** and **Next**. If you don't, click **Next** and skip to step 15.

14. Type in the optional information you want included, pressing **Tab** to move from field to field. You can include as much or as little information as you want. When you're done, click **Next**.

15. Quicken gives you a summary of your account, as shown in the following figure. The first summary window shows your account name, description, and balance. Click **Next** to see the online services, optional, and tax information. (We'll talk about the tax information for Quicken accounts later in this chapter.)

16. Click **Done** and your new savings account register appears.

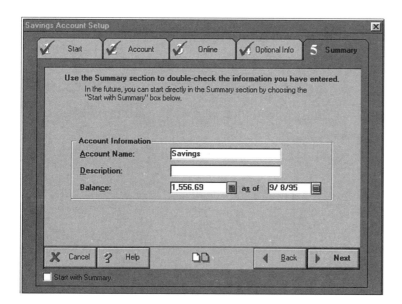

*A savings account summary.*

# Set Up a Credit Card Account

It seems like half of my Quicken accounts are credit card accounts. I could set one up in my sleep. Here's how to do it:

1. Select **Create New Account** from the Activities menu.

2. Click **Credit Card**.

3. You'll see the Start tab in the Credit Card Account Setup window. Click **Next**.

4. Quicken suggests Credit Card as the name for the account. This probably isn't descriptive enough, so type the real name of your credit card. Click **Next**.

5. Quicken asks if you have your last credit card statement. If you do, click **Next** and go on to step 6. If you don't, click **No** and **Next**. Quicken tells you it will set up the account with a balance of $0.00 as of today's date. Click **Next** and jump to step 8.

6. In Statement Date, use the Calendar icon to enter the date of your credit card statement. Press **Tab**.

7. In Balance Due, type how much you owe on your credit card. Quicken will use this as the opening balance of your Quicken credit card account. Click **Next**.

8. Now Quicken wants to know if you have signed up to use QuickBanking with your credit card account (QuickBillPay is not available for credit card accounts). If you haven't, click **Next** and skip to step 13. If you have, click **Yes** and **Next**.

9. From the Financial Institution drop-down list, select the name of the bank you're using for QuickBanking. Click **Next**.

10. Type your credit card account number and click **Next**.

11. Type your Social Security number or Tax Identification Number. Enter the same number you used when you signed up for the online service. Press **Tab**.

12. Type the nine-digit routing number from your welcome letter and click **Next**.

13. If you want, type the credit limit for your card and click **Next**.

14. Quicken asks if you want to include optional information about your credit card account, such as the name, address, and phone number of your bank. If you do, click **Yes** and **Next**. If you don't, click **Next** and skip to step 16.

15. Type in the optional information you want included, pressing **Tab** to move from field to field. You can include as much or as little information as you want. When you're done, click **Next**.

16. Quicken gives you a summary of your account, as shown in the following figure. The first summary window shows your account name, description, and balance. Click **Next** to see the QuickBanking, optional, and tax information.

*A credit card account summary.*

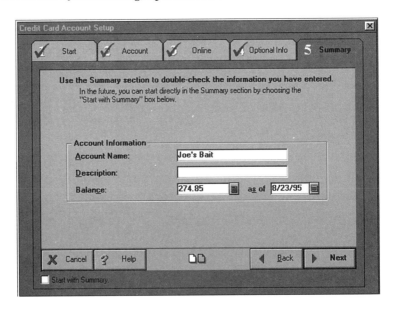

17. Click **Done** to see your new credit card account register.

## For Every Rule, There's an Exception

Not all accounts are created equal, and Quicken requires different information for different accounts.

➤ QuickBanking and QuickBillPay are only available for checking, savings, and money market accounts. Credit card accounts allow QuickBanking, but not QuickBillPay.

➤ For investment accounts, Quicken will ask you, "Are you using this account to track a single mutual fund?" Creating an investment account to track a single mutual fund lets you reconcile the account by share balance. Click **Yes** or **No**.

➤ Also for investment accounts, it asks "Would you like to include a linked cash account for cash management?" Click **Yes** if your real (as opposed to Quicken) investment account has features such as check writing, cash or debit cards, or automatic funds transfer.

# It's April 15. Do You Know Where Your Money Is?

Dealing with the IRS isn't anyone's idea of a rollicking good time, but the feds give migraines to people like me who work at home and don't have a big brother corporation to hand them W-2s, W-4s, and WD-40s.

Fortunately for me and anyone else who has an income, there are software programs, such as TurboTax, that are like having a tax accountant in your den. You can set up your Quicken accounts so the pertinent information can be transferred directly to your tax software.

At the account Summary, click the **Tax Information** button. Here you can check whether the account is tax-deferred. And—this is the really cool part—you can specify exactly which tax schedule line item should be assigned to transfers into and out of your account (see the figure below). For example, if you will deposit Social Security income in your account, select Form 1040:Soc. sec. income from the Transfers In: drop-down list.

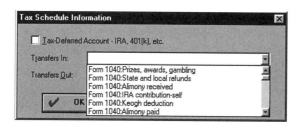

*Quicken is like extra-strength ibuprofin at tax time.*

The New Account Setup for investment and asset accounts has a special Taxes section where you can select tax schedules, instead of doing it at the Summary. To learn more about how Quicken helps you with your taxes, see Chapter 17.

# Making Your Accounts Roll Over and Do Tricks

Don't think that once you set up an account, everything about it is set in stone and it will sit there, impassive, for all eternity. *Au contraire*, you can always add more accounts, enter or change the additional information, edit the information in the account summary, and delete accounts. You do all this from the Account List, which also lets you see all your accounts at a glance.

You can get to the Account List in one of three ways: select **Account** from the Lists menu, click on the **Accts** icon in the main iconbar, or click on **Account List** in the HomeBase window.

As shown in the following figure, the Account List gives you a recap of your accounts and an iconbar of things to do to them.

*Use the Account List to view your accounts and add, edit, and delete accounts.*

Iconbar

Account Recap

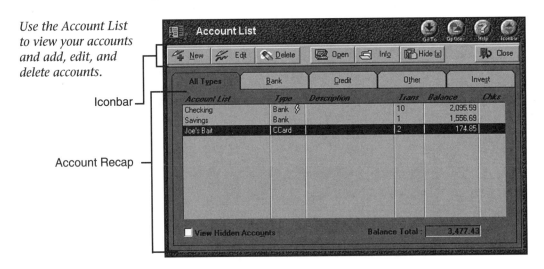

## The Account Recap

The account recap tells you the name of the account, the type, the description (if you entered one when you set up the account), the number of transactions that have taken place, and the current balance. If you have checks to be printed from that account (see Chapter 8), there will be a check mark in the Chks column.

The Balance Total is the balance of all the accounts in the recap. In the preceding figure, it shows the balance of the two bank accounts minus the amount owed to Joe's Bait.

You can see the same information on a specific type of account by clicking **Bank** (checking and savings), **Credit** (credit cards), **Other** (cash, money market, asset, and liability), or **Invest**.

## The Iconbar

Let's roll through the iconbar to learn what you can do to your accounts:

➤ **New** creates a new account just as you did in the previous section.

➤ **Edit** brings up the New Account Setup Summary so you can change or add to it.

➤ **Delete** erases an account and you'll never see it again. But don't worry about clicking **Delete** accidentally; a dialog box makes you type "yes" and click **OK** before Quicken deletes the account. If you click **Cancel**, Quicken reassures you that the account was not deleted.

➤ **Open** opens the account register so you can enter transactions.

➤ **Info** shows the optional information from New Account Setup so you can change or add to it.

➤ **Hide[x]** hides an account from the Account List. This is useful if you want to see the **Balance Total** for all accounts except one or two. To see the hidden account again, click **View Hidden Accounts** at the bottom left of the Account List.

➤ **Close** closes the Account List.

**Check This Out...**

**Think Before You Delete** If you do decide to delete an account, remember that everything that references that account—transfers to and from other accounts, budgets, reports, planners—will be irreversibly affected. In other words, you'd better be darn sure you know what you're doing.

Congratulations. You're well on your way to getting your life organized. Now go call your mother.

## The Least You Need to Know

This chapter got you started on the real meat (or the eggplant, if you're a vegetarian) of using Quicken. Some samples from our menu:

➤ There are eight different types of Quicken accounts, and you can have as many or as few as you need.

➤ Quicken leads you step by step through setting up a new account.

➤ Use the Account List to view basic information about your accounts and to add, edit, and delete accounts.

# Chapter 5

# Account Registers: The Nuts and Bolts of Quicken

## In This Chapter

➤ Entering transactions in account registers

➤ Whoops! What to do if you screwed up

➤ Playing the field and looking for a date

Once you've got your accounts set up, it's time to get to the nitty-gritty of organizing your finances: entering transactions in the account registers. It doesn't do much good to set up Quicken accounts if you don't put anything in them. Transactions are how you keep track of what goes in and out of your accounts when, to whom, and why. When you move on to some of Quicken's more advanced functions, the transactions become especially important. Quicken uses them to create budgets, reports, and graphs, and in the Financial Calendar.

In this chapter, you'll learn how to navigate an account register, enter and edit transactions, and search for one transaction among many.

## A Place for Everything and Everything in Its Place

Every account that you set up has its own *register*. The register contains details about the transactions in the account: date, payee, amount, memo, and category. If you've ever recorded a check in a checkbook (you do record all the checks you write, don't you?), you have already been using a register. This will be old hat for you.

To open your account register, click on the **Register** icon in the main iconbar or the HomeBase window. Quicken opens the register that you used last, or the last account you set up. The following figure shows the register for a checking account.

*All the account registers are similar to the checking account register.*

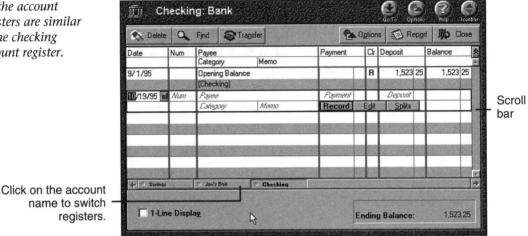

Scroll bar

Click on the account name to switch registers.

Here are some tips to getting around the account register:

➤ All of the accounts you set up are listed along the bottom of the register. To switch to the register for another account, click on the account name.

➤ When you first open a register, the Qcards will tell you exactly what to enter in each field. (See Chapter 3 for a description of Qcards.)

➤ The first line in the register shows your opening balance and the date. You can see the current account balance (labeled **Ending Balance**) in the lower right corner (unless it's hidden by the Qcard).

➤ The second line has a heavy black box around it, which means this is the line you're using. You'll always enter a new transaction in the last line in the register. When you record the transaction, Quicken automatically sorts them by date, earlier dates first.

➤ As you enter transactions, you can scroll through them by clicking on the scroll bar at the right of the register.

➤ Move from field to field in the register by pressing **Tab**.

# Entering Transactions in the Register

Stretch your fingers and grab a cup of coffee. Now you're going to enter all the transactions that have taken place since the date of your opening balance.

First, we'll go step-by-step through entering transactions in a checking account register. The registers for savings and money market accounts are identical to the checking account register, so you'll learn how to use all three registers in one fell swoop.

The registers for the other Quicken accounts (credit card, cash, asset, liability, and investment) are similar to the checking account register, with a few variations. After we've gone through the checking account register, I'll describe the differences you'll find in the other registers.

## The Basic Account Registers: Checking, Savings, and Money Market

Take note of the date and opening balance for your Quicken checking account. Get out your checkbook and write a check to Beverly R. Roath—just kidding. (Hey, it was worth a shot.) In your checkbook, find the first transaction after the opening date for your Quicken account; this is the first transaction you'll enter in Quicken. Ready? Here goes:

1. Click on the **Calendar icon** on the right side of the Date field, then click on the date of the transaction. Press **Tab**.

2. The **Num** field has a drop-down list to enter the check number or another description for the transaction, shown in the following figure. Click on the arrow to see the drop-down list.

   ➤ Click **ATM** for an automatic teller machine transaction.

   ➤ Click **Deposit** for a deposit transaction.

   ➤ Click **EFT** (which stands for electronic fund transfer) for a transaction that has been sent with QuickBillPay or QuickBanking.

   ➤ Click **Next Chk#** to record the next check number. For the first transaction, Quicken enters a check number of 101, so you'll want to type the actual check number for your transaction.

**Don't Procrastinate** Keeping the account registers up-to-date can be time-consuming, especially if you graduated from the Hunt and Peck School of Typing or have a lot of accounts. To keep from being buried under a mountain of receipts and statements, update your registers regularly.

**Whiz Through the Days** To advance the date by one day, press the + key on your number pad. To decrease the date by one day, press the - key.

45

*The Num field drop-down list.*

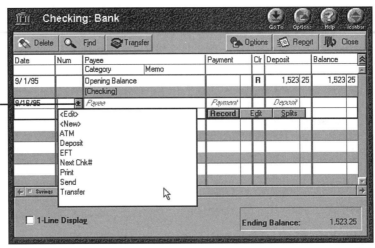

Click on the arrow to see the drop-down list.

**Whiz Through the Check Numbers** To advance the check number by one, press the + key on your number pad. To decrease the check number by one, press the - key.

➤ Click **Print** for a transaction for which you'll print a check. After you print the check, Quicken changes **Print** to the check number.

➤ Click **Send** for a payment that will be sent through QuickBillPay (Quicken will change **Send** to **EFT** after it's been transmitted).

➤ Click **Transfer** when you transfer funds to another account with QuickBanking (Quicken will change **Transfer** to **EFT** after it's been transmitted).

➤ Click **New** to add your own transaction description to the drop-down list. Type the name of the description (up to five characters) and click **OK**.

➤ Click **Edit** to change the name of a transaction description that you entered (you can only change descriptions that you added, not any of Quicken's).

When you've entered the transaction description or check number in the Num field, press **Tab**. (For more information on printing checks and using QuickBillPay and QuickBanking, see Chapter 8.)

3. In the Payee field, type the name of the person or company you wrote the check to, or a description of a deposit. Each time you type a new payee, Quicken will add the name to a drop-down list.

When you click on the arrow in the Payee field for a new transaction, Quicken displays the Payee drop-down list, along with the amount of the check and the category, as shown in the following figure.

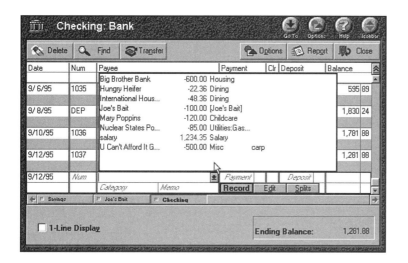

*An example of a Payee drop-down list.*

If the transaction you're entering is for one of the payees in the list, click on it and Quicken inserts the name, amount, and category in the register. Another weapon in the fight against carpal tunnel syndrome! If you need to, you can change the amount and category as described below.

4. In the Payment field, type the amount of the check. Use the number pad on your keyboard to enter numbers faster. Click on the Calculator icon to use the Calculator, if you need it. Press **Tab**.

5. You don't need to worry about the Clr field right now. You'll use it to mark the transactions that have cleared your bank when you balance your account, which we'll talk about in Chapter 9.

> **Check This Out...**
>
> **An Introduction to Memorized Transactions** The transactions in the Payee drop-down list are called *memorized transactions*. You'll learn more how to work with them in Chapter 7.

6. If you chose Deposit in the Num field, Quicken jumps to the Deposit field after you enter the payee. Type in the amount of the deposit, or use the Calculator icon. Press **Tab**.

7. Click on the arrow in the Category field and select a category from the drop-down list. Categories record exactly what the transaction was for. Categories are a big part of what makes Quicken the wonder that it is. Chapter 6 talks about them in detail.

8. In the Memo field, type in a note about the transaction, if you want to jog your memory later about the transaction. This is optional. Press **Tab**.

9. Click **Record** or press **Enter** to save the transaction. Quicken beeps so you'll know the transaction was saved.

Congratulations! You've entered your first transaction in Quicken. As you enter more, you'll find it goes very quickly. Later in this chapter we'll talk about the **Edit** button in the register, which lets you make changes to transactions. (I'll describe the Splits button in Chapter 7.)

## Credit Card Account Registers

The credit card register looks just like the checking, savings, and money market registers, except it has a Ref field instead of a Num field. Your credit card statement may give a reference number for each charge. If you want, you can type the reference number in the Ref field, but it's optional. There's no drop-down list for this field.

## Cash Account Registers

➤ The cash account register (shown in the following figure) has a Ref field instead of a Num field to enter a reference for the transaction. Chances are you won't need one.

➤ Type in the amount you spent in the Spend field.

➤ Likewise, type an amount in the Receive field when you add to your cash reserves.

*The cash account register.*

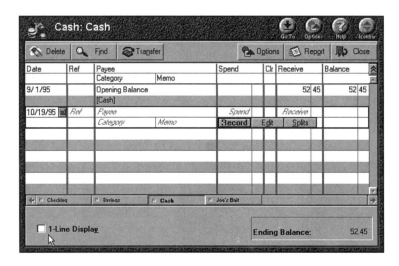

## Asset and Liability Account Registers

The following figure shows an asset account register, but the asset and liability account registers have the same look. The fields that are different from the checking register are:

➤ Record a depreciation or decrease in the Decrease field.

➤ Record an appreciation or increase in the Increase field.

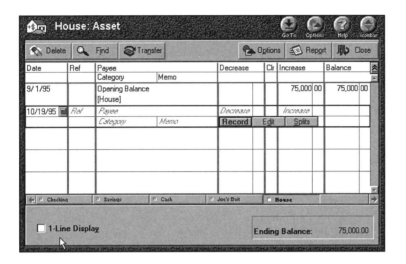

*The asset and liability account registers are identical.*

# Investment Account Registers

The investment account register (shown in the following figure) is a little trickier, but if you can read your account statement, you shouldn't have a problem. The following fields are included in the investment account register:

➤ **Action**    A drop-down list shows an assortment of investment actions, such as "buy security" and "dividend." Click **Help** to learn more about investment actions. You can also click the **Action** button on the top of the register to select an investment action.

➤ **Security**    Type in the name of the security. Quicken will add it to a drop-down list so you can select it again later.

➤ **Price**    Enter the price per share.

➤ **Shares**    Type in the number of shares.

➤ **Basis**    If you entered a price and number of shares, Quicken calculates the dollar amount for you in this field. Otherwise, you can enter the amount of the transaction after subtracting any commissions or fees.

➤ **Mkt Value**    Enter the total commission, fees, and front load, and Quicken will add it to the amount of the transaction.

> **Check This Out...**
>
> **Insight Into Your Investments**
> Investor Insight is a Quicken feature that lets you get up-to-the-minute stock quotes, mutual fund price changes, and investment news stories. Investor Insight also works in tandem with your Quicken investment accounts. To learn more about Investor Insight and investment accounts, read Chapters 25 and 26.

**49**

*Investment account register.*

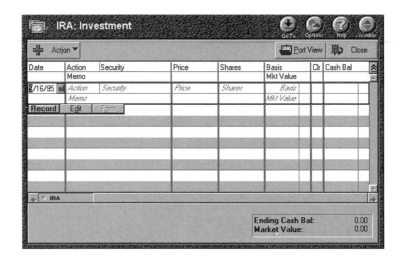

# Don't Panic! Fixing Mistakes

When balancing my checkbook the old-fashioned way, I've found mistakes five pages back in the register and then had to use a bottle of white-out to fix a month's worth of balances. Don't you just hate it when that happens? Toss that white-out out the window, because modifying registers with Quicken is a breeze.

➤ To change any field in a transaction, click on the field and enter the new information. For example, to change the payee, click on the **Payee** field and select another payee from the drop-down list or type a new name. To change the amount of a check, click on the **Payment** field and type a new amount. Click **Record** and Quicken saves the changes.

If you make a mistake when editing a transaction, click the **Edit** button and then select **Restore Transaction**. Quicken changes the transaction back to the way it was before you made the changes. However, you have to select **Restore Transaction** before you click **Record**. Once you click **Record**, Quicken saves whatever changes you made.

**You Don't Need to Insert Lines for Earlier Transaction Dates** If you want to enter a transaction from an earlier date, you don't need to insert a blank transaction. Quicken automatically sorts all the transactions by date, no matter when you enter them.

➤ To erase a transaction, click on any field in the transaction and click the **Delete** button. Quicken asks if you're sure you want to delete it; click **Yes**.

➤ To copy a transaction, click on any field in the transaction. Click the **Edit** button and select **Copy Transaction**. Then click on a new register line, click the **Edit** button, and select **Paste Transaction**.

➤ If you want to insert a blank register line above a transaction, click on the transaction. Click on the **Edit** menu (not the Edit button) and select **Insert Transaction**. Quicken inserts a blank register line above the selected transaction.

➤ If you void a check, click on the corresponding transaction in the register. Click on the **Edit** menu and select **Void Transaction**. Quicken deletes the transaction amount from the balance, but puts **VOID** in the Payee field in front of the payee name so you still have a record of the transaction.

# In Search Of Lost Transactions

Joe, of Joe's Bait and Department Store, insists you're three months behind on your credit card payments, but you know you paid him. How can you prove it without scrolling through three months of transactions?

**Faster Ways to Delete, Insert, and Void Transactions** Instead of selecting Delete, Insert, and Void Transaction from the Edit menu, you can use Ctrl+key combinations. To delete a transaction, click on it and press **Ctrl+D**. To insert a blank transaction, press **Ctrl+I**. To void a transaction, press **Ctrl+V**.

I'm so glad you asked. You can search for a name, amount, category, or any other information in an account register.

1. Click the **Find** button in the account register window. The following figure shows the Find dialog box.

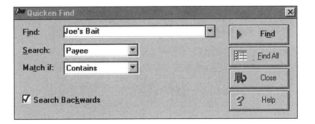

*Finding a transaction in the register.*

2. Type **Joe's Bait**, or whatever you want to search for.

3. If you only want to search in a specific field, select the name of the field from the Search: drop-down list. For example, select **Payee** to look for Joe's Bait in the Payee field. If you don't select a field from the drop-down list, Quicken will look in all the fields.

4. To find the most recent transaction for Joe's Bait, click **Find**. Quicken jumps to that transaction in the account register.

You can also search for all the transactions for Joe's Bait in every account. Click **Find All**, and Quicken lists every transaction for Joe's Bait in all the accounts, as shown in the following figure.

*Find All lists every
transaction in all
your accounts.*

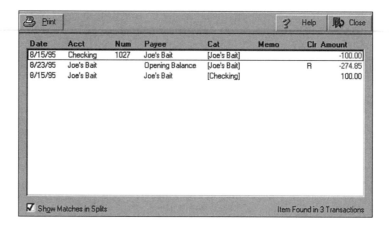

If you know the date of the transaction, you can search just for the date:

1. Click the **Edit** button on the account register and select **Go to A Specific Date**.

2. Click on the Calendar icon to enter the date you want to find.

3. Click **OK**, and Quicken jumps to the first transaction for that date in the register.

## The Least You Need to Know

➤ You record account transactions in the register. The registers for all the different types of accounts are variations on a checkbook register.

➤ Qcards tell you what to enter in each field.

➤ You can easily make changes to fields. You can also copy, paste, delete, insert, and void transactions.

➤ Avoid excessive scrolling with the Find and Go To features.

# Chapter 6

# Cruising in the Fast Lane: Categories and Classes

## In This Chapter

➤ Tracking your money with categories

➤ Assigning categories to transactions

➤ Using the Categories & Transfer List to customize categories and subcategories

➤ Creating supercategories for budgets and reports

➤ Give your transactions some class

Have you ever looked at your account balance, done a double-take, and cried, "Where did all my money go?" After you've read this chapter, you'll know exactly where it went.

*Categories* allow you to keep track of exactly how much you spend on your mortgage, car, groceries, and trips to Bora Bora. So instead of piling up stacks of receipts and trying to sort them out at the end of the month, you assign one or more categories to every transaction.

With *classes*, you can specify where, to what, or to whom your categories apply. For example, if you write checks for both personal and business expenses, you can specify that a dinner out was for business. Or you can set up a class for a job project.

# The Categorical Imperative

Remember when you went through New User Setup, it asked you whether you wanted home or business categories, or both. This is because Quicken has a predefined list of common home and business categories that you can use or modify as you want.

When you click on the arrow in the Category field in an account register, a drop-down list displays the categories divided into income and expenses, as shown in the following figure.

*The drop-down category list displays when you click on the arrow in the Category field.*

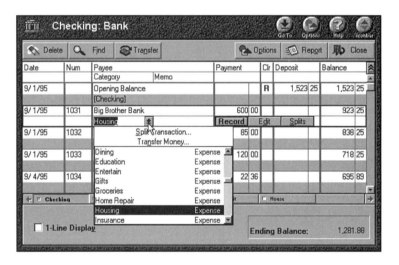

To assign a category to a transaction, scroll through the list until you find the one you want (income categories are listed first, expense categories second) and click on it. The category then appears in the Category field of your register.

You should assign categories to every transaction. Quicken will use the categories to create budgets, reports, and graphs. By assigning a category to every transaction, you'll get an accurate account of your finances.

# The Category & Transfer List

Quicken's predefined categories cover the bases for most situations, but you can get rid of the categories you don't want, change them, and add new ones that fit your spending habits. After all, how is Quicken supposed to know you spend $50 a month on fishing lures?

Quicken saves all the categories in a window called the Category & Transfer List. When you add, edit, and delete categories in the Category & Transfer List, Quicken updates the category drop-down list in the account registers so you're always working with a current list.

You can get to the Category & Transfer List, shown in the following figure, by selecting **Category & Transfer** from the Lists menu, or by pressing **Ctrl+C**.

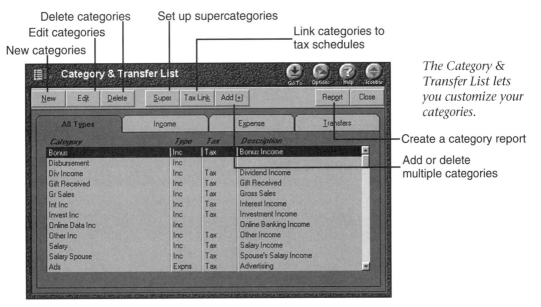

*The Category & Transfer List lets you customize your categories.*

The Category & Transfer List shows you the type of category (income, expense, or subcategory), whether the category is taxable, and its description. You can see all types of categories, or just the income, expense, or transfer categories by clicking on the tabs along the top of the list. (We'll talk about transfers in Chapter 7.)

## Add Categories

To add new categories to the list:

1.  In the Category & Transfer List window, click the **New** button. The Set Up Category dialog box appears as shown in the following figure.

**You Won't Learn About Tax Link in This Chapter** Quicken has a feature that lets you link categories to specific line items on income tax forms, which is what the Tax Link button in the Category & Transfer List is for. However, you won't learn about it here. Chapter 17 describes all of the ways you can use Quicken to help with your taxes.

*Adding a new category to the Category & Transfer List.*

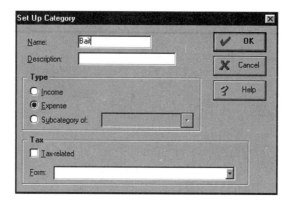

2. Type in the name of the category, such as **Bait**.

3. Enter a description of the category (optional).

4. Check whether it's an Income or an Expense category.

5. Click **OK**. You've got a new category.

## Subcategories

On the Category & Transfer List, scroll down to the Auto category. Indented under it, there are Fuel, Insurance, Loan, and Service; these are *subcategories* of the Auto category. You can add your own subcategories to categories if you like.

To differentiate minnows from leeches in your Bait category:

1. Click on the **New** button. The Set Up Category dialog box appears, shown in the following figure.

*Adding a subcategory to the Category & Transfer List.*

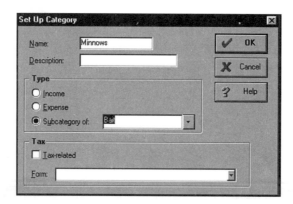

2. In the Name: field, type **Minnows**.

3. Enter a description (optional).

4. Click the **Subcategory of:** option button.

5. Select **Bait** from the drop-down list.

6. Click **OK**. Repeat the steps for leeches, big glow-in-the-dark purple worms, and any other weird lures you buy.

When you select a subcategory from the drop-down list in your account register, both the main category and the subcategory will appear in the Category field, like this:

Bait:Leeches

# Delete Categories

To delete a category you don't think you will use, click on the category in the Category & Transfer List and click the **Delete** button.

Be careful when deleting categories! If you have assigned the deleted category to transactions in your account registers, Quicken deletes the category from the transactions. In other words, those transactions will no longer have a category assigned to them. (The transactions themselves are **not** deleted—just the category.) Quicken also deletes the category from any reports, graphs, and planners you created. A warning window asks, "You are about to permanently delete a category." Click **OK** to go through with it; click **Cancel** to keep the category.

To delete a subcategory, click on it in the Category & Transfer List and click **Delete**. Quicken will ask if you want to merge the subcategory with the parent. If you click **No**, Quicken will delete the subcategory from the Category & Transfer List and from all transactions, but will retain the main category in any transaction where the subcategory appeared. For example, I delete the subcategory Leeches and do not merge it with the Bait category. In the transactions in my Joe's Bait account, Quicken deletes the subcategory Leeches but saves the category Bait.

If you click **Yes**, Quicken deletes the subcategory from the Category & Transfer List and from all your transactions. Although the main category is still available in the Category & Transfer List, Quicken will also delete the main category wherever it appeared with the subcategory you deleted. For example, I delete the subcategory Leeches and click **Yes** merge it

**Can I Delete a Category That Has Subcategories?**
Yes, but you have to be sneaky about it. If you try to delete a main category that has subcategories, Quicken will beep at you and refuse to do it. You can, however, delete each subcategory individually and then delete the main category.

with the Bait category. In the transactions in my Joe's Bait account, Quicken deletes the subcategory Leeches and the category Bait where it appeared with the Leeches. It does not, however delete Bait from other transactions where Bait is either alone or with another subcategory, such as Minnows.

## Delete Multiple Categories

So you scan the Category & Transfer List and realize that not very many of them work for you. You don't have to laboriously click on each category you don't want and then click the **Delete** button.

Instead, click on the **Add** button to see the Add Categories dialog box. The category list is on the left. Select only the categories you want to keep and click **Add>>**. The selected categories jump to the right. If you decide you don't want a category in the Categories to Add column, select it and click **<<Remove**. It jumps back. Keep clicking and watch the categories leap around like Mexican jumping beans. When you've got all the categories you want in the Categories to Add column, click **OK**, and Quicken regenerates the Category & Transfer List with just those you selected.

## Edit Categories

You can change the specifics of a category by clicking the **Edit** button. The Edit Category dialog box looks just like the Set Up Category dialog box and shows the category's name, description, and type. Change what you want and click **OK**.

## TA-DUM! Supercategories!

Supercategories don't really have anything to do with comic book heroes. A *supercategory* is a way to group categories to get a more general overview of where your money goes. Unlike categories and subcategories, you don't assign supercategories to transactions in your account register. Instead, you can use supercategories in budgets and cash flow reports to see the total amount you spent on or received from a group of categories.

For example, let's say that besides your Bait category, you've got one for rods and reels, one for your boat, and one for gifts you give to your spouse to make up for all the time you spend at the lake. You can set up a Fishing supercategory and group the Bait, Rods and Reels, Boat, and Spousal Gifts categories under it. Then when you create a budget, Quicken will add up all the amounts for the four categories and show the total you spent on fishing.

As another example, you could create a supercategory "Food" that includes the Dining and Groceries categories. Then your budget or cash flow report will show the total amount you spent on food.

When you click on the **Super** button in the Category & Transfer List window, the Manage Supercategories dialog box appears, as shown in the following figure.

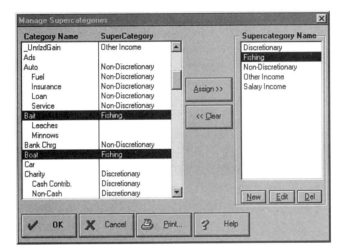

*Supercategories are used as umbrellas for your categories.*

To add a new supercategory, click the **New** button. Type in the supercategory name and click **OK**.

To group categories under a supercategory, click on the supercategory name. Then in the Category Name list, click on the category you want (hold down the **Ctrl** key to select more than one), and click **Assign>>**. The supercategory displays next to the category name.

If you don't want a category to be grouped under a supercategory, click on the category name and select <<**Clear**.

Although you create supercategories in the Category & Transfer List window, you won't see them listed with the categories and subcategories. The only place to see them is in the Manage Supercategories dialog box, and in budgets, budget reports, and cash flow reports. (Chapter 12 describes reports and Chapter 15 describes creating budgets.)

## Category Reports

You can create an instant report that lists all the transactions for a category and totals the amounts. Just select the category you want from the Category & Transfer List and click the **Report** button at the top right of the window. The following figure shows a sample report for the Dining category.

*The category report shows each transaction for a category and their totals.*

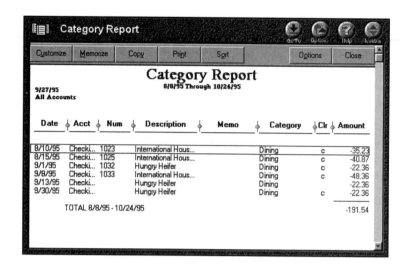

You'll learn more about using reports in Chapter 12.

# Pay Attention, Class

Now that you've conquered categories, you're ready to move on to classes. You probably won't use classes as often as categories, but they're convenient little buggers to have around. Remember that classes let you specify where, to what, or to whom your categories apply. You can assign a class and a category to transactions in your account register. As an example, we'll set up a class to categorize your fishing expenses for a trip to Tahiti to catch goldfish.

# How Classes, Categories, and Supercategories Work Together

All these sub- and supercategories and classes can get rather confusing. I'll try to sort it all out for you.

To carry out our fishing example, we have:

➤ a Bait category

➤ Minnows and Leeches subcategories

➤ a Tahiti Trip class

➤ a Fishing supercategory

In the account register, you assign the Bait category to a transaction when you buy bait. You use the subcategories (Minnows and Leeches) to specify what type of bait you buy.

Then you can assign the Tahiti Trip class to a transaction when you buy bait for your trip to Tahiti. If you buy bait for another trip or reason, you can either not assign a class to that transaction or create another class.

When you create a budget or cash flow report, you use the Fishing supercategory to see the total for those transactions that include the Bait category, Leeches and Minnows subcategories, and Tahiti Trip class.

## Adding, Editing, and Deleting Classes

Unlike categories, Quicken does not provide any predefined classes. But working with classes is essentially the same as working with categories.

Select **Class** from the **Lists** menu, or press **Ctrl+L**, to bring up the Class List, shown in the following figure. Notice that it has some of the same icons as the Category & Transfer List.

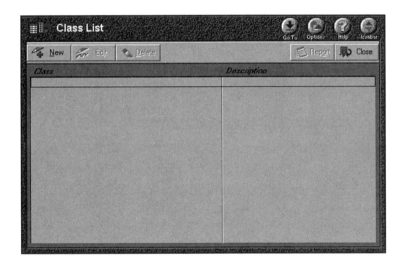

*The Class List is similar to the Category & Transfer List.*

To add a new class:

1. Click on the **New** button. The Set Up Class dialog box appears, as shown in the following figure.

*Adding a new class.*

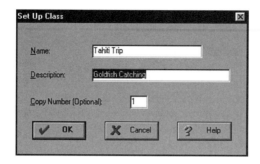

2. Type in the name of the class. For our example, type **Tahiti Trip**.

3. Enter a description of the class (optional), such as Goldfish Catching.

4. Click **OK** or press **Enter**. Your new class shows up in the Class List.

### What Does the Copy Number Do?

If you receive multiple copies of some tax forms, such as W-2s, you can assign a number for each copy of the form. For example, if you have two jobs and get two W-2s, you can set up a class for Job 1. Type **1** in the Copy Number field of the Set Up Class dialog box to assign the first W-2 to Job 1. Then set up a class for Job 2 and type **2** in the Copy Number field.

You edit and delete classes the same way you do categories; select the class you want and then click the **Edit** or **Delete** button. Remember that deleting a class will delete it from all the registers, reports, graphs, and planners.

## Assigning Classes to Transactions

Now flip back to your account register. Before you assign a class to a transaction, you first have to give it a category. Then there are two ways to give it a class:

➤ Open the Class List and double-click on the class you want. It then appears in the Category field of the account register, like this:

Bait/Tahiti Trip

If you've chosen a subcategory too, the Category field will look like this:

Bait:Minnows/Tahiti Trip

➤ If that's too much clicking, select the Category field in the account register and type a slash (/) and the first few letters of the class. Quicken will fill it in. Don't forget the slash, or Quicken will beep at you.

## Class Reports

When you get back from your intrepid goldfish adventure, you can tell at a glance how much it set you back. From the Class List, select **Tahiti Trip** and click the **Report** button. The report will show every transaction you assigned to the Tahiti Trip class.

# The Least You Need to Know

Categories and classes help you get the most bang for your buck. Some of the things you saw in the chapter include the following:

➤ Categories help you keep track of where your money goes. Quicken uses them for reports, budgets, graphs, and planners.

➤ Use the Category & Transfer List to add new categories and subcategories, edit and delete categories, create supercategories, and view category reports.

➤ Classes specify where, to what, or to whom your categories apply.

➤ Working with classes is nearly identical to working with categories.

# Chapter 7

# Fine Tuning with Splits, Transfers, and Memorized Transactions

## In This Chapter

➤ Assign several categories to a transaction with splits

➤ The shell game: transferring money between accounts

➤ Working with memorized transactions

You ought to breeze right through this chapter because you've already been introduced to the things I'm going to talk about: splits, transfers, and memorized transactions. Now that you've got your accounts in place, these gadgets make it easier to work with them.

When you entered transactions in your register in Chapter 5, you saw a Splits button in the account register. *Splits* let you assign more than one category to a single transaction, and specify how much you spent on each category in the split.

Chapter 6 dealt with the Category & Transfer List, where we talked about categories but skipped over transfers. In this chapter you'll learn how to transfer funds between your Quicken accounts.

Also in Chapter 5, I gave you a brief introduction to memorized transactions. When you type a new name in the Payee field, Quicken records the name, amount, and category in the Payee drop-down list so you can select it again later. The names, amounts, and categories are *memorized transactions*, and in this chapter you'll learn how to work with them in the Memorized Transaction List.

# Do the Splits

In Chapter 6 we talked about assigning a category to a transaction. But on your last trip to Joe's Department Store and Bait Shop, you spent $26 on a Deluxe Bagel Beauty wide-slot toaster, $134 on tennis shoes with flashing lights, and $17.50 on bait for your Tahiti excursion (now you just have to figure out how to get those worms through customs). How do you include categories for small appliances, clothing, and bait in one transaction?

With a split. Splits let you keep track of different amounts for different categories in one transaction. This is how it works:

1. Enter the transaction in your register, including the total amount spent in the Payment column (in our example, $177.50). If it's a split deposit, put the total in the Deposit column.

2. Tab over to the Category column.

3. Click on the **Splits** button. The Splits window displays to let you enter several categories for this one transaction.

4. Select a category from the drop-down list.

5. Include a memo, if you want.

6. Type in the amount you spent on the category.

7. Repeat steps 4-6 for up to 30 categories.

8. Click **OK**.

The following figure shows the Splits window for our example.

*Splits allow you to record more than one category for a transaction.*

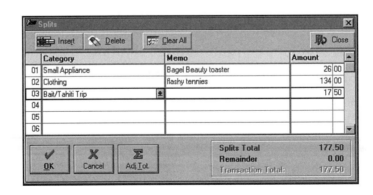

# The Splits Window

The Splits window has buttons to help you work with your split transaction: Insert, Delete, Clear All, and Adj. Tot.

➤ Click **Insert** to insert a new line above the current line.

➤ Click **Delete** to erase the current line.

➤ If you want to get rid of all the categories and amounts and start over, click **Clear All**. A confirmation window will pop up to make sure you really want to do that.

➤ If you enter all your categories and discover that the total is different than the amount you entered in the register, click **Adj. Tot.** The register amount changes to match the total of the splits.

➤ Click **Close** or **Cancel** to close the Splits window without recording the split.

When you're done, the Category field in the register shows —Splits—, a green checkmark and a red X to indicate that there's more than one category for this transaction (see the following figure). Click on the checkmark to see the Splits window again and make any changes. The red X clears the split categories from the transaction, just like the Clear All button in the Splits window.

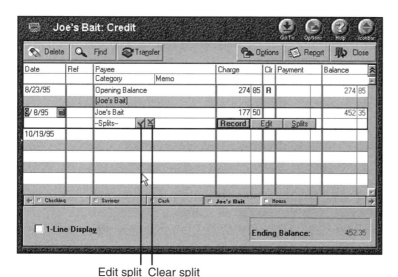

*The account register shows which transactions are splits.*

Edit split  Clear split

# Throw Your Money Around

In Chapter 6 you met up with the Category & Transfer List. What I didn't tell you then is that the Category & Transfer List also shows the names of all the accounts you've set up so you can transfer funds between accounts. For example, you write a check to Joe's Bait & Department Store for all the wild worms you charged and record it in your checking account register. With a *transfer*, you tell Quicken to record the payment in the Joe's Bait account register at the same time. That way you don't have to enter the same transaction twice.

You can also record cash transfers between accounts; for example, if you withdraw $100 from your savings account and deposit it into your checking account.

## Transferring Money Between Accounts

There are two ways to transfer money between accounts: with a transaction and with the Transfer button in the account register window. We'll cover transferring with a transaction first.

To transfer money between accounts with a transaction, record the check to Joe's just as you would any other in your checking account register. In the Category field, scroll down to the bottom of the drop-down list and you'll find your other accounts listed in brackets.

When you select [Joe's Bait] from the list, two things happen. First, [Joe's Bait] appears in the Category field of your checking account register. Second, Quicken inserts a new transaction in your credit card register with the date, the payee name, the amount of the check shown as a payment, and [Checking] in the Category field (see the following figure).

*Quicken records a transfer in both accounts.*

Transfer from checking—

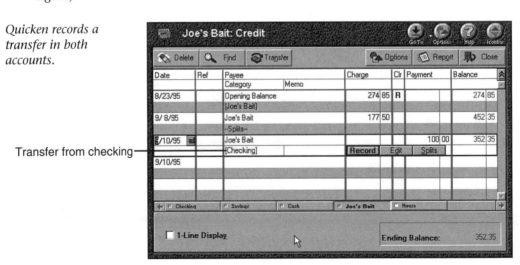

The second way to transfer money between accounts is to click on the **Transfer** button in the account register window. The following figure shows the Transfer Money Between Accounts dialog box.

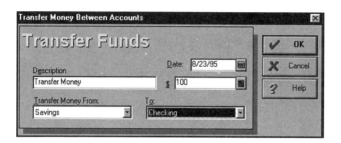

*You can also use the Transfer button to transfer money between accounts.*

In the Transfer Money Between Accounts dialog box:

1. In the Date field, click on the **Calendar icon** to enter the date of the transfer.

2. In the $ field, type the amount of the transfer.

3. The Transfer Money From: field shows the account register that was open when you clicked the **Transfer** button. If you're transferring funds from a different account, select the account name from the drop-down list.

4. In the To: drop-down list, select the account to which you're transferring the money.

5. Click **OK**. Quicken records the transfer in both account registers.

You can transfer money between all types of accounts. It doesn't matter whether you record the transfer coming or going. In other words, if you're transferring money from a savings to a checking account, you can enter the transaction in the savings account as a withdrawal, select [Checking] from the category drop-down list, and let Quicken record it in the checking account as a deposit. Or you can record the checking account deposit, select [Savings] from the category drop-down list, and let Quicken deduct it from your savings.

## Finding Where Your Money Went

You recorded your transfer transaction in one account and want to see the reciprocal transaction in the second account. You could switch registers and scroll through the transactions until you find it, muttering to yourself that there's got to be an easier way. Take heart, there is:

1. If it's not already highlighted, click on the transaction you entered.

2. Click on the **Edit** button.

3. Select **Go to Transfer** from the menu.

4. The second account register pops up with the transfer transaction highlighted. Repeat the process to jump back.

# No Mnemonic Devices Needed

In Chapter 5, I showed you that when you enter your transactions in your account register, Quicken creates a drop-down list in the Payee field so you don't have to retype the name.

This drop-down list also shows the amount of the transaction—a minus sign (-) indicates a payment; a plus sign (+) indicates a deposit—and its category or split. This is a *memorized transaction*. Quicken creates them automatically every time you enter a transaction, or you can do it yourself.

## Turning Off Automatic Memorized Transactions

Quicken automatically memorizes every transaction you enter in your account registers. After a while, this can make the Payee drop-down list quite lengthy, and you'll probably decide you don't need to memorize each and every transaction you enter. You can turn off the option for automatic memorized transactions by following the steps below:

1. Click the **Options** button in the window border (the Options button is available for every window).

2. In the Options window, click the **Register** icon.

3. In the Register Options window, click the **QuickFill** tab, shown in the following figure.

*Turning off automatic memorized transactions.*

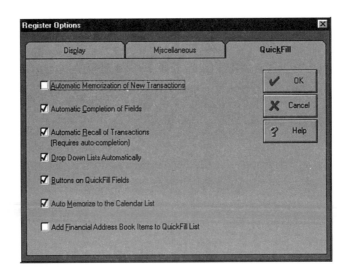

4. Click **Automatic Memorization of New Transactions** to turn it off, and click **OK**.

5. Click **Close** to close the Options window.

After you turn off the automatic memorization, the Payee drop-down list holds the same memorized transactions that it did before. But Quicken won't automatically add new transactions to the list; you'll have to memorize a transaction yourself. The next section tells you how to do it.

# The Memorized Transaction List

With the Memorized Transaction List (shown in the following figure), you can add, edit, and delete memorized transactions to change what appears in the Payee drop-down list. You can also create a report on memorized transactions. To work with the Memorized Transaction list, select **Memorized Transaction** from the **Lists** menu or press **Ctrl+T**.

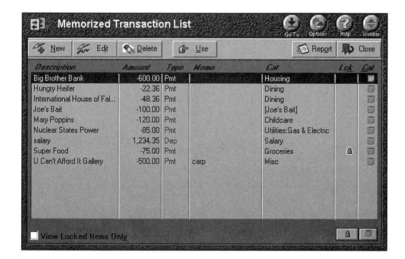

*The Memorized Transactions List.*

## Adding and Editing Memorized Transactions

There are two ways to add a memorized transaction to the list: either in the account register or in the Memorized Transaction List.

To memorize a transaction in the register, click on the transaction and select **Memorize Transaction** from the **Edit** menu, or press **Ctrl+M**. The transaction then appears in the Payee field drop-down list and in the Memorized Transaction List.

To add a memorized transaction in the Memorized Transaction List:

1. Click the **New** button in the Memorized Transaction List. The following figure shows the Create Memorized Transaction dialog box.

*Adding to the Memorized Transaction List.*

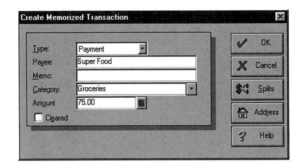

2. From the Type: drop-down list, select the transaction type (for example, a payment or deposit). Press **Tab**.

3. Type in the payee name and press **Tab**.

4. If you want to include a memo for the transaction, type it in the Memo field.

5. From the Category drop-down list, select a category for the transaction. If it's a split transaction, click the **Splits** button to open the Splits window.

6. Type the amount of the transaction and click **OK**. Quicken adds the transaction to the Memorized Transaction List and to the Payee drop-down list.

You can change any or all of the details for a memorized transaction by clicking on it in the Memorized Transaction List and clicking the **Edit** button.

## Deleting Memorized Transactions

After you've used Quicken for a while, the Memorized Transaction List can become rather long and cumbersome. You'll want to cull the transactions you use only occasionally or don't use at all anymore so it's easier to find the important ones.

To delete a memorized transaction, select it in the list and click the **Delete** button. A warning window gives you the option to cancel if you want. Otherwise, click **OK** to delete the transaction.

Deleting a memorized transaction deletes it from the Memorized Transaction List and the Payee drop-down list. It does **not** erase any transactions from the register.

# The Use Button

Clicking the Use button on the Memorized Transaction List is the same as selecting a transaction from the Payee drop-down list. Quicken inserts the memorized transaction in the last line of your register with the current date. You must have an account register open before you can click the Use button to add a memorized transaction.

# Lock and Unlock

Take a gander at the Memorized Transaction List and you'll see a Lck column along the right side of the window and a padlock icon on the bottom right. Lck stands for lock, not lick, so get your mind out of the gutter. *Unlock* means that when you use a memorized transaction and change the amount in the register, Quicken will replace the old amount with the new in the Memorized Transaction List. *Lock* saves the old amount, even if you change it in the register.

The transactions that Quicken memorizes are unlocked and the Lck column is blank. When you memorize a transaction manually, it is locked and the padlock icon appears in the Lck column. You can lock and unlock a transaction amount by selecting it in the list and clicking the padlock icon on the bottom right.

Click **View Locked Items Only** on the bottom left to see only the transactions that are locked.

# Memorized Transaction Reports

You discover that you're grossly exceeding your dining-out budget, so you want to see just how much you've spent at the International House of Falafel.

In the Memorized Transaction List, select Int'l House of Falafel and click the **Report** button. The report lists all the transactions for the International House of Falafel, with the date, amount of the transaction, and the total spent, as shown in the following figure. It looks like you'd better learn how to make falafel at home.

*A memorized transaction report.*

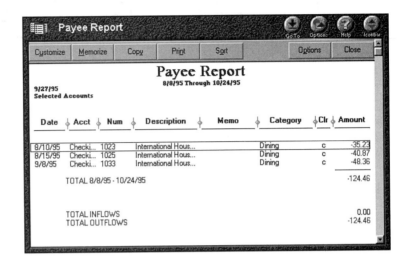

## The Least You Need to Know

In the era B.Q. (Before Quicken), you had to plod through your registers and bank statements like a '58 Volkswagen Beetle. With splits, transfers, and memorized transactions, you're zooming down the Autobahn in a Ferrari.

➤ Do the splits to record more than one category for a transaction.

➤ When you transfer money between accounts, you only have to record one transaction, select an account from the Category & Transfer List, and Quicken records it in both accounts.

➤ Quicken automatically memorizes a transaction when you enter it in the register. You can add, edit, and delete memorized transactions in the Memorized Transaction List.

➤ Memorized transaction reports list each instance when a memorized transaction was recorded in the account registers, including the dates and amounts of the transaction.

# Checks and Balances

Every household has a division of labor. My husband does most of the home repairs (which are endless in this bottomless money pit we call a home) and mops up the water in the basement after a heavy rain. I clean enough to keep the house from being declared a societal menace by the Department of Health, and twice a month I sit down and pay the bills.

I yearn for the day when I can tell the computer to scrub the toilets, but in the meantime Quicken's check-writing feature takes some of the drudgery out of bill-paying.

To write checks with Quicken, you'll need to order checks from Intuit Marketplace to use with your printer. (You can try shoving your checkbook in your printer, but I don't think it will work.) If you have a modem, you can use QuickBanking and QuickBillPay to do it all electronically. I'll talk about both features later in this chapter.

# Working with Checks

To write checks, select **Write Checks** from the Activites menu or press **Ctrl+W**. The following figure shows the Write Checks window.

*Use the Write Checks window to work with checks.*

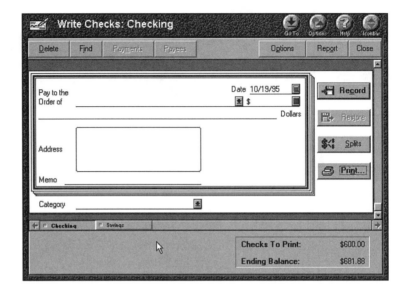

When you write checks on Quicken, Quicken automatically saves the transaction in your checking account register; essentially you're entering the transaction in the Write Checks window instead of the account register. The advantage is that you can then print the check on your printer from the same window.

When you select Write Checks from the Activities menu, Quicken assumes that you want to write checks from your checking account. Notice that along the bottom of the window, Quicken lists other accounts besides checking from which you might write checks. Just click on the account name to write checks from that account.

You fill out a check in much the same way that you enter transactions in an account register.

1. The check shows the current date. If you want to postdate the check, click on the Calendar icon in the date field and select a new date. Press **Tab** to move to the Pay to the Order of field.

2. There are three ways to fill in the Pay to the Order of field:

   ➤ Click on the arrow in the Pay to the Order of field to see a drop-down list of memorized transactions appears—the same drop-down list as the Payee field in your account register. Select a payee name from the drop-down list and Quicken fills out the Pay to the Order of, Amount, and Category fields for you.

> ➤ Go to the **Lists** menu and select **Memorized Transaction**. Click on the trans-action you want in the list and click **Use**. Quicken closes the Memorized Transaction List and enters the name, amount, and category in the check.

> ➤ Type in the payee name and press **Tab**. After you've entered the amount and category, Quicken adds the name to the Memorized Transaction List.

3. If you used a memorized transaction, Quicken fills in the amount. To change it or enter a new amount, type in the amount or use the Calculator to have Quicken enter the sum, then press **Tab**. Quicken automatically writes out the numerical amount (for example, Seventy-Five and 00/100) on the second line.

4. If you included an address when you created the memorized transaction, Quicken enters it here so you can mail the check in a window envelope. See Chapter 11 for more information on creating and using addresses. Press **Tab** to move through the Address field.

5. The Memo field serves the same purpose as the memo line in your checkbook. If you want, type in a note about the check and press **Tab**.

6. If you used a memorized transaction, Quicken entered the category for you. If you need to, click the arrow in the Category field (below the check) to select a new category from the drop-down list, or click **Splits** to choose more than one. The category won't print on the check, but it will be recorded in your register.

7. Click the **Record** button. Quicken saves the check in your account register and displays a blank check in the Write Checks window.

Big deal, you say, you can do most of that with your boring old paper checkbook. Be patient, there's more. You'll see the benefits soon enough.

## Deleting and Restoring a Check

Clicking the Delete button deletes the current check from the Write Checks window and from the account register. Quicken asks if you're sure; click **Yes** to delete the check and the register transaction.

If you want to delete a check after you've printed it, you should delete the transaction from the account register, since the check will no longer be visible in the Write Checks window. Or you can void the transaction to keep a record of it in the register. Chapter 5 describes how to delete and void transactions.

If you haven't recorded the check yet and want to start over, click **Restore**. If the check was blank when you started, Quicken restores a blank check. If the check was filled out, Quicken erases the changes you made and shows the original check.

## Finding a Check

The Find button locates a specific check and displays it in the Write Checks window. To find a check:

1.  Click **Find**.

2.  Next to Find:, type what you want Quicken to find. This could be the payee name, the amount of the check, the memo, whatever.

3.  Quicken automatically searches all fields in the register. If you want to shorten the search by specifying what field it's in, select the field from the Search: drop-down list.

4.  The Match if: drop-down list shows Contains. This means Quicken will find any checks that contain what you entered in Find:, but you can limit the search even further. For example, you can have Quicken find a word that starts with a certain letter or letters, or an amount that's greater or less than the amount you entered in Find:.

5.  Search Backwards is checked, which means Quicken will search backward through the check register to find the most recent checks first. Click on the checkmark to have Quicken search from the beginning of the register. After you click **Find**, click **Yes** to have Quicken continue searching from the beginning of the register.

6.  When you click **Find**, Quicken displays the most recent check in the Write Checks window. Clicking **Find** will *only* find transactions for checks that you wrote in the Write Checks window; it will not find transactions that you entered directly in the account register.

7.  If you click **Find All**, Quicken will list all the transactions for the search, whether you entered them in the Write Checks window or not.

## Check Reports

The **Report** button on the Write Checks window displays a report that lists every transaction for the payee from all accounts, with the date, category, and amount so you can see how much you've paid and when. Chapter 12 discusses reports in detail.

## Printing Checks

The easiest way to print checks is to enter them all in the Write Checks window first and then print the lot of them. If you quit Quicken without printing checks and forgot which ones you need to print, there are two ways to tell. In the Account List, there's a checkmark in the Chks column next to the account from which you need to print checks. In your account register, checks that need to be printed have PRINT in the Num field.

# Set Up Your Printer

Before you start printing you need to tell Quicken how to use your printer.

1. From the File menu, choose **Printer Setup**, then **Check Printer Setup**.

2. If it's not already, select the printer you want to use from the Printer drop-down list. If your printer isn't listed, you need to install the *printer driver* for your printer. The manual that came with your printer will tell you how to do that.

3. Auto-detect tells Quicken to detect whether your printer uses continuous-feed paper or single sheets. You shouldn't need to change this option.

4. From the Check Style drop-down list, choose the type of check you'll print (standard, voucher, or wallet), depending on what you ordered from Intuit Marketplace.

5. If your printer uses single sheets, you can print a partial page of checks. Under Partial Page Printing Style, select the icon (left, centered, or portrait) that shows how to place paper in the printer's feeder. If you're not sure, check your printer manual.

6. Click **OK**.

# Print Checks

When you're ready to start printing, click the **Print** button in the Write Checks window. The Select Checks to Print window pops up, as shown in the figure below:

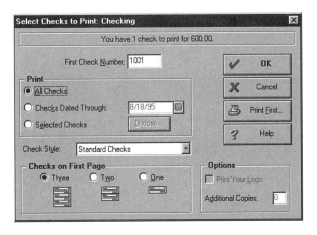

*The Select Checks to Print window.*

The bar at the top of the window tells you how many checks you have to print and their total amount. To print the checks:

1. Make sure the First Check Number matches the first number on your page of checks. When you're done printing, Quicken then enters the check numbers in the register.

2. You can either print all checks, checks up to a certain date, or selected checks.

   ➤ Click **All Checks** to print all of them.

   ➤ Click **Checks Dated Through:** and select a date from the Calendar to print checks up to that date.

   ➤ To print a few selected checks, click **Selected Checks** and the **Choose** button. From the list of checks to print, click in the **Print** column next to the ones you want (you'll see a yellow checkmark) and click **Done**.

3. If it's different from what you chose in the Check Printer Setup window, select a new check style from the Check Style: drop-down list.

4. Click on the number of Checks on First Page so it matches your sheet of checks.

5. You can print just the first check to test it by clicking the **Print First** button.

6. To print all the selected checks, click **OK**.

Now, wasn't that better than getting writer's cramp from writing all those checks by hand?

## Shop'Til You Drop

As I mentioned at the start of the chapter, you can order checks for your printer through Intuit Marketplace. You can also buy business forms, window envelopes, deposit slips, stationery, stamps, software, and other assorted doodads.

To shop from the comfort of your desk chair, select **Order Checks** from the **Activities** menu. The following figure shows the Intuit Marketplace window.

You can learn about the products before ordering by clicking the **Catalog** icon.

When you click on the product icon you want, Quicken will ask you questions about your order, such as the type of paper and quantity. When you order checks, have your checkbook ready so you can enter the information exactly as it appears on your current checks. Let's go through a sample check order so you know how it works.

### Decorate Your Checks

The standard Quicken check is pretty dull. You can liven it with fonts (type styles), pictures, and even your company logo. Chapter 19 describes how to customize your checks.

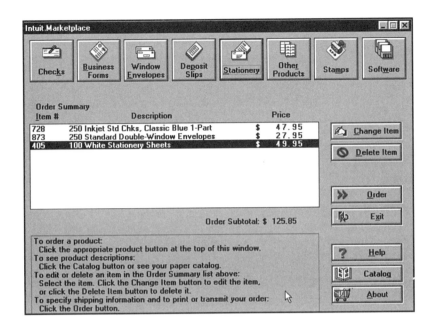

*The couch potato's shopping extravaganza.*

1. Click the **Checks** icon.

2. Type in your bank account number. Click **Continue**. Type your account number again to verify it. Click **Continue**.

3. Check the type of paper you want for the checks. Continuous paper has the sheets attached to each other and perforated tracks. Single sheet paper comes in separate sheets. If you're not sure which one your printer uses, check your printer manual. Most newer printers use single sheets. Click **Continue**.

4. Check whether you're using an InkJet, BubbleJet, or other type of printer, such as a laser printer. Again, if you're not sure, check your printer manual. Click **Continue**. The following figure shows the Size and Style dialog box.

5. Check the size of checks you want. Standard is three 8-1/2" x 3-1/2" checks on a page. Voucher is one 8-1/2" x 3-1/2" check on a page, with a tear-off voucher for accounts payable or payroll. Wallet is a 6" check with a 2-1/2" side stub. If the wallet option is dimmed, that means it's not available for the kind of paper you selected.

6. Click on the style you want from the menu. If you want to know what each style is, click the **Catalog** button.

7. Click the number of checks you want under Quantity. Quicken shows the price for the size, style, and quantity you selected. Click **Continue**. The following figure shows the Your Name and Address dialog box.

*Selecting the check size, style, and quantity.*

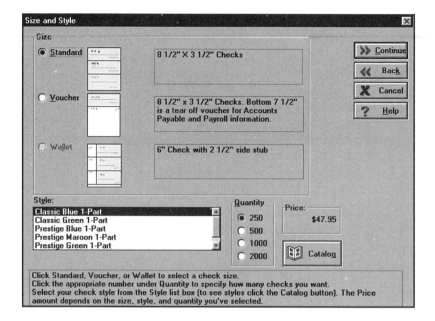

8. Type in your name, address, and any other information, such as a phone number, you want printed on the checks. If you want a line to appear in bold on the checks, click **Bold** next to the line.

9. You have three options if you want to get fancy with your checks:

➤ To have one of Intuit's prepared logos printed on the checks, click **Free Logo** and select a logo from the drop-down list. Check the catalog to see what they are.

➤ Click **Monogram** and type in a letter to have a baroque initial on the checks.

➤ For a one-time $35 setup charge, you can send Intuit your original artwork to print on the checks. Check this option if you want to use your own business logo. For more information on using original artwork, click **Help**.

If you don't want a logo on the checks, click **None** and then click **Continue**.

10. Type the name and address of your bank and click **Continue**.

11. Type the bank fractional number exactly as it appears on your checks. The bank fractional number is usually in the upper right or upper middle of your check and looks like this: 12-3456/1234567890. Press **Tab** to move to the next entry box as you type the number. Click **Continue**.

12. Enter the starting check number. Click **Continue**.

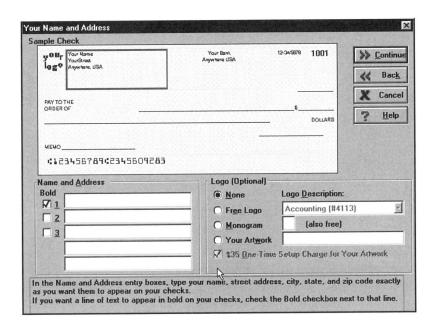

*Selecting what you want printed on the check.*

13. Choose whether you want one signature line or two. Click **Continue**.

14. Quicken displays all the check information so you can verify it. If you need to correct something, click **Back**. If it's correct, click **OK**. Quicken then helpfully suggests that you order window envelopes to go with your checks. In trade circles, this is known as suggestive selling.

As you order products, Quicken lists them in the Order Summary on the Intuit Marketplace window. Click **Change Item** to go back through the order process and alter your order. Click **Delete Item** to remove it from the summary.

When you're shopped out, click **Order**. You'll need to enter shipping and payment information, and choose whether to place the order by modem, mail, or fax. You'll also need to enter your local sales tax rate and your credit card number. When you click **OK**, Quicken will show you the details of your order in the Preview Order window so you can verify it before sending it out.

If you're ordering by modem, click **Transmit** in the Preview Order window and Quicken will automatically dial Intuit Marketplace and send your order through your modem. If you're ordering by mail or fax, click **Print** in the Preview Order window to print out the order form.

Thank you for shopping at Intuit Marketplace. Have a nice day!

# Take Your Money on a Trip Down the Information Superhighway

Lately you've been hearing a lot of brouhaha about the so-called information superhighway, which will someday allow us to do everything by computer. We'll never have to leave our homes again.

Now whether you look at this as a marvelous technological advance or a paranoid's fantasy, there are some advantages. With QuickBanking, you'll never have to make a mad dash to get a deposit in before the bank closes, or stand in line for twenty minutes when the guy ahead of you brings in $50 worth of pennies. With QuickBillPay you can say goodbye to that fuzzy feeling on your tongue from licking too many envelopes and stamps; let your modem do the mailing.

With QuickBillPay, you can write checks in the Write Checks window and then send them to your bank through your modem. Your bank then sends them on to the payee. With QuickBanking, you can transfer funds between accounts and get information about your accounts, such as balances and checks cleared, also with your modem.

To use QuickBanking and QuickBillPay, the first thing you need is a modem. If you don't have one, skip this section because it won't mean anything to you. Or go out and buy one; they cost as little as $50. You will also have to enroll in the online services with your bank or Intuit Services Corporation, and you will need an Intuit Membership.

To get to QuickBanking or QuickBillPay, click on **Online Banking** or **Online Bill Pay**, respectively, in the HomeBase window.

## Enroll in QuickBanking and QuickBillPay

When you click on **Online Banking** or **Online Bill Pay** in the HomeBase window and you haven't enrolled yet, Quicken will remind you to enroll. Click on the **Help** button to see a list of financial institutions that have partnered with Quicken to provide these services. Then call the bank to set it up.

If your bank isn't listed, you can still use QuickBanking and QuickBillPay through Intuit Services Corporation. Their number is in the Help window.

Once you've enrolled, you'll receive a welcome letter in the mail that gives you details about your account and using QuickBanking and QuickBillPay. When you set up a new Quicken account, the Set Up New Accounts window will ask you for information from this letter, as described in Chapter 4.

To add the online information to an account you've already set up, select the account from the Account List and click **Edit**. Click **Enable QuickBanking** and/or **Enable**

**QuickBillPay** and click **Next**. Quicken then will ask you for the information from your welcome letter. When you're done, a lightning bolt in the Account List shows that this is an online account.

## Join the Club

Next you need an Intuit Membership so that Intuit knows you've signed up for the QuickBanking and QuickBillPay services. After you've enrolled, click on **Online Bill Pay** or **Online Banking** in the HomeBase window, and Quicken will ask you if you want to set up a new Intuit Membership or use an existing membership. If you choose the latter, it will ask you to enter your membership number and password.

For a new membership, Quicken will ask for your name, address, and phone number. Then you'll need to enter a password and your mother's maiden name, which Intuit will use to verify your identity if you need to change your password.

When you click **OK**, Quicken will dial into Intuit with your modem, send the information, and display your membership number. You are now an official member. Your secret decoder ring will arrive in six to eight weeks. Just kidding.

## Pay Your Bills with QuickBillPay

Once you've gotten through all that rigmarole, you can finally use QuickBillPay to pay your bills.

1. From the HomeBase window, click **Online Bill Pay**. Quicken brings up the Online Bill Payment window.

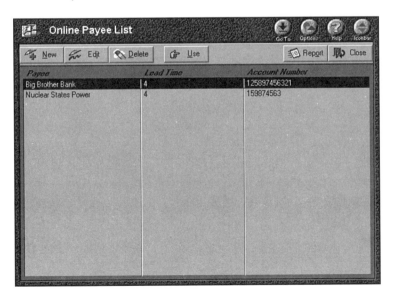

*Paying bills online.*

2. Click the **Checks** icon in the Online Bill Payment window to get to the Write Checks window. Notice that the Print button has been replaced with Send.

3. Type in the payee name and press **Tab**.

4. For online checks, Quicken maintains a list of payees separate from the Memorized Transaction List. When you enter a new name, Quicken will ask if you want to add that name to the list. Click **Yes**.

5. You will then need to enter the payee's name, address, account number, and phone, and click **OK**. The next time you write a check to that payee, just type in the first few letters of the name and Quicken will insert the rest of the information in the check.

6. Fill out the rest of the check as you would any other.

7. Click **Send**. Quicken has your modem dial your bank and sends the check.

## QuickBanking

With QuickBanking, you can get transaction information from your bank or transfer funds between accounts. Click **Online Banking** in the HomeBase window and Quicken will ask you to enter your Intuit membership number and your password. Click **OK** and you'll see the window shown in the following figure.

*Use your modem to get transaction information or transfer funds.*

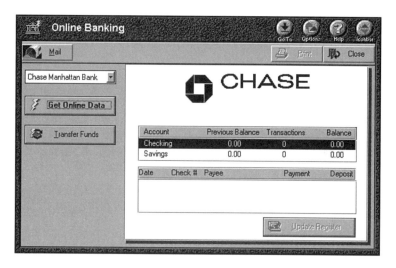

When you select **Get Online Data**, Quicken uses your modem to call your bank, retrieve information about your account, and send it back to your computer. You can see which transactions have cleared the bank and your most recent balance.

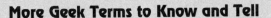

### More Geek Terms to Know and Tell

The process of getting information from another location and sending it to your computer with a modem is called *downloading*. Reverse it—send information from your computer to another someplace else—and it's called *uploading*. Toss those words around at your next cocktail party and impress everyone with your technological savvy.

To transfer funds between accounts, both funds must be online accounts. Here's how to transfer funds:

1. Click **Transfer Funds**.

2. Enter the amount to be transferred.

3. With the drop-down lists, select the accounts to transfer the money from and to.

4. Click **Send** and let your modem do the talking. Quicken will hang up your modem when it's done transferring the funds.

5. In the QuickBanking window, click **Update Register** and Quicken will record the transfer in your account registers.

## Surfing the 'Net

Quicken's latest whiz-bang feature is access to the Internet, that conglomerate of inter-connected computers that spans the globe. Click on the **QFNet** icon in the iconbar, and after you register, it will bring you to the Quicken Financial Network on one spot in the Internet called the World Wide Web. The following figure shows Quicken's "home page" on the World Wide Web.

*Quicken gives you access to the Internet.*

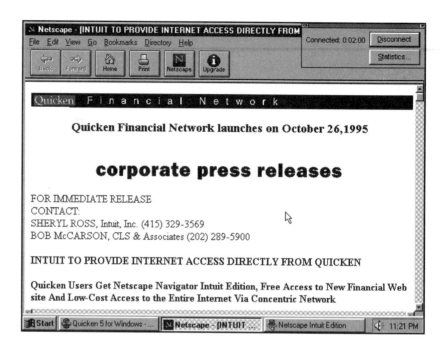

Here you can get information about Quicken and financial news from Intuit. Click **Upgrade**, and for a monthly fee, you can get wider access to the Internet—e-mail, news groups, flame wars, and all those other mysterious pastimes you've heard about. So grab a surfboard and hang ten on the 'Net.

Now that you've taken a short jaunt down the information superhighway, I bet you're rife with anticipation for 500 interactive channels.

## The Least You Need to Know

Quicken makes paying bills almost fun. And since it's all electronic, it hardly seems like real money!

➤ Write checks in seconds with memorized transactions.

➤ You can print a group of checks, checks up to a certain date, or a few selected checks at a time.

➤ Intuit Marketplace has checks for your printer, plus a cornucopia of related merchandise.

➤ Forget the printer altogether with QuickBanking and QuickBillPay.

# Chapter 9

# Make Peace with Your Bank: Reconcile Your Accounts

I know that as soon as you get your bank statement, you eagerly rip it open and balance your account to the last penny. Yeah, right. As long as you're not overdrawn, the statement goes in the shoe box or the circular file.

But now that you've invested in Quicken and spent the time setting up your accounts, expend the extra bit of effort to make sure what you have agrees with what the bank says you have. You'll feel better. I promise.

When you reconcile your Quicken accounts, Quicken performs all the calculations and shows you a list of cleared and uncleared transactions, so it's easier to find things you may have missed. It also gives you the totals for cleared deposits and withdrawals, so you can compare them with the totals on your bank statement. Balancing an account with Quicken is much faster and easier than doing it the old way.

# Paging Jimmy Carter: The Reconciliation Process

While you usually think of balancing only your checkbook, it's a good idea to reconcile your other accounts as well. I've found if I don't reconcile my credit card accounts, I forget to include the interest charged and I think I owe less than I actually do. It's a pleasant fantasy, but doesn't coincide with reality.

Quicken has slightly different reconciliation processes for three groups of accounts: checking, savings, and investment accounts; credit card accounts; and asset, liability, and cash accounts. I'll give you examples from each group, and then give some helpful suggestions if you still can't get the darn thing to balance.

## Balancing Bank and Investment Accounts

For this group, I'll use a checking account as an example. The same process applies for savings and investment accounts. Step by step, here's how to balance a bank account with Quicken:

1. Open your account register.

2. For each transaction listed on your statement—payments, deposits, and transfers—click in the Clr column. Quicken puts a **c** (stands for cleared if you're wondering) in the column. Click **Record** or press **Enter** after you clear each transaction.

   You do not need to enter separate transactions for interest earned or service charges. You'll take care of that in a minute.

3. Once you have all your transactions marked, click on the **Recon** icon in the main iconbar. You'll see the dialog box shown in the following figure.

*Reconciling a bank account.*

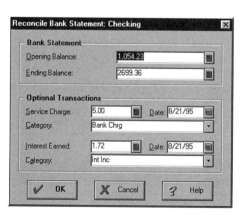

4. The opening balance is entered for you. If this is the first time you've balanced the account, this is the opening balance you entered when you set up the account. If

you've reconciled the account before, the previous ending balance on your bank statement becomes the current opening balance.

5. Type in the ending balance shown on your bank statement.

6. If there's a service charge, enter the amount and the date in the Service Charge and Date fields, and choose Bank Chrg from the Category drop-down list. Quicken will enter it in the register for you.

7. If you receive interest on this account, enter the amount and the date in the Interest Earned and Date fields, and choose Int Inc (interest income) from the Category drop-down list. Quicken also includes this is the register.

8. Click **OK**. Quicken displays a list of the payments and deposits that have cleared. In the bottom right corner, you can see the cleared balance, the bank ending balance, and the difference, as shown in the following figure.

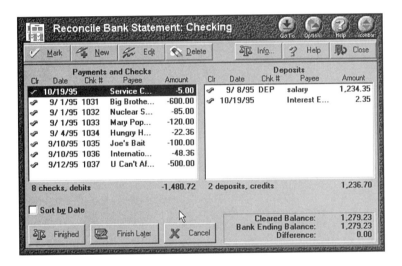

*The Reconcile Bank Statement window.*

9. If the difference is 0.00, reward yourself with a large bowl of chunky chocolate chip ice cream. Your account balanced. Click **Finished** and Quicken congratulates you with a cheery picture of a sunrise (I guess a smiley face would have been a bit much). It also asks you if you want to create a reconciliation report, which we'll get into at the end of this chapter.

When your account has balanced, Quicken changes the **c** in the Clr column of the register to **R**, for reconciled.

10. If the difference is something other than 0.00, you've got more work to do. I'll talk about how to get that sucker to balance in the section appropriately called "#*@%&! It Won't Balance!" later in this chapter.

**Check This Out...**

### Not Tonight, Dear, I Have a Headache

If your account didn't balance and you don't want to deal with it right away, click **Finish Later**. Quicken saves the transactions cleared, the ending balance, service charge, and interest for the next time you want to reconcile. When you want to get back to it, open the account register and click the **Recon** icon in the main iconbar.

## Balancing Credit Card Accounts

Just as you did with your bank account, open the credit card account register, mark the transactions that have cleared, and click **Recon**. The figure below shows the reconcile window for credit card accounts.

*Reconciling credit card accounts.*

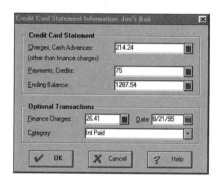

1. Enter the total charges and cash advances shown on your credit card statement. Do not include interest or finance charges here; you'll enter that in a minute.

2. Enter the total amount of payments and credits from your statement.

3. Enter the ending balance.

4. For interest paid and other finance charges, type in the amount and date and select **Int Exp** from the Category drop-down list.

5. Click **OK**. Again, you'll see a list of the charges and payments cleared, the cleared balance, statement balance, and the difference.

6. Click **Finished** and Quicken tells you your outstanding balance and asks if you want to pay some or all of it. Talk about staying on top of your bills!

7. If you don't want to pay it now, click **Cancel**. If you do, select the account you want to use for the payment (checking is the *default*) and click whether you want to use a printed check or a handwritten check.

8. If you chose a printed check, Quicken brings up the Write Checks window with the name of the credit card account in the Pay to the Order of field. Quicken assumes you want to pay the entire balance and enters it in the Amount field. If you're not prepared to be that responsible, change the amount. (See Chapter 8 for more information about writing checks.)

9. If you chose a handwritten check, Quicken switches to the checking account register and shows the transaction as a transfer to your credit card account. Change the amount if you don't want to pay the full balance.

## Balancing Asset, Liability, and Cash Accounts

Open the account register, mark the transactions that have cleared, and click **Recon**. The figure below shows the Reconcile window for asset, liability, and cash accounts.

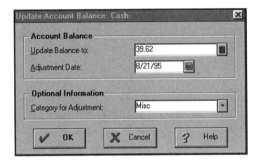

*Reconciling asset, liability, and cash accounts.*

Reconciling asset, liability, and cash accounts simply involves updating the balance in the account to match your statement or the cash you have on hand.

For cash accounts, enter the amount of cash in your wallet. If it's different than the balance in your cash account, you can choose a category to account for it. If you have no idea where the $8.38 went, that's what the Misc category is for.

If your asset or liability account has a fluctuating value, Quicken will make the adjustment here. Choose a category such as **UnrlzdGain** (unrealized gain) to explain the adjustment.

When you click **OK** for any of the three accounts, Quicken enters the amount and category of the adjustment in the account register.

# *%&! It Won't Balance!

You followed the steps to reconcile your bank account, but the difference is something other than 0.00 and the happy sun didn't congratulate you. Before you tear your hair out and hurl a brick through your monitor, try a few tricks to find the mistake.

## Check Your Opening Balance

If this is the first time you've reconciled the account, the first thing to check is whether the opening balance in the account register matches the opening balance in your bank statement. If it doesn't, click **Recon** again and change the opening balance to match your statement. Continue through the other reconciliation steps described above and, hopefully, this time the difference will be 0.00.

## Check the Cleared Items

First, make sure that you've entered all the transactions that have not yet cleared the bank. Then scroll through the list of transactions in the Reconcile window and check that they match your statement. You may have:

➤ Missed marking a transaction. In the list of transactions, click in the Clr column to mark it.

➤ Forgotten to record a transaction. To add a transaction to the register, click the **New** button.

➤ Missed entering a service charge.

➤ Entered a service charge twice. Remember that you entered a service charge in the Reconcile window; make sure you didn't also record a separate transaction for it.

➤ Mistakenly marked an item as cleared. Click the yellow checkmark in the list of transactions to unmark it.

➤ Entered a deposit as a payment or a payment as a deposit. I do that all the time.

➤ Entered the wrong amount for a transaction. To edit a transaction from the Reconcile window, select the transaction from the list and click the **Edit** button. Quicken will switch to the account register. When you're done editing the transaction, click **Recon** to continue reconciling the account.

As you mark, unmark, and edit transactions the balance difference will change. When it reaches 0.00, click **Finished** and bask in the sunshine.

## It's the Bank's Fault!

If your bank screwed up, click **Finished**. The Adjust Balance window will tell you the amount you're off; click **OK** and Quicken will adjust your balance by that amount. Call your bank and politely inform them that they're a bunch of dimwits. The adjustment will appear on your next bank statement.

## Fudge It

If you've exhausted all the possibilities and still can't find the mistake, or if it's such a small amount that you don't really care, click **Finished**. The Adjust Balance window will tell you the amount you're off; click **OK** and Quicken will adjust your balance by that amount. A Balance Adjustment transaction will appear in your account register.

> **It's Off Again!** Since Quicken already entered the adjustment as a cleared item, the balance will be off by the same amount the next time you reconcile. Just click **Finished** and let Quicken make the adjustment.

# Reconciliation Reports

When you're done reconciling, Quicken will ask you if you want to create a reconciliation report. (To create the report at any time, choose **Reconciliation** from the **Reports** menu.) The reconciliation report lists the cleared and uncleared transactions from your register and the ending balance. The figure below shows the Reconciliation Report Setup dialog box. It's a good idea to attach this report to your bank statement and file it away with the bank statement.

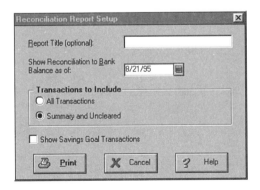

*Set up reconciliation reports.*

If you want, type in a title for the report. The date field specifies the date of the ending balance shown in the report.

If you click All Transactions, the report will show the details of all the transactions, in addition to a summary (number and amount) of the cleared transactions. Summary and Uncleared shows only the summary information of the cleared transactions, plus details of the uncleared transactions.

Click **Print**. If you want to see the report before you print it, click **Preview**. Otherwise, click **OK** to print the report. (See Chapter 12 for more details on reports.)

# The Least You Need to Know

Reconciling your accounts need not be an excruciating process. For one thing, Quicken does all the math for you, and that's 90% of the battle.

➤ To balance an account, open the account register and click **Recon** in the main iconbar. Enter the information requested, and let Quicken do the rest.

➤ With credit card accounts, Quicken gives you the option of paying the balance immediately.

➤ If your account doesn't balance, take a careful, systematic look at the transactions to find the mistake.

➤ If that still doesn't work, you can always fudge it.

# No More Excuses for Late Payments

I know what it's like trying to sort through those bills; every one is due on a different day. Most are monthly, but then there are those odd ones that pop up every three or six months. If you put it off at all, you find yourself scrambling to catch up before you start getting nasty notices calling you a deadbeat. It's enough to make you want to chuck it all and spend the rest of your life foraging for berries on a Pacific island somewhere.

With the Financial Calendar, you can see a month's worth of transactions at a glance, mark when bills are due, write notes to yourself, and even have Quicken warn you when you need to make payments and write checks.

And—prepare to say "Wow!"—when you reach the date of a scheduled transaction, Quicken will automatically enter it in your account register. However, you still need to remember to write or print the check yourself. Quicken isn't quite that good.

# Open the Financial Calendar

Click the **Calendar** icon in the main iconbar to see the Financial Calendar, which is shown in the following figure.

Click the Calendar icon to display the Financial Calendar.

*Keep track of what's due when with the Financial Calendar.*

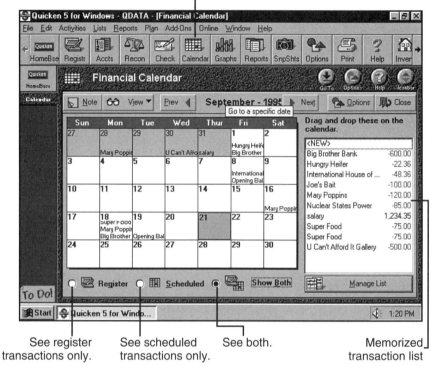

See register transactions only.

See scheduled transactions only.

See both.

Memorized transaction list

The calendar automatically shows the current month. To see other months, click the **Prev** and **Next** buttons at the top of the calendar.

### It's August, not December!

If the Financial Calendar isn't showing the correct date, make sure the date on your computer is set right. To change the date (as well as the time), click the **Start** button on the Windows 95 taskbar, choose **Settings**, then choose **Control Panel**. Double-click on the **Date/Time** icon and change the date (or time) in the Date/Time Properties dialog box.

When you include a transaction in the Financial Calendar to be reminded of it, it's called a *scheduled transaction*. When you first bring up the Financial Calendar, Show Both is selected, which means it's showing the transactions recorded in your register for the current month and any scheduled transactions (which you don't have yet). That can get rather crowded, so click **Register** or **Scheduled** to see one or the other alone.

# Adding a Scheduled Transaction

Now you get to practice the fine art of dragging and dropping. A list of memorized transactions is on the right of the calendar, under Drag and drop these on the calendar. (See Chapter 7 to learn how to work with memorized transactions.) To schedule a transaction, click on it in the list, hold the mouse button down, and drag it to the date where you want it.

## The Transaction I Want Isn't in the List

If you want to schedule a transaction that's not on the list, drag <NEW> to the calendar, and proceed as described below. Or click **Manage List** (at the bottom of the list) to see the Memorized Transaction List, where you can memorize more transactions.

When you release the mouse button ("dropping" the transaction on the calendar), the New Transaction dialog box appears, as shown in the following figure.

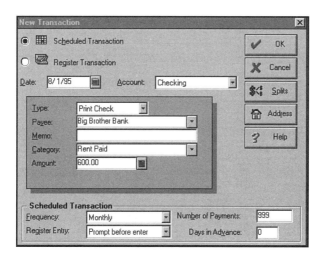

*Adding a new scheduled transaction to the calendar.*

After dragging and dropping the transaction onto a date, follow these steps:

1. Click either **Scheduled Transaction** or **Register Transaction**. Quicken will record either on the date you choose. The main difference between the two types of transactions is that a scheduled transaction will be recorded in your account register regularly and indefinitely; a register transaction is recorded only once. You might want to add a register transaction for a one-time or occasional bill for which you need reminding.

2. Check the date shown to make sure it's what you want.

3. Select the account for the transaction from the Account: drop-down list.

4. From the Type: drop-down list, select whether the transaction is a payment, deposit, print check, or online payment.

### Online Repeating Transactions

If you select Online Pmt from the Type: drop-down list, it's called a *repeating online transaction*. Quicken will send the transaction with QuickBillPay (or QuickBanking for deposits) on the date you specify. Remember to turn on your computer and modem and have Quicken running on that date. See Chapter 8 for more on QuickBillPay and QuickBanking.

5. If you dragged and dropped a memorized transaction, Quicken filled in the payee, category, and amount. If you need to change them, or if you dragged <New> to the calendar to schedule a new transaction, enter a payee name. Quicken will add it, the amount, and the category to the Memorized Transaction List.

6. Type in a memo (optional) if you want a note about what the transaction is for.

7. Select a category from the Category drop-down list.

8. Enter the amount of the payment or deposit.

9. If you chose Print Check for the type, click the **Address** button on the right side of the dialog box to enter a payee address that Quicken will print on the check.

10. If you selected Scheduled Transaction in step 1 (these options are not available for register transactions), do the following:

    ➤ From the Frequency: drop-down list, select how often you want the transaction to be scheduled.

    ➤ For any frequency more than once, the Number of Payments: the field shows 999. Leave it at 999 if you have an indefinite number of payments, or you can change it to reflect the length of a loan, such as 60 months for a five-year loan. You can then have the joy of seeing this number decrease as you make payments.

➤ Select an option from Register Entry. "Prompt before enter" means that Quicken will alert you before it enters the transaction in your register. Choose "Automatically enter" if you don't want a prompt.

➤ If you enter a number in the Days Advance field here, which is optional, Quicken enters the transaction in the register as a postdated transaction the specified number of days before the scheduled transaction date. For example, if you schedule a transaction for the 15th and put 5 in Days in Advance, Quicken will record the transaction on the 10th, but will postdate it for the 15th.

11. Click **OK**, and the new transaction appears on the calendar.

## When Do I Get Paid?

If you're using Quicken for your business, you may also want to schedule transactions for payments due from your customers. You can then create an accounts receivable report to see who owes you money. See Chapter 12 for details.

# Changing a Scheduled Transaction

When you click on a scheduled transaction in the calendar, a window pops up so you can work with the scheduled transaction, as shown in the following figure. You can edit the information you entered in the New Transaction dialog box (such as the payment amount or type), delete the scheduled transaction, record it in your account register before the scheduled date, or add a new scheduled transaction to the date.

*Working with scheduled transactions.*

Here's what you can do from this window:

➤ **New** brings up the New Transaction window that we just talked about. It's the same as dragging and dropping <New> from the list of memorized transactions on the right.

➤ **Delete** erases the transaction from the calendar. For example, if you delete the scheduled transaction for Joe's Bait, Quicken will delete it from all future months. However, it won't erase any transactions for Joe's Bait that are already in your register; Quicken just won't automatically record any new ones. Delete also won't affect any of the other scheduled transactions in the calendar.

➤ **Register** records a register transaction in your register before the scheduled date.

➤ **Pay Now** records a scheduled transaction in your register before the scheduled date.

➤ **Edit** lets you change the information you entered when you scheduled the transaction. But the Edit Scheduled Transaction dialog box (shown in the following figure) that appears when you click the button has one additional feature, Group Transactions, which we'll talk about next. So read on, MacDuff.

*The Edit Scheduled Transaction dialog box.*

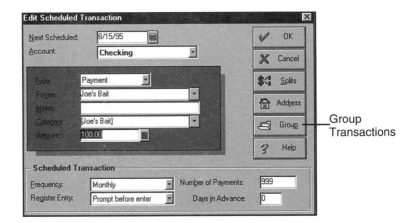

## Group Transactions

If you're like me, most of your bills are clustered at the beginning and the middle of the month. You can group several transactions together to have Quicken pay them all at the same time. Here's how:

1. Click the **Group** button on the right side of the Edit Scheduled Transaction dialog box.

2. Quicken displays the Create Transaction Group dialog box. Look over the transaction information (date, account, frequency, and so on) and make any changes.

3. Type in a name for the group and click **OK**.

4. Quicken shows you the list of memorized transactions in the Assign Transactions to Group dialog box. To add a transaction to the group, click on it in the list and click **Mark**.

**102**

5. Repeat step 4 for all of the transactions you want included in the group.

6. Click **Done**. On the date for the group, the calendar shows (Group 1). When the date rolls around, Quicken will record all of the transactions in the group at once.

## The Scheduled Transaction List

You can also add, edit, delete, and pay scheduled transactions from the Scheduled Transaction List. To get to it, select **Scheduled Transaction** from the **Lists** menu. The following figure shows the Scheduled Transaction List.

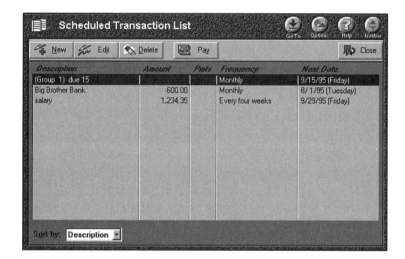

*The Scheduled Transaction List.*

The New and Edit buttons display the Create Scheduled Transaction and Edit Scheduled Transaction dialog boxes that you saw in the Financial Calendar. Ditto the Pay and Delete buttons.

With the Sort by drop-down list at the bottom of the Scheduled Transaction List, you can sort the scheduled transactions by description, amount, or the next scheduled date.

## What the Groucho Glasses Are For

The View button with the Groucho glasses lets you see the Financial Calendar in one of four ways: the calendar alone, the calendar with the memorized transaction list, the calendar with an account graph, or the calendar with both.

When you click on View, you see two options: Show Memorized Txns and Show Account Graph. A checkmark indicates whether that feature is showing. Click on the name to turn the feature on and off.

Show Memorized Txns shows the memorized transaction list, which we've already gone over. I don't think the account graph is terribly useful, but it looks really cool. When you click on Show Account Graph, this is what you see:

*A graphic account of
your money.*

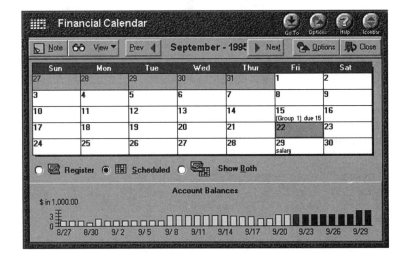

The account graph (shown at the bottom of the Financial Calendar window) shows the total actual balances for all your accounts, plus postdated and scheduled transactions, so you can see what kind of hole you're digging yourself into. The account graph shows the current month, with actual balances for past dates in yellow and future projected balances in blue. Click on a date in the calendar, and the account graph displays the balance for that day in green. It shows the accounts in thousands of dollars. Since my accounts are better measured in hundreds, I don't like to be reminded of my depressing lack of cash flow. But if you've got more bucks than I do, you might enjoy it.

# A String on Your Finger

Quicken provides a host of reminders to keep all this stuff straight. When you start Quicken, it reminds you which scheduled transactions are due in the coming weeks. You can also write notes to yourself and save them in the Financial Calendar.

## Reminders at Startup

The next time you start Quicken after scheduling transactions, a reminder window appears listing the transactions that are due.

➤ To record a transaction, click on it in the list and click **Record**.

➤ To edit a transaction, click on it in the list and click **Edit**. Quicken displays the Edit Scheduled Transaction dialog box described earlier in this chapter.

➤ To delete a transaction, click on it in the list and click **Delete**. The transaction is deleted from the reminder window and the Financial Calendar.

➤ If you don't want to do anything with the transactions, click **Done** and Quicken will display the same list in the reminder window the next time you start up.

# Calendar Notes

Tired of scraps of paper scattered hither and yon with reminders that you can never find when you need them? Take note: you can write notes to yourself in the Financial Calendar. Just do this:

1. In the calendar, click on the date you want to be reminded.

2. Click the **Note** icon in the iconbar at the top of the Financial Calendar window. The following figure shows the Note dialog box.

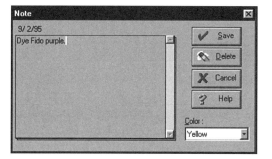

*Remind yourself with calendar notes.*

3. You have the option of changing the background color for the note. If you don't like bright yellow, choose another color from the Color drop-down list.

4. In the yellow (or other color) box, type whatever you want. It doesn't have to have anything to do with finances; you can remind yourself to dye Fido purple next week if that's what turns your crank.

5. Click **Save**.

In the calendar, a little yellow (or whatever color you chose) box appears on the date when you wrote the note. Click on the box to see the note.

# Constant Reminders

Whenever you have scheduled transactions due, checks to write, and/or notes to yourself, "To Do!" appears in the bottom left corner of your screen. It's there whether you're using the Financial Calendar or not. Click **To Do!**, and Quicken will tell you what's waiting to be done, as shown in the following figure.

*Quicken reminders: calendar notes, checks to print, and bills to pay.*

Click To Do!

You can see notes for a different week or month with the Show Notes for: drop-down list. If there are other activities scheduled, the appropriate icon located on the bottom of the Quicken Reminders window is highlighted. Just click on the icon when you want to print checks, record scheduled transactions in your account registers, or bank online.

The Options button at the top of the Quicken Reminders window lets you customize when and how Quicken reminds you of things to do. To change the reminder options, click the Options button and do one of the following:

➤ If you want Quicken to remind you of upcoming scheduled transactions whenever you turn on your computer instead of just when you start Quicken, click **Turn on Billminder**. You can then enter how many days in advance to be reminded, from 0-30.

➤ Click **Show Reminders on Startup** (of Quicken) and **Show Calendar Notes** to turn those options on and off.

106

# The Least You Need to Know

The Financial Calendar helps you organize your bills so you always know what you need to pay when. Here are some of the things you can do with it:

➤ View a month's worth of transactions from your account registers at a glance.

➤ Schedule transactions in the calendar. Quicken will then remind you when it's due and automatically record it in the account register.

➤ Group transactions to record several on the same date.

➤ See a graph of actual and projected account balances.

➤ Write notes to yourself that won't get buried under the debris on your desk.

➤ See the reminders when you start your computer or when you start Quicken.

# Chapter 11

# The Check's in the Mail: The Financial Address Book

## In This Chapter

➤ Organize your addresses with the Financial Address Book

➤ Customize the Financial Address Book

➤ Print addresses

In Chapter 8, I mentioned that you can print payee addresses on your checks, and that, for electronic payments, Quicken maintains a list with the payee's name and address. Now I'm going to tell you how it all works.

With the Financial Address Book, you can keep track of the addresses and phone numbers for your creditors, plus those for your bank, broker, bookie, and whomever else you want. The Financial Address Book creates a central list that you can sort, search, and print. You can also sort the addresses into groups of friends, relatives, and business associates.

## Starting the Financial Address Book

Although the Financial Address Book interacts with your Quicken file, it's saved separately from your accounts. You can open the Financial Address Book either from your Windows 95 desktop or from within Quicken. Here's how:

➤ To open the Financial Address Book from the desktop, click on the **Start** menu. Go to **Programs**, then **Quicken**, and finally, click on **Financial Address Book.**

➤ If you've already opened Quicken, click on the **AddrBk** icon in the main iconbar. The figure below shows the Financial Address Book window.

*Manage your addresses with Financial Address Book.*

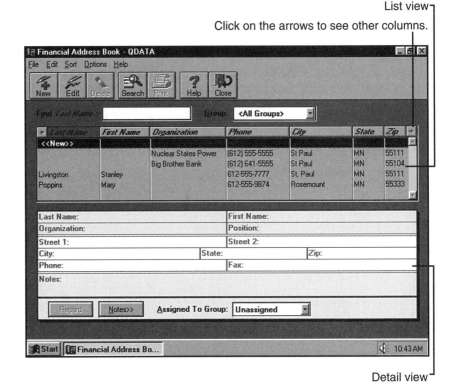

The Financial Address Book window is divided into two parts: List view and Detail view. The List view lists the addresses saved in the Financial Address Book. The Detail view shows the details of an address selected in the list, such as the address, phone number, and so on. I'll tell you how to change what you see in the window later in this chapter.

The first time you open the Financial Address Book, Quicken imports any addresses you've created in the Memorized Transaction List, the Scheduled Transaction List, and the Electronic Payees List. If you haven't entered any addresses, the Financial Address Book is empty and you can start from scratch.

# Adding Addresses

Because the Financial Address Book interacts with your Quicken file, there are three ways to add addresses to the Financial Address Book: from the Memorized Transaction List, from the Scheduled Transaction List, and in the Financial Address Book itself. (See Chapter 8 for details on entering addresses for electronic payees.)

## From the Memorized or Scheduled Transaction List

When you include an address with a memorized or scheduled transaction, Quicken saves it both to the appropriate list and to the Financial Address Book. To add an address:

> **It's Beeping at Me** If you click **Address** and get the message, "Transaction must be a check to have an address," you'll have to change the payment type in the Edit Transaction dialog box. Select **Print Check** from the Type: drop-down list and try again.

1. Switch to Quicken by clicking on it in the taskbar, or open Quicken from the **Start** menu.

2. Select **Memorized Transaction** or **Scheduled Transaction** from the **Lists** menu.

3. Click on the transaction to which you want to add an address and click **Edit**.

4. In the Edit Transaction dialog box, click **Address**.

5. Type in the address, phone number, and any other information you want included.

6. Click **OK** twice.

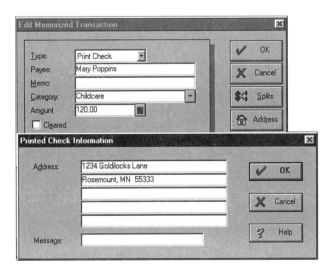

*Adding an address to a memorized or scheduled transaction.*

Two things happen next. When you bring up Financial Address Book again, you'll see the address listed. And, when you write a check for the memorized or scheduled transaction, Quicken automatically puts the address on the check.

# In the Financial Address Book

To add a new address to the Financial Address Book:

1. Click the **New** button in the iconbar or double-click on **<<New>>** in the List view.

2. In the Detail view, click in the **Last Name** field, if necessary, type the last name, and press **Tab**.

3. Continue entering as much or as little information as you need. Move between the fields by pressing **Tab**. The following figure shows a new address added to the Financial Address Book.

*Adding a new address to the Financial Address Book.*

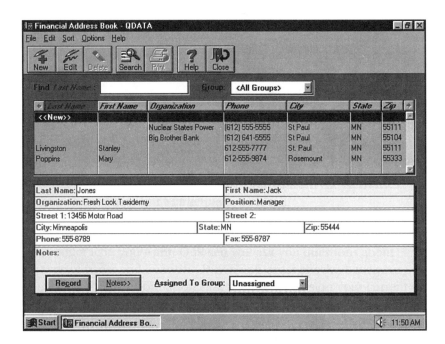

4. At the bottom of the Detail view, there's a space for notes. If your note is long, click on the **Notes>>** button. The Notes section expands to cover the entire Detail view section.

5. When you're done, click **Record**, and the address is added to the list.

# Editing and Deleting Addresses

People move, situations change, and from time to time you'll need to update the Financial Address Book to keep it current. To edit an address:

1. Click on the address to edit in the List view.

2. Click **Edit** in the iconbar of the Financial Address Book window. Financial Address Book highlights the last name in the Detail view.

3. Make the changes for the address in the Detail view. Move between the fields by pressing **Tab**.

4. Click **Record**. If you created the edited address in Quicken, the Financial Address Book automatically updates the memorized or scheduled transaction where you created it.

To delete an address:

1. Click on the address in the List view. You can select more than one address to delete by pressing the **Ctrl** key as you click. To select a range of addresses, click the first address in the range, hold down the **Shift** key, and click the last address.

2. Click **Delete** in the iconbar or press the **Delete** key.

3. The Financial Address Book will ask you if you're sure. Click **Yes**. The address will be deleted from the Financial Address Book and, if you created it in Quicken, from the memorized or scheduled transaction where you created it.

> *Techno Talk*
>
> **Editing Electronic Payee Addresses** You cannot update electronic payee addresses in the Financial Address Book; you must edit them in Quicken. I don't know why. It's just the way it is. To change an electronic payee address, select **Online Payees** from the Lists menu and click **Edit**.

# Grouping Addresses

The Financial Address Book lets you group addresses so you can search and print just the addresses from a specific group. For example, if you want to send out announcements to all your friends of your prize goldfish catch in Tahiti, you can print labels just for the addresses in the friends group, ignoring your family and coworkers.

The Financial Address Book provides five groups: family, friends, work, Quicken, and unassigned. All the addresses you create in Quicken are assigned to the Quicken group. Addresses that you create in the Financial Address Book (without going into Quicken) are unassigned until you give them a group. You can have up to 100 different groups. I'll show you how to add groups to the Financial Address Book later in the chapter.

## Assigning an Address to a Group

You can assign an address to a group either when you first enter it or anytime afterward. Just click on the address in the List view and select the group you want from the Assigned to Group: drop-down list in the Detail view. An address can only be assigned to one group.

If you want to see the addresses assigned to a group in the List view, select the group you want from the Group drop-down list located on top of List view. The List view then shows only the addresses assigned to that group. To see all the addresses in all the groups, select <**All Groups**> from the Group drop-down list.

## Adding Groups to the Financial Address Book

You are a charter member of the Society for the Preservation of Lawn Tennis and are responsible for the group's mailings. You need to create a group for the members' addresses. No problem. Quicken lets you add more groups to the Financial Address Book. Here's how:

1. From the Options menu, select **Set Up Groups**. The following figure shows the Set Up Groups dialog box.

*Adding new groups to the Financial Address Book.*

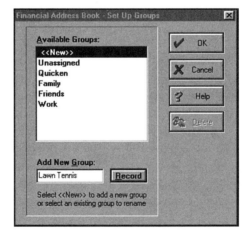

2. Type **Lawn Tennis** or any name you want for your group in the Add New Group: field.

3. Click **Record** or press **Enter**.

4. Continue adding groups, if you want. When you're done, click **OK**. The new groups will be added to the Group and Assigned to Group: drop-down lists.

## Renaming a Group

Lawn tennis has become so hopelessly passé, even you can't save it. The Society for the Preservation of Lawn Tennis has become the Kato Kaelin Fan Club. The membership is the same, but you need to rename the group.

1. From the Options menu, select **Set Up Groups**.

2. Click on the group name in the list. The Add New Group: field changes to Rename Selected Group To:.

3. Type **Kato Fans** or the new name for your group in the Rename Selected Group To: field.

4. Click **Record** and **OK**.

# I Don't Like It Like That

If you don't like the way the Financial Address Book looks, you can change the columns in the List view, the fields you see in the Detail view, the way the Financial Address Book sorts addresses, and hide the iconbar.

## Changing Columns in the List View

The Financial Address Book is preset to show Last Name, First Name, Organization, Phone, City, State, and Zip in the List view, in that order. If this doesn't work for you, you can add, remove, and change the order of the columns.

1. From the Options menu, choose **Change Column Order**. You'll see the Change Column Order dialog box, shown in the following figure.

*Add, remove, and change the order of columns in the List view.*

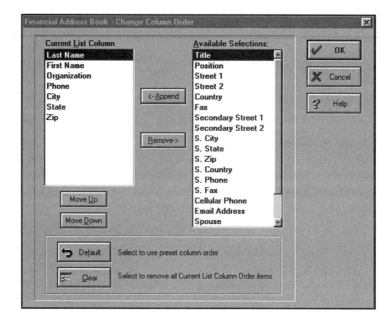

2. To change the order of the columns, click on the column name in Current List Column: and click **Move Up** or **Move Down**, depending on where you want it. Keep clicking to move it more than one position.

3. To add a new column, click on the name of the new column you want to add in Available Selections: and then click <-**Append**. The new column is added to the end of the current list.

4. To remove a column, click on the column name you want to remove in Current List Column: and then click **Remove->**.

5. If you want to remove all of the columns in the current list so you can add all different columns from the Available Selections list, click **Clear**.

6. If you change your mind about your changes, click **Default** to return to the preset columns.

7. When you're done messing around with the columns, click **OK**.

## The Available Selections Are All That's Available

While you can choose columns from the Available Selections list to appear in Financial Address Book, you cannot create new columns of your own making.

# Changing the Detail View

The information you can enter for an address depends on the fields showing in the Detail view. You may need a little or a lot of detail. To change what you see in Detail view:

1. Select **Show/Hide Fields** from the Options menu. The following figure shows the Show/Hide Fields dialog box. The fields that are available but hidden from the Detail view are in gray.

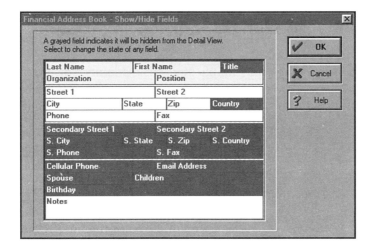

*Changing the Detail view.*

2. To hide a field, click on it. The field turns gray. The only fields that you cannot hide are the Last Name and Organization fields.

3. To show a field that's hidden, click on it. The field turns yellow or white.

4. Click **OK**. You'll see your changes reflected in the Detail view.

# Sorting Addresses

In the List view, the Financial Address Book automatically sorts the fields by last name. You can sort them by first name, organization, city, or any other column.

1. Click on the **Sort** menu.

2. If you want the Financial Address Book to sort by first name, organization, or city, select the appropriate option from the menu. The list view then sorts by your selection.

3. If you want to sort by another column, select **By_** from the **Sort** menu.

4. In the Current List Column Order: drop-down list, click on the column you want to sort by.

5. Click **OK**.

### Why Would I Want to Change the Sort Order?

If you keep track of contacts for your business, you may have a list of companies but not people's names. In that case, you'd want to sort by organization. Or if you're doing a bulk mailing, you'll need to print the labels sorted by zip code.

## Hiding the Iconbar

If you have oodles of addresses, you can hide the iconbar to give the List view more room. To hide the iconbar, select **Show Iconbar** from the Options menu. Select it again to show the iconbar.

# Dr. Livingston, I Presume?

The search feature makes it easy to find a specific name and address. To find Dr. Livingston without buying a pith helmet:

1. Click the **Search** button in the iconbar. The following figure shows the Search dialog box.

*Looking for Dr. Livingston.*

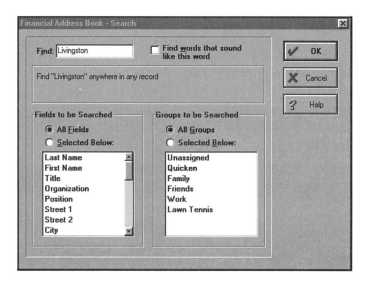

2. Type the word you want to look for in the Find: field. If you're not sure of the exact word, click the checkbox labeled Find words that sound like this word and the Financial Address Book will also look for similar words.

3. The Financial Address Book automatically searches all fields and all groups. If you know the word is in a specific field and/or group, click **Selected Below:** and select the field and group you want to search from the drop-down list.

4. Click **OK**. The List view shows all the names and addresses the search found.

# Printing Addresses

Once you've got your addresses in place, you can print all or some of them in five different formats:

➤ An address book with complete addresses

➤ A phone list with names and phone numbers

➤ Mailing labels

➤ Envelopes

➤ Rolodex cards

The thing to remember is that the Financial Address Book will print whatever is in the List view at the time you print, so make sure the List view shows the addresses you want to print.

➤ To print all addresses, choose <**All Groups**> from the Group drop-down list located above List view.

➤ To print one group, select the group name from the Group drop-down list.

➤ To print one address, click on it in the List view.

Before you start printing, it's a good idea to use Print Preview to set up the format and make sure it will print the way you want it.

1. Select **Print Preview** from the File menu. The following figure shows the Print Preview dialog box.

*Selecting printing options.*

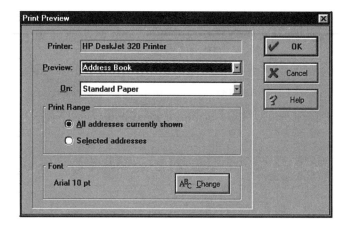

2. From the Preview drop-down list, choose the format you want: address book, phone book, labels, rolodex, or envelope.

**I Don't See My Labels in the List** The On: drop-down list shows Avery labels. If you're printing with a different brand, just make sure the size is the same as the selected Avery label.

3. The Financial Address Book will select the kind of paper that goes with the format. If, for example, you're using different size labels than what's shown, you can change it by selecting the correct size from the On: drop-down list.

4. You only need to change the Print Range to Selected addresses if you're printing one address.

5. Font shows the print type Address Book will use. Click **Change** to choose a different font.

6. Click **OK**.

7. If you're printing labels, the Financial Address Book will display a Print Labels dialog box that gives you the option of printing mailing labels or return labels. If you want to print return labels, click **Print One Page of Return Labels** and type the return address. Click **OK**.

8. The Print Preview window shows a full page of addresses in the format you chose, as shown in the following figure. Click **Zoom In** to get a closer look. If there's more than one page, click **Next Page**.

9. When you're satisfied, click **Print**. The Print dialog box will show the format you selected in the Print Preview dialog box. If you need to change it, you can do it here or click **Cancel** and go back to Print Preview. Click **OK** to start printing.

If you have trouble printing, Chapter 20 discusses common printing problems and what to do about them.

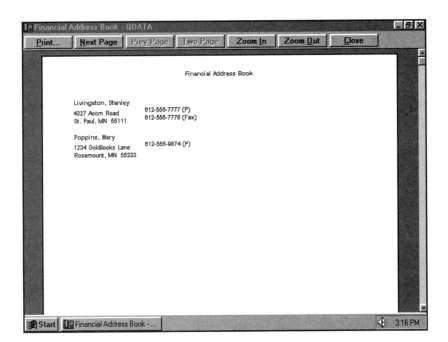

*Viewing your addresses before you print them.*

# The Least You Need to Know

The Financial Address Book is a handy way to manage your addresses. You can keep track of all your addresses here, not just financial addresses.

➤ The addresses you enter for memorized transactions, scheduled transactions, and electronic payees are automatically recorded in the Financial Address Book.

➤ When you edit a Quicken address in the Financial Address Book, the address is automatically updated in the Memorized or Scheduled Transaction List. Electronic payees are an exception; you have to edit them in Quicken.

➤ You can group your addresses to make it easier to sort and print them. The Financial Address Book will keep track of up to 100 groups.

➤ You can change the columns in the List view and the fields you see in the Detail view, sort addresses by any column, and hide the toolbar.

➤ Use the Search feature to find a specific name and address.

➤ The Financial Address Book lets you print an address book, a phone list, labels, rolodex cards, and envelopes.

# Part 2
# Reports, Graphs, Planners, and Things That Make You Say "Ooh"

*Part 2 talks about Quicken's fantastic features, the things that elicit comments like "Wow! Cool!" Detailed reports and 3-D color graphs are a mouse-click away. Budgets and forecasts help you determine your financial standing in the coming year. Quicken's Loan and Refinance Planners evaluate loan terms and mortgage refinancing. The tax-related features ease the pain at tax time. And for long-range planning, Quicken calculates what you need to save for your kids' college education and your retirement, and helps you create savings goals.*

*These features take the mystery and confusion out of financial management and planning. Fasten your seat belts. You're about to experience some financial wizardry.*

# Chapter 12

# Everything You Ever Wanted to Know About Your Money: Running Reports

## In This Chapter

➤ Reports for home, business, investments, and just about everything else

➤ Creating, customizing, and printing reports

➤ Tell Quicken to memorize the reports you use often

When I sit down to think about it, which isn't often, I'm amazed at the complexity of my family's finances. Besides the standard bills, I'm *still* paying off school loans and a car loan, and we recently added a home equity loan to our collection. Credit cards are a black hole; every time we get close to paying the suckers off, the car needs new tires or the furnace needs a new pump. Being self-employed adds a new twist to the plot. And we're a young, barely middle-class, suburbanite couple who think stocks, bonds, and mutual funds are for our parents' wealthier friends.

So beyond setting up accounts and scheduling transactions in the Financial Calendar, how can you keep track of all the pieces to your financial puzzle? One word: reports.

# Reports for Every Imaginable Situation

In previous chapters we touched on simple reports for categories, classes, memorized transactions, checks, and reconciliation. But click on **Reports** in the iconbar and you'll see that Quicken can create reports for every circumstance you can think of, and a few you can't.

*Quicken offers reports for home, business, investments, and EasyAnswers.*

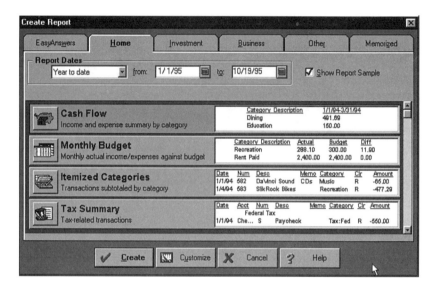

To find the report you want, click on the tab along the top of the Create Report dialog box and scroll through the list of reports. I'll discuss the different reports in each tab briefly. See the section "Creating Reports" for the scoop on how to put together a Quicken report.

## EasyAnswers Reports

The EasyAnswers reports give you quick answers to specific questions, such as how much you spent on a particular category or how much you've saved this year compared to last. The following figure shows the EasyAnswers tab.

The questions are self-explanatory; what you see is what you get. Use the drop-down lists to change what the report will show. For example, the first question asks, "Where did I spend my money Last Year?" Change Last Year to Current Month to see where it all went this month.

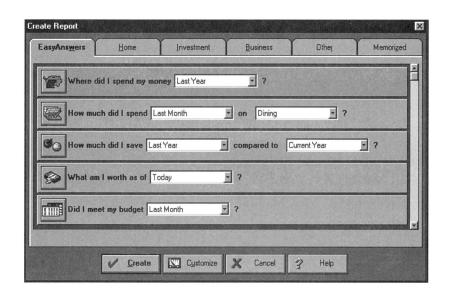

*The EasyAnswers reports give you quick answers to simple questions.*

# Home Reports

The Home tab gives a list of common reports for home use. Here's a brief description of each of the reports:

➤ **Cash Flow**   Summarizes income and expenses by category. It will show category subtotals and your total "inflow" and "outflow."

➤ **Monthly Budget**   Compares your actual income and expenses, by month, against your budget. Before you can use a budget report, you first have to set up a budget, which I'll talk about in Chapter 15.

➤ **Itemized Categories**   Subtotals transactions by category. Unlike the Cash Flow report, the Itemized Category report lists all the transactions for each category and shows a subtotal.

➤ **Tax Summary**   Lists tax-related transactions.

➤ **Net Worth**   Shows the balances of each account and calculates your net worth.

➤ **Tax Schedule**   If you assigned transactions to tax schedule line items, this report gives you a subtotal of the transactions for each line item. Very convenient at tax time.

➤ **Missing Checks**   Displays the transactions from your checking account and tells you if there are any missing or duplicate checks.

➤ **Comparison**   Compares income and expenses by period. For example, you can compare how much you spent this year compared to last.

# Investment Reports

Investment reports let you see your investments in a new light.

➤ **Portfolio Value**   Shows the value of all the securities in your investment accounts.

➤ **Investment Performance**   How well is that stock doing? This report shows the return on your investment.

➤ **Capital Gains**   I always think of George Bush when I hear this term. Anyway, this report shows the gains on a security you sold.

➤ **Investment Income**   Summarizes your investment income and expenses by category.

➤ **Investment Transactions**   Lists the transactions in your investment accounts by date.

# Business Reports

Three of the business reports in this tab, Cash Flow, Missing Checks, and Comparison, are the same as home reports, except they'll use the accounts and categories you set up for your business. The other reports are as follows:

➤ **P&L Statement**   Shows profit and loss by category.

➤ **P&L Comparison**   Compares the amounts for each category by date.

➤ **A/P by Vendor**   Lists the bills to pay, by creditor. You need to have the transactions scheduled in the Financial Calendar before you can create this report.

➤ **A/R by Customer**   Lists the payments due by customer. Quicken gets this information from the Financial Calendar.

➤ **Job/Project**   If you set up classes to track income and expenses for specific job projects, this report lists income and expenses by class.

➤ **Payroll**   Lists payroll income and expenses by employee name. To use this report, you have to set up categories and accounts specifically for payroll. The payroll report will only recognize categories and accounts that have "payroll" in the name.

➤ **Balance Sheet**   Lists your assets and liabilities. The report will include bank and other accounts, not just asset and liability accounts.

# Other Reports

The Other tab gives a few reports not listed elsewhere:

➤ **Transaction**   Lists the transactions from all or some accounts.

➤ **Summary**   Summarizes transactions by category.

➤ **Comparison**   Actually, this is listed elsewhere. Here it is again.

➤ **Budget**   Shows actual annual income and expenses compared to your budget.

➤ **Account Balances**   Summarizes your account balances.

Whew. I think that covered every possible configuration. They did leave out a report for what happens when you try to launder half a million in cash through a Bermuda front company before it winds up in an unmarked Swiss account. If you find this to be a glaring omission, let Intuit know and maybe they'll include it in the next version. Then change your name to Guido.

# Creating Reports

Nothing could be simpler. Creating a report involves exactly three clicks: on the tab containing the report you want, on the report itself, and on the **Create** button. Presto! You have a report which appears on your screen. The following figure shows a sample Cash Flow report.

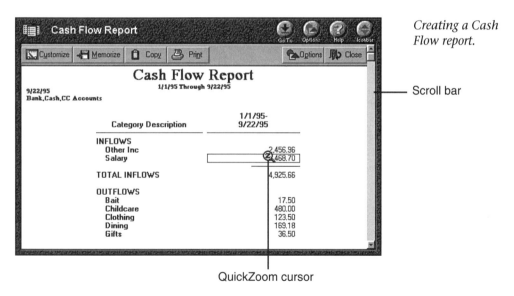

*Creating a Cash Flow report.*

Scroll bar

QuickZoom cursor

Click on the scroll bar to see the rest of the report that's not visible in the window. The following sections talk about the Customize, Memorize, Copy, Print, Options, and Sort buttons. (The Sort button is only available for reports that list transactions, such as Itemized Category reports.) But first I'll describe a handy Quicken feature, QuickZoom, which lets you see details about a specific transaction or other item in a report.

## QuickZoom Reports

When you move your cursor over certain items in the report, the cursor changes into a magnifying glass. This means that when you double-click on the item, Quicken will display a QuickZoom report that gives you more detail about that item or transaction.

For example, in the Cash Flow report, the cursor turns into a magnifying glass when it moves over the amounts in the right column. Double-click on the amount for Salary, and Quicken displays a QuickZoom report that details the Salary transactions, as shown in the following figure.

*A QuickZoom report detailing salary transactions.*

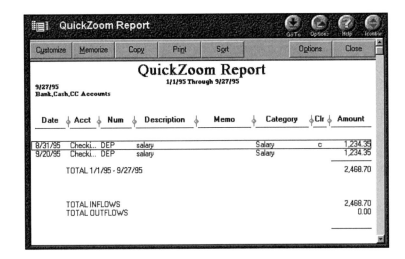

The items for which Quicken can create a QuickZoom report vary among the different types of reports. Whenever you move the cursor over an item and the cursor turns into a magnifying glass, you can create a QuickZoom report for that item.

## Copying Reports

If you want to include the report in a spreadsheet or word processing document, click the **Copy** button in the report window and Quicken copies the report to the Windows clipboard. You can then paste the report into a spreadsheet or word processing document. See Chapter 18 for more details on copying Quicken information to other software applications.

## Sorting Transactions in Reports

The Sort button is only available in reports that list individual transactions, as opposed to transaction summaries, such as the Itemized Category or Tax Summary report. Clicking the **Sort** button displays the Select Sort Criteria dialog box, shown in the following figure.

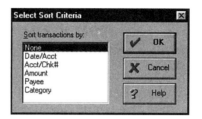

*Sorting transactions in a report.*

In the Select Sort Criteria dialog box, click on the field you want to sort by and click **OK**. For example, click **Payee** to sort the transactions alphabetically by payee name.

# Can I Change It?

Of course. You can customize the report's dates and layout, its settings, and the accounts, classes, categories, and transactions included in the report.

### What About the Reports in the Other Chapters?

I told you before that you could get more information on reports in Chapter 12. Well, this is it. Everything that I talk about from here on out also applies to the reports for categories, classes, memorized transactions, checks, and reconciliation that I mentioned in the other chapters. However, you cannot create these reports from the Create Report dialog box; you have to create them from their respective windows. For example, you can only create a category report from the Category & Transfer List.

## Dates

The first and easiest thing to change is the date of the report. When you click on a report in a tab, it tells you the period for the report (year, month, or quarter) and the starting (from) and ending (to) dates. By changing the period and dates, you can have the report cover as much or as little ground as you want. To change the dates:

1. Select the report you want.

2. Under Report Dates, select a new period for the report to cover from the drop-down list. Quicken will put the starting and ending dates for the period in the From: and To: fields.

*Changing the dates a report covers.*

Select a time period. ——

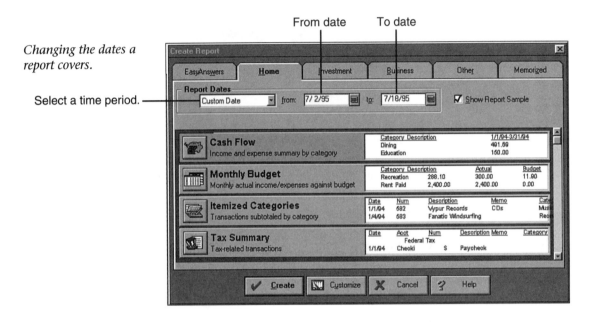

If you choose Custom Date from the menu, you can enter more precise starting and ending dates. For example, if you want the report to cover the period from July 2 to July 18, choose Custom Date.

3. If you chose Custom Date, click on the calendar in the From: field to select the starting date for the report, such as 7/2/95.

4. For a Custom Date, click on the calendar in the To: field to choose the ending date for the report, such as 7/18/95.

# Column Widths

Another common change you may want to make is the width of the columns. Some reports have column markers, as shown in the following figure.

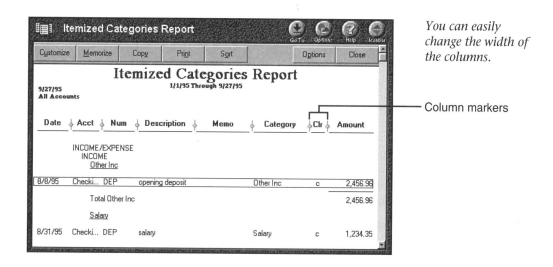

*You can easily change the width of the columns.*

Column markers

To change the width of a column, create the report, then click on the column marker and drag it to its new position. If some text in that column was hidden, it will show as much as the new width allows.

## Settings

After you've created a report, you can change how it displays the accounts and categories, and the default date ranges.

1. Create the report.

2. Click the **Options** button. The following figure shows the Report Options dialog box.

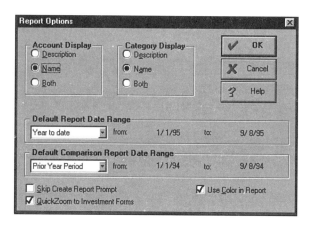

*Changing the report options.*

3. Under Account Display, select whether you want the report to show the account name, a description of the account, or both. You must have entered an account description when you created the account for it to display here.

4. Under Category Display, select whether you want the report to show the name of the category, its description, or both. Quicken's predefined categories have descriptions. If you created the category, you must have entered a description for it to show on the report.

5. The Default Report Date Range specifies the range of dates Quicken will automatically show in the Create Report dialog box. The current default is Year to date, so when you select a report, it automatically uses dates from the beginning of the year to the current date.

   For example, if you choose Quarter to date from this drop-down list, then whenever you select a report, Quicken automatically displays dates from the beginning of the quarter to the current date. You can still change it for individual reports, but if you consistently use reports for a period other than Year to date, you may want to change the default.

   If you choose Custom Date from the drop-down list, you can enter more precise from and to dates. See the section above on changing dates for more information.

### Techno Talk

### Just What the Heck Is a Default?

You'll hear this term a lot when working with computers. A default is an option that Quicken, or any other program, automatically uses when you perform a function. For example, when you print, Quicken uses the default printer. There can be default type styles, margins, dates, you name it. You never have to change a default for the program to work; Quicken selects the most common options for the defaults so you don't have to.

6. For reports that compare amounts between dates, the Default Comparison Report Date Range sets the range of dates Quicken will automatically use for the comparison. For example, if you chose Quarter to date for the Default Report Date Range, you may want to choose Last Qtr from this drop-down list to compare the amounts between the current quarter and last quarter.

The other options are things you probably won't need very often, but here's a quick summary of what they do:

➤ **Skip Create Report Prompt** When you select a report type from the Reports menu, Quicken normally will display the Create Reports dialog box before it creates the report. For example, you select the **Reports** menu, the **Home** submenu, and then **Cash Flow** to create a Cash Flow report. Quicken will display the Create Reports dialog box; then you have to click Create to create the report. If you select Skip Create Report Prompt in the Report Options dialog box, Quicken will create the Cash Flow report without first displaying the Create Reports dialog box.

➤ **QuickZoom to Investment Forms**   If this box is checked, double-clicking on a transaction in an investment report will take you to the investment form you completed for that transaction. If this box is not checked, double-clicking on a transaction in an investment report will take you to the entry in the investment account register for that transaction.

➤ **Use Color in Report**   When this box is checked, Quicken displays the report title and negative amounts in color. When it's not checked, the report title and negative amounts are in black.

## Customize Options

To customize the other options, click on the **Customize** button either in the Create Reports dialog box or the window of a report you've already created. The specifics will vary from report to report, and detailing all of them would make this book 800 pages long. As an example, I'll talk about customizing a Cash Flow report, which is fairly representative of them all.

## The Display Tab

In the Display tab, you can change the report layout and customize how the report displays the information, as shown in the following figure.

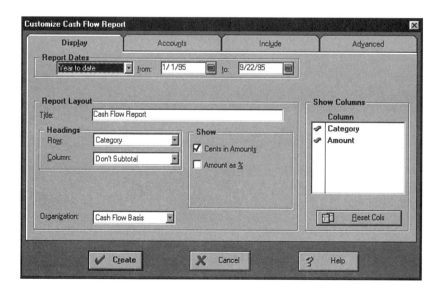

*Changing the report's display options.*

Here are the options you can change in the Display tab:

➤ **Report Dates**  You can change the dates the report covers here just as you did in the Create Reports dialog box.

➤ **Title**  Type a new title for the report.

➤ **Headings**  From the Row: drop-down list, select what information you want in the report's rows. For example, the Cash Flow report automatically shows your income and expenses by category. Select **Account** from the Row: drop-down list, and it will show your income and expenses by account instead of by category.

From the Column: drop-down list, select what information you want in the report's columns. For example, the Cash Flow report normally doesn't have a subtotal column. Select **Month** from the Column: drop-down list, and the Cash Flow report will display categories that subtotal your income and expenses each month.

➤ **Organization**  From the Organization: drop-down list, select how you want the report organized. For example, you can organize the Cash Flow report by Cash Flow Basis, Income and Expense, or Supercategory.

➤ **Show**  You can choose whether to show cents in amounts and/or show the amounts as a percentage.

➤ **Show Columns**  A yellow checkmark indicates which columns appear in the report. Click on a column name to deselect it, then click **Reset Cols** to format the report.

## The Accounts Tab

In the Accounts tab, you can select which accounts to use to generate the report's information, as shown in the following figure.

Here are the options you can change in the Accounts tab:

➤ The accounts included in the report have a yellow checkmark next to them. Click on the account name under Selected Accounts to deselect and exclude it from the report.

➤ Click the **Clear All** button to clear all the accounts so you can select just a few.

➤ Click the **Mark All** button to select all the accounts.

➤ You can include a group of a certain account type. For example, if you only want to include bank accounts in the report, click the **Clear All** button, then click the **Bank** button under Account Type. Quicken will select your bank accounts and include only them in the report.

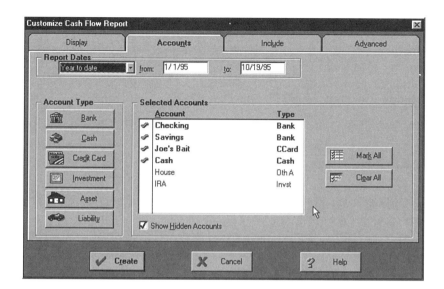

*Selecting accounts to include in a report.*

## The Include Tab

In the Include tab, you can select which categories and classes to include in the report. You can also tell Quicken to include only the payees, categories, classes, and/or memos that contain a certain word or phrase. The following figure shows the Include tab.

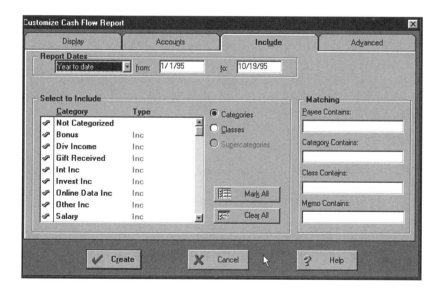

*Selecting categories and classes to include in a report.*

Here are the options you can change in the Include tab:

➤ Under Select to Include, click on the category names to deselect them and exclude them from the report (hold down the Shift key to deselect a range of categories). Click **Classes** and do the same to select which classes to include in the report. (The Supercategories option is only available for budget reports.)

➤ Click the **Clear All** button to clear all the categories or classes so you can select just a few.

➤ Click the **Mark All** button to select all the categories or classes.

➤ Under Matching, you can include only the payees, categories, classes, and/or memos that contain a certain word or phrase. For example, to include all transactions to Joe's Bait, type **Joe's Bait** in the Payee Contains: field.

## The Advanced Tab

The Advanced tab lets you specify which transactions to include in the report. The following figure shows the Advanced tab.

*Specifying which transactions to include in a report.*

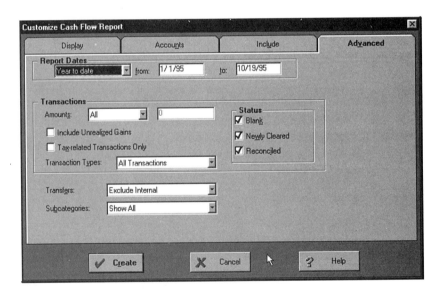

➤ You can include only those transactions that are less than, equal to, or greater than a certain amount. For example, to include only those transactions that are greater than $100 in the report, select **Greater than** from the Amounts: drop-down list and type **100** in the text box next to the drop-down list.

➤ You'll use the Include Unrealized Gains checkbox only if you have investment accounts. For transaction reports, click **Include Unrealized Gains** to have Quicken create new transactions in the report (not in the account register) that represent price fluctuations for securities. For summary reports, click it to include unrealized gains in the report.

➤ Click **Tax-related Transactions Only** to include only those transactions that are from a tax-deferred account and those that have a category assigned to a tax schedule (see Chapter 17 to learn about tax-related categories).

➤ From the Transaction Types: drop-down list, select whether to include payments, deposits, unprinted checks, or all transactions in the report.

➤ The options under Status let you decide whether to include transactions that have or have not been cleared in your account registers. Click **Blank** to include transactions that have not been cleared (there's nothing in the Clr column of the account register). Click **Newly Cleared** to include those that have been cleared but not reconciled (they have a **c** in the Clr column). Click **Reconciled** to include those that have been reconciled (they have an **R** in the Clr column). You can select one, two, or all three of these options.

➤ In the Transfers: drop-down list, select whether to include transfers in the report.

➤ In the Subcategories: drop-down list, select whether to include subcategories in the report. If you selected only certain categories to include in the Include tab, the report will only show the subcategories for those selected categories.

When you're done customizing the report, click the **Create** button at the bottom of the Customize Report dialog box to create the report with the options you selected.

# Printing Reports

If you want to save a paper copy of the report you've created, here's how you can print it:

1. Once you create a report and it is displayed on-screen, click on the **Print** button.

2. Print Preview lets you see exactly how the report will look before you print it. To see Print Preview, click **Preview** in the Print Report window. The Print Preview window shows one or two full pages of the report, depending on the length of the report.

3. Unless you have superhuman vision, it's difficult to see the specifics of the report. Click **Zoom In** to get a closer look.

4. If the report is longer than one page, click **Next Page** and **Prev Page** to see all the pages of the report.

5. When you're satisfied, click **Print**.

If the report is lengthy, it may take a while to print, depending on the speed of your printer. If you have trouble printing, Chapter 20 discusses common printing problems and what to do about them.

# Memorized Reports

As you use Quicken, you may find that you use the same report over and over. If you've customized it, you don't need to change the same options each time you create the report. Instead, create the report once and have Quicken memorize it.

Once you've created a report and changed the options you want, click the **Memorize** button to bring up the Memorize Report window (see the following figure).

*The Memorize Report window.*

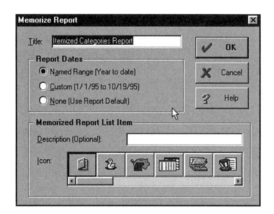

1. If you want, give the report a new, flashy title in the Title: field. If you're memorizing two of the same type of report (such as Cash Flow), you should give each one a different title to keep them straight. The title is shown at the top of the report when you create and print it.

2. Click on one of the options under Report Dates to specify how Quicken will determine what dates to use when you recall the report.

   ➤ **Named Range**  Click **Named Range** to have Quicken memorize the report with the date range period from the Create Report window. For example, if you created the report for the period Year to date, then the report will cover the period from the first of the current year to the date when you recall the report.

   ➤ **Custom**  If you chose Custom Date for the report period, click here to have Quicken memorize the report with the dates you entered in the From: and To: fields of the Create Report window.

   ➤ **None**  Quicken uses the Default Report Date Range from the Report Options window.

3. In the Description field, type something to remind you what this report is for, especially if you memorize more than one of the same type of report. For example, if you have two Cash Flow reports covering different date ranges, you could enter "Month to Date" for one and "Year to Date" for the other.

4. Click on an icon to associate with the memorized report. You might want to choose the piggy bank for a Cash Flow report or the Uncle Sam hat for a Tax Summary report. I don't know what you'd use the rubber ducky for. An Itemized Categories report for bath supplies?

5. Click **OK** and Quicken will memorize the report.

## Recalling a Memorized Report

The Create Reports dialog box has a Memorized tab. The reports you memorize will be listed here so you can select them when you need them again.

Click the **Memorized** tab and you'll see the memorized report's title, description, and icon. To recall a memorized report, click on it and click **Create**. You can customize it just as any other report.

The Memorized tab has a few options not available to the standard reports. Click **Edit** to give the memorized report a new title, description, or icon. Click **Delete** to delete the memorized report from the Memorized tab.

## The Least You Need to Know

Reports are one of the features that make Quicken more than a glorified checkbook. If you can click a mouse button, you can feel like a professional money manager.

➤ The Create Reports dialog box lists every report you'll ever need.

➤ To create a report, click three times and repeat, "There's no place like home. There's no place like home."

➤ Each report has a number of options you can customize to satisfy your whims.

➤ Use memorized reports so you don't have to customize a report every time you use it.

# Chapter 13

# Make Your Money Look Pretty with Graphs

---

**In This Chapter**

➤ Snapshots without a Polaroid

➤ Invasion of the Graphs! 3-D! In Color!

➤ Creating, customizing, and memorizing graphs

---

You've seen those computer commercials that show an overdressed yuppie creating elaborate graphs and charts with the click of a button. You thought it was just a Madison Avenue fantasy. Now you know their secret: they were using Quicken in those commercials.

## A Quickie Accounting of Your Cash

Not only can you create cool graphs with a click, you can get an instant overview of your finances. *Snapshots* show expense comparisons, net worth, categories where you're over your budget, the value of your investment portfolio, notes from the Financial Calendar, and a lot of other stuff.

To see snapshots, select **Snapshots** from the Reports menu. The following figure shows a sample Snapshot window, also called a page.

*A snapshot of your financial picture.*

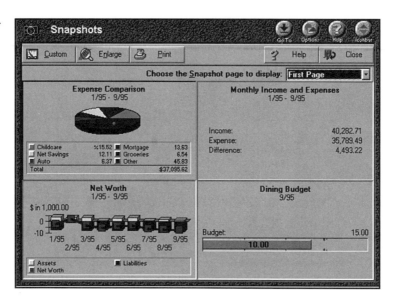

Each snapshot shows a different picture of your finances. When you first open the Snapshots window, Quicken displays four snapshots: Expense Comparison, Monthly Income and Expenses, Net Worth, and a category budget. But there are many more snapshots available. First, I'll list all the snapshots available, and then I'll tell you how to change what snapshots you see in the Snapshots window.

Here's a brief description of each snapshot that Quicken provides:

➤ **Expense Comparison**   A pie graph that displays your top six expense categories as a percentage of your total expenses.

➤ **Monthly Income and Expenses**   A bar graph that compares your monthly income and expenses over time.

➤ **Net Worth**   A bar graph that displays the value of your assets, liabilities, and net worth over time.

➤ **Net Worth Trend Line**   Shows the same information as Net Worth, but as a line graph.

➤ **Actual vs. Budgeted Net Income**   A bar graph that compares your actual and budgeted income over time. You have to set up a budget (see Chapter 15) before you can display this and the following three snapshots.

➤ **Actual vs. Budgeted Categories**   A bar graph that shows the categories where you missed your budget by the greatest amount.

➤ **Budget Goal**   Displays the current status of your budget for a selected category.

➤ **Supercategory Budget**   Displays the current status of your budget for a selected supercategory.

➤ **Savings Goal**   Shows your progress toward a savings goal. You have to define a savings goal before you can use this option (see Chapter 15).

➤ **Portfolio Value by Account, Portfolio Value by Goal, Portfolio Value by Security, and Portfolio Value by Type**   Bar graphs that show your portfolio's value by account, goal, security, and type, respectively.

➤ **Annual Total Return by Account, Annual Total Return by Goal, Annual Total Return by Security, and Annual Total by Return Type**   Bar graphs that display the average annual return of your portfolio by account, goal, security, and type, respectively.

➤ **Calendar Notes**   Shows the notes from the Financial Calendar for the current week.

# Customizing the Snapshots Window

Like just about everything else in Quicken, you don't have to be content with what it gives you. Click the **Custom** button in the Snapshots window to change which snapshots appear in the Snapshots window, customize each snapshot, change the number of snapshots that appear on a page, and add another page of snapshots. The following figure shows the Customize Snapshots dialog box.

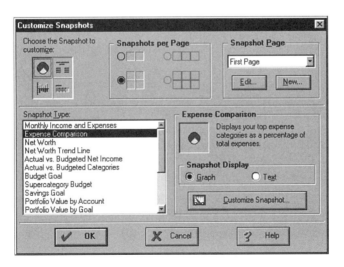

*Customizing snapshots.*

## Choose Which Snapshots to Use

When you click on a square under Choose the Snapshot to Customize:, its type is highlighted in the Snapshot Type: list. If you don't have a portfolio and don't need a portfolio value snapshot, click on the portfolio value square, and select a new snapshot from the Snapshot Type: list to replace it.

## Customize an Individual Snapshot

You can also customize each individual snapshot. When you click on a snapshot's square under Choose the Snapshot to Customize:, the bottom right corner explains what the snapshot is. What you can customize varies from snapshot to snapshot, but the following table gives you an overview on how to change the various options. In the next section, I'll show you how to select specific accounts, categories, classes, and securities to include in the snapshots.

### Customize Snapshot Options

| Customize Option | Available For: | How to Use: |
| --- | --- | --- |
| Snapshot Display | All snapshots except Budget Goal, Super-category Budget, Savings Goal, and Calendar Notes | Click **Graph** to display the information as a graph; click **Text** to display it as text. |
| Date Range | All snapshots except Calendar Notes | From the menu, select the period you want the graph to cover; for example, Year to Date or Month to Date. |
| Show Subcategories in Graph | Monthly Income and Expenses, Expense Comparison, Actual vs. Budgeted Net Income, Actual vs. Budgeted Categories | Click to have the graph display subcategories along with the categories. |
| Graph Supercategory Budgets | Actual vs. Budgeted Net Income, Actual vs. Budgeted Categories | Click to graph super-categories along with categories. |
| Choose Supercategories | Supercategory Budget | From the list, click the supercategories to graph. |

| Customize Option | Available For: | How to Use: |
| --- | --- | --- |
| Choose Category | Budget Goal | From the list, select the categories for which you have a budgeted goal. |
| Accounts | All snapshots except the budget snapshots and Calendar notes. | From the list, select the accounts from which the graph will gather information. |
| Categories | Monthly Income and Expense, Expense Comparison, Net Worth snapshots, Actual vs. Budget snapshots | From the list, select the categories to include in the graph. |
| Classes | Monthly Income and Expense, Expense Comparison, Net Worth snapshots, Actual vs. Budget snapshots | From the list, select the categories to include in the graph. |
| Securities | Portfolio Value snapshots | From the list, select the securities to include in the graph. |

### Income and Expense Filter? Is That Like a Water Filter?

When you select accounts, categories, classes, and securities for snapshots and reports, Quicken calls them *income and expense filters* because they filter what information the reports and snapshots use.

# Selecting Accounts, Categories, Classes, and Securities

Quicken automatically includes all accounts, categories, classes, and securities in the various snapshots. Some snapshots, as described in the table, allow you to select specific accounts, categories, classes, or securities if you want to narrow down what the snapshot shows. The process is the same for all of these things.

1. From the Customize Snapshot dialog box, click on the appropriate button (**Accounts, Categories, Classes,** or **Securities**).

147

2. Click on the yellow checkmark to remove the account, category, class or security from the snapshot.

3. To remove all of them, click **Clear All**.

4. If you change your mind and want to include all of them, click **Mark All**.

5. Click **OK**. The snapshot will only include those selected.

## Change the Number of Snapshots Per Page

Quicken automatically displays four snapshots per page. You can choose two, three, or six snapshots per page by clicking on the page icons under Snapshots per Page. Fewer snapshots will be larger and show more detail in the Snapshots window.

## Add Another Page

Quicken initially displays one page of snapshots. If you want to see more than four snapshots, you'll need to add another page.

1. Click the **New** button under Snapshot Page in the Customize Snapshot dialog box.

2. Type a name, something clever like **second page**.

3. Click **OK**. The following figure shows the Customize Snapshot dialog box for the second page.

*Adding a second page of snapshots.*

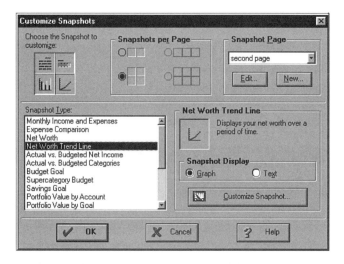

4. Click on a square under Choose Snapshot to customize:.

5. From the Snapshot Type: list, select what you want the snapshot to show.

6. Repeat steps 4 and 5 until the page is full.

7. You can customize each snapshot as you did for the first page.

8. Click **OK**.

When you add another page, the Snapshots window will ask you which page to display.

## Deleting a Page of Snapshots

If you decide later that you don't need both pages, you can delete one. To delete a page:

1. In the Snapshots window, click **Custom**.

2. In the Customize Snapshots dialog box, click **Edit**.

3. In the Edit Snapshot Pages dialog box, click **Delete**. The page and the snapshots it contained are deleted.

# Graphic Descriptions

Snapshots show simple graphs for a quick overview. Quicken provides four other types of graphs that offer more flexibility: Income and Expense, Budget Variance, Net Worth, and Investment graphs.

➤ **Income and Expense graphs**   Show your income and expenses, by category, over a period of time. They also display each category as a percentage of your income.

➤ **Budget Variance graphs**   Compare actual spending and income with your budget. You have to create a budget before you can use a budget variance graph (see Chapter 15).

➤ **Net Worth graphs**   Resemble income and expense graphs, except that they use your account balances instead of specific categories. This gives you a broader overview of your finances.

➤ **Investment graphs**   Summarize your investment portfolio and the price history of your securities, either by type, goal, security, or investment account.

# Creating Graphs

To create a graph, click on the **Graphs** icon in the HomeBase window. The following figure shows the Create Graph dialog box that appears.

*Creating a graph.*

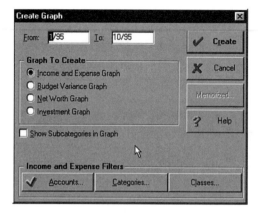

1. In the From: field, type the beginning date for the graph. Notice that the graphs use whole months, such as 1/95; Quicken won't accept a specific date like 1/15/95. Press **Tab**.

2. In the To: field, type the ending date for the graph.

3. Under Graph to Create, click next to the name of the graph you want.

4. Select what information the graph will use:

   ➤ For Income and Expense, Budget Variance, and Net Worth graphs, Quicken automatically uses all accounts, categories, and classes. If you only want to use certain ones, click on the appropriate button and select the accounts, categories, or classes from the list. See the section on "Selecting Accounts, Categories, Classes, and Securities" earlier in this chapter.

   ➤ For Investment graphs, you can select the investment accounts and securities to use.

   ➤ For Income and Expense graphs and Budget Variance graphs, click Show Subcategories in Graph to include subcategories along with categories.

   ➤ For Budget Variance graphs, click Graph Supercategory Budgets to include supercategories.

5. Click **Create**.

The following figure shows a sample Income and Expense graph.

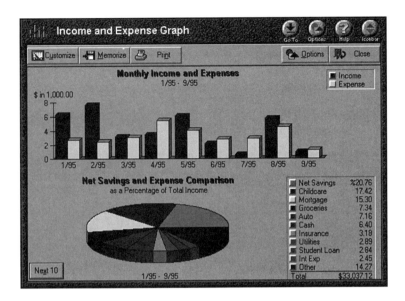

*A sample Income and Expense graph.*

## What You See When You Create a Graph

The sample graph has both a bar graph and a pie graph; the other types of graphs may have one or the other or both. Some other features:

➤ The title of the graph explains what it is and gives the dates.

➤ Each graph has a key that describes what each color in the graph represents.

➤ When you move the mouse cursor over the key, the cursor turns into a magnifying glass. Double-click on one of the items in the key and Quicken will create a QuickZoom graph that details that one item. (QuickZoom works in snapshots, too.)

➤ To see the exact value of a bar or pie slice in the graph, move the mouse cursor to the bar or pie slice and hold down the left mouse button. The value displays until you release the mouse button.

➤ You can hide a bar or pie slice by pressing the **Shift** key and clicking on the bar or pie slice with the left mouse button.

➤ If there is too much information to include in one graph, Quicken will display the top five or ten items in the graph and a button that says Next 5 or Next 10. Click on the button to display the other items.

## Changing the Graph

After you've created a graph, you can change the way it looks and the information shown without creating a new graph.

The Customize button displays the same options as the Create Graph dialog box, so you can change the date range and the income and expense filters. When you click OK, Quicken will redisplay the graph with the new information.

The Options button changes the way the graph looks and prints. The following figure shows the Graph Options dialog box.

*Changing what a graph looks like.*

The following describes ways you can change the appearance of your graph:

➤ **Display Patterns on Screen**   Quicken uses black-and-white patterns instead of color for the graphs. If you don't have a color printer, click this option to make the graph easier to print.

➤ **Create All Graphs in Separate Windows**   If the graph has both a pie and a bar graph, this option will put each in a separate window. Click this option if you want to print just the pie or the bar graph.

➤ **Draw in 2-D**   Quicken automatically creates 3-D graphs. 2-D graphs are faster to draw and print. If printing a graph makes your printer grind to a near halt, try printing it in 2-D.

The following figure shows the sample Income and Expense graph with black-and-white patterns in 2-D.

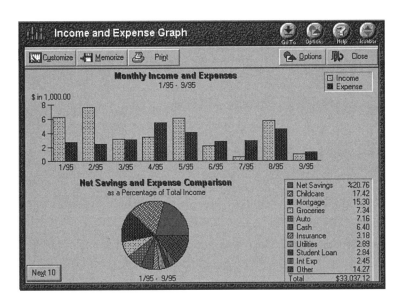

*A black-and-white graph in 2-D. Not quite as ornate, but easier to print.*

## Printing the Graph

Click the **Print** button to print the graph. There's no print preview for graphs; what you see on your monitor is how it will print. If you have trouble, try changing one of the options described above or refer to Chapter 20.

## Memorized Graphs

Let's say you set up three classes to track income and expenses for three different job projects. You then create an Income and Expense graph for each class. By memorizing the graphs, you can continue to track the projects separately without recreating the graphs each time. To memorize a graph:

1. Create the graph as described above, selecting the accounts, categories, and classes you want included.

2. Click the **Memorize** button.

3. Under Graph Name:, change the name so that the name of each graph is unique.

4. Click **OK**.

To recall the graph, click **Graphs** in the main iconbar and click **Memorized**. Quicken will display a list of the memorized graphs. Select the one you want and click **Use**.

*Memorizing a graph.*

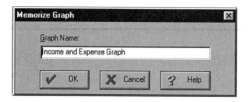

# The Least You Need to Know

Snapshots and graphs show your money in 3-D, with lots of pretty colors. You may be broke, but you sure look good.

➤ Snapshots give an instant overview of your finances.

➤ You can decide which snapshots to use and what information they'll include.

# Chapter 14

# Support the Debtor Economy: Working with Loans

## In This Chapter

➤ Loan accounts manage your payments

➤ Change the terms of the loan and Quicken does the math

➤ Can you afford another loan? Use Loan Planner to find out

I've heard it said that the United States is a debtor economy. So whenever I break out the credit cards or take out another loan, I get that warm, patriotic feeling, knowing I am supporting my country. Actually, I wish I had been born rich instead of good-looking. Just kidding.

Quicken has two features to help you manage your loans. You can set up loan accounts to keep track of the payments, interest, and remaining principal. The Loan Planner lets you evaluate the terms of a loan before you take it out.

## Setting Up a Loan

You can set up loans on Quicken for any kind of installment loan: car, mortgage, home equity, and so on ad infinitum. For credit card debt, however, you'll want to set up a credit card account since you probably don't make the same payments every month.

When you set up a loan, Quicken creates a liability account if you're making payments on the loan, or an asset account if you're receiving payments. You can also use an existing account for the loan. But the process for setting up a loan is different from creating a regular account. To set up a loan:

1. Select **Loans** from the Activities menu. The View Loans window displays.

2. Click **New** in the View Loans window. Quicken's EasyStep feature takes you through the process. The following figure shows the Loan Setup window.

*Use EasyStep to set up a loan.*

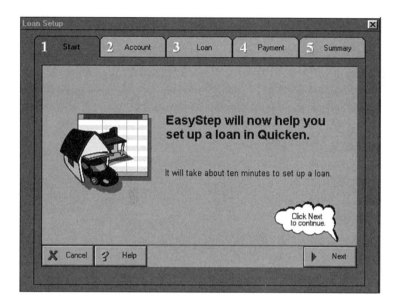

3. To start setting up the loan, click **Next**.

4. If you are making payments on the loan, click **Borrow Money**. If someone is paying you (you lucky dog), click **Lend Money**. Click **Next**.

5. If you want Quicken to create a new account for the loan, click **New Account:** and type a name for the account. If you want to use an existing account, click **Existing Account:** and select the account from the drop-down list. Click **Next**.

6. EasyStep asks if you have made any payments on the loan. If you have, click **Yes**, regardless of whether you've recorded them in Quicken. If you haven't, click **No**. Click **Next**.

7. Next to Opening Date:, use the calendar icon to select the date when you took out the loan.

8. Next to Original Balance:, type or use the calculator to enter the amount of the loan as shown in the following figure. Enter the full amount you borrowed, even if you've made payments. Click **Next**.

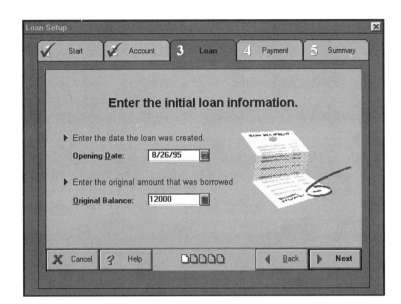

*Enter the date you took out the loan and the amount you borrowed.*

9. EasyStep asks if the loan includes a balloon payment. A *balloon payment* is a payment at the end of the loan that's much larger than your regular payments. Click **Yes** or **No**, then **Next**.

10. From the menu, select the time period of the loan (years, months, weeks, or payments), then type in the number. For a five-year loan, you could enter either 5 Years or 60 Months. Again, enter the original length, even if you've made payments. Click **Next**.

11. Next you'll need to enter how often you make payments. If you make payments at regular intervals, click **Standard Period:** and select the payment period from the drop-down list, such as monthly or quarterly. If you have some other kind of arrangement, click **Other Period:** and type in the number of payments you make per year. Click **Next**.

12. Quicken needs to know the loan's *compounding period*, which is how often the interest is recalculated. You may have to check the fine print or call your lender for this. Select the compounding period from the menu and click **Next**.

   If you have made payments on the loan and clicked Yes in step 6, continue on to step 13. If you have not made any payments and clicked **No** in step 6, skip to step 15.

13. Do you know the current balance of loan on which you've made payments? If not, click **No** to let Quicken calculate it for you. Click **Next** and skip to step 15. If you may know the current balance, click **Yes** and **Next**.

14. If you clicked **Yes** in step 13, use the calculator to enter the Current Balance Date. Then enter the Current Balance Amount. Click **Next**.

15. Use the calendar icon to enter the date of the first payment (or next payment, if you've already started paying it). Click **Next**.

16. If you know the amount of the next payment, including principal and interest, click **Yes** and **Next**. If you don't know, click **No** to let Quicken calculate it for you. Click **Next** and skip to step 18.

17. If you clicked Yes in step 16, enter the Payment Amount, as shown in the following figure. Include only the principal and interest in the payment amount; if there are other charges, such as fees or insurance, we'll take care of those later. Click **Next**.

*Enter the payment amount, including principal and interest.*

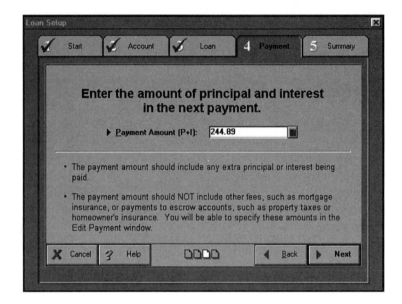

18. Type the interest rate for the loan. Use either whole numbers or decimal amounts; for example, type 8 for eight percent or 9.25 for nine and one-quarter. If you have an adjustable rate loan, enter the interest rate that applies to the next payment. Click **Next**.

19. Use the Summary to double-check the information you entered. You can make any changes here. Click **Next** to go through the entire summary. On the last page of the summary, click **Done**.

20. If you had Quicken calculate the current balance or payment amount, Quicken tells you it performed the calculation. Click **OK** and Quicken inserts the balance or payment amount in the Summary. Check it out. Click **Done**.

# Set Up the Loan Payment

When you've completed EasyStep, Quicken displays the Set Up Loan Payment dialog box (shown in the following figure), which you'll use to tell Quicken how to handle the loan payments.

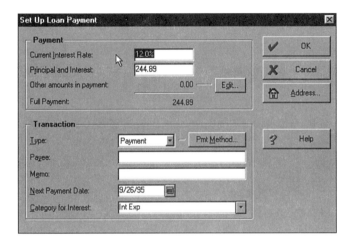

*Add details about the loan payment.*

From here you can add other amounts besides the principal and interest to the payment, select a payment type and method, include the payee name and memo to print on the checks, and enter an address for the payee.

1. Beyond the principal and interest, our mortgage payment includes property taxes and homeowners insurance premiums. If you want to include such additional costs in the payment, click **Edit** next to Other Amounts in Payment. If you don't, skip to step 3.

2. Quicken displays the Splits window, just like you use for your account registers. Enter the amount and category for the additional costs and click **OK**. (For more on splits, see Chapter 7.)

3. From the Type: drop-down list, select how you're going to make the payment: Payment (such as a handwritten check), Print Check to print a check from Quicken, or Online Pmt to use QuickBillPay.

4. Click **Pmt Method**.

5. Under Payment Type, click whether you want to use a memorized transaction, a scheduled transaction, or a repeating online payment.

**It Won't Let Me Select Repeating Online Payment**

Before you can select the repeating online payment option, first you have to create a new repeating online payment for the loan in the Financial Calendar. For more info, see Chapter 10.

6. If you selected a scheduled transaction:

   ➤ From the Register Entry: drop-down list, select whether you want Quicken to prompt you before it records the transaction, or record it automatically, without prompting.

   ➤ From the Account to Pay from: drop-down list, choose which account to use to make the payment.

   ➤ If you want Quicken to record the transaction before the scheduled date, type the number in Days in Advance:. Click **OK**.

7. Next to Payee:, type the payee name so Quicken can record it in your account register.

8. If you want, enter a memo that will also be recorded in the register.

9. If the next payment date is wrong, use the calendar to enter a new one.

10. Quicken automatically puts the interest in the Int Exp (interest expense) category. If you want to use a different category for the interest, select it from the drop-down list.

11. If you chose Print Check for the payment type, click **Address**, type the address, and Quicken will print it on the check. This address will also be recorded in the Financial Address Book.

12. When everything's kosher, click **OK**. Quicken returns you to the View Loans window, which now looks like this:

The loans you set up are listed in the Loan: drop-down list at the top of the window. To see or edit another loan, select it from the drop-down list.

*Viewing the details of your loan.*

# Things You Can Do with Your Loan

No, you can't pawn it off on someone else, unless you know someone really stupid. Believe me, I've tried. But you can see the payment schedule and a graph of the loan, change the payment amount and interest rate, and delete a loan you've paid off.

## See the Payment Schedule

The Payment Schedule tab shows the date, principal, interest, and remaining balance for each payment. Payments you've made are shown in yellow; future payments are in blue. If you edit the payment amounts or interest rate, the payment schedule will reflect the changes.

**Techno Talk**

### Amortization: It's Not Just for Bankers Anymore

Amortization is another of those words that are not as complicated as they sound. Amortization is simply the division of a loan payment into principal and interest. As you pay the loan, the amount of each payment that goes to the interest declines and the amount that goes to the principal increases.

Now we've both learned something new.

## See the Loan in Graphic Form

It's another invasion of the graphs! They're everywhere! They're everywhere!

Ahem. Sorry. Click on the **Payment Graph** tab. It displays the future loan balance in blue, the interest accumulated in green, and payments made in yellow.

## Edit the Loan Details

Switch back to the Loan Summary tab, click **Edit Loan**, and Quicken brings you back to the EasyStep Summary. Now you can change the opening date, original balance, length of the loan, the compounding period, and the payment period.

Click **Next** to change the current balance, payment amount, the payment due date, and the interest rate. (The View Loans window also provides buttons for changing the payment and interest rate). Click **Done** and Quicken updates the loan and returns you to the View Loans window.

## Change the Payment Information

When you click Edit Payment, you'll see the same information as the Set Up Loan Payment dialog box described earlier in this chapter. Only this time the Pay Now button is active, so you can change the payment information and make a payment in one fell swoop.

## Change the Interest Rate

If you have an adjustable rate loan, you'll need to change the interest rate from time to time. Click **Rate Changes** to add, edit, and delete interest rates. The rate changes recorded here will not affect any transactions already recorded in the registers.

➤ If you want to keep track of how the interest varies over time, click **New** to add a new interest rate while saving the old one. Enter the new rate and the date it takes effect. Quicken calculates the loan information according to the effective date, so recent dates will supersede previous dates. You can either enter your payment amount or have Quicken calculate it for you.

➤ Click **Edit** to change the interest rate without saving the previous rate. Enter the new rate and its effective date. You can either enter your payment amount or have Quicken calculate it for you.

➤ Delete erases the selected rate.

When you're done changing the interest rate, click **Close**.

162

# Delete a Loan

One of the best feelings in the world is making that final loan payment. Celebrate with a pint of Ben & Jerry's New York Super Fudge Chunk ice cream, and you've achieved Nirvana.

When you delete a loan, Quicken gives you the option of saving the associated asset or liability account. If you save the account, Quicken will continue to include the payments in graphs and reports for the period of the loan, so you can see how the loan payments affected your finances. If you don't save the account, it's as if the loan never existed. To delete a loan:

1. Select the loan from the Loan: drop-down list in the View Loans window.

2. Click **Delete**.

3. Quicken asks if you want to save the associated account for the loan. Click **No** or **Yes**.

If you save the account, the loan is deleted from the View Loans window but the account remains in the Account List. You can still access the account register, use the information in reports and graphs, or delete it later.

# Making Loan Payments

When you created the loan, you set up the loan payment as either a memorized transaction, a scheduled transaction, or an repeating online payment. You also chose a payment method of either Payment, Print Check, or Online. The three different types of transactions and payment methods work slightly differently.

## Memorized Transaction Payments

With memorized transactions, you can make a payment either from the View Loans window, the account register, or the Write Checks window.

For all three payment types (Payment, Print Check, and Online), you can make a payment from the View Loans window.

Click the **Make Payment** button and Quicken asks if this is a regular payment or an extra payment. If it's an extra payment, how about sending some of that extra cash over this way? I'm in the book.

No matter what your choice, the Make Payment dialog box gives the specifics so you can check it over before paying. Make sure it's paying from the right account (the default is checking). Click **OK** and Quicken automatically records the payment in the checking and loan account registers. If you chose Print Check, Quicken adds the loan payment to the list of checks to print. If it's an online payment, Quicken dials your modem and sends it through.

If you've handwritten the check, you can also record the memorized transaction in the checking account register just as you would any other transaction. Quicken will also record the payment in the loan account register.

For printed checks and online payments, you can also use the Write Checks window to write, print or send, and record the check.

## Scheduled Transaction and Repeating Online Payments

Quicken handles these like any other scheduled or repeating online transactions; when the date arrives, it sends the payment and records it in the account registers. Or, for scheduled transactions without online banking, it's up to you to write or print the check.

If you want to make a payment before the scheduled date, you can either do it from the Financial Calendar (see Chapter 10) or from the View Loans window, as described above for memorized transactions.

# Is It Really a Good Deal?

It seems like every other minute banks, credit unions, car dealerships, and other institutions eager to have a crack at your wallet are announcing new loans or financing packages that will solve your financial worries. Then, in print so small or in a voiceover so fast only Superman could discern them, they gloss over the real terms. So how can you tell if the deal's as good as it sounds?

The Loan Planner lets you play out hypothetical situations in three ways: you can enter a loan amount, interest, and number of payments and let Quicken calculate what your monthly payments would be. Or you can do it backwards. If you know what kind of payment you can afford, enter the payment, interest, and length of the loan and let Quicken calculate the total loan you could get. For both calculations, you can then see a payment schedule that shows what the principal, interest, and balance are over the life of the loan.

The Loan Planner is designed to let you try out a myriad of rates, amounts, and lengths to see what works best for you. When you're done, you can print the payment schedule, but otherwise the figures you entered become mere dust in cyberspace. The Loan Planner does **not** affect any loans you set up on Quicken or any of your other accounts.

# Calculating Loan Payments and Amounts

To use the Loan Planner:

1. Select the **Plan** menu and select **Financial Planners**, then **Loan**. The figure below shows the Loan Planner dialog box.

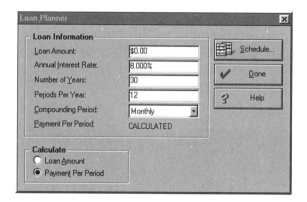

*Use the Loan Planner to try out different interest rates, payments, and loan lengths.*

2. Notice that under Calculate, Payment Per Period is clicked. Ergo, Quicken will calculate the loan payment. If you want to calculate the loan amount, click **Loan Amount**.

3. If you chose Payment Per Period, type in the loan amount and press **Tab**.

   Steps 4-7 apply to both calculations.

4. Type the annual interest rate as either a whole number (8) or a decimal (9.25) and press **Tab**.

5. Type the number of years the loan spans and press **Tab**.

6. Type the number of payment periods per year and press **Tab**.

7. From the Compounding Period: drop-down list, select how often the interest rate is recalculated and press **Tab**.

8. If Quicken is calculating the loan amount, enter the amount of the payments.

9. When you've completed the fields, press **Tab**. The payment per period or loan amount is shown in the appropriate field.

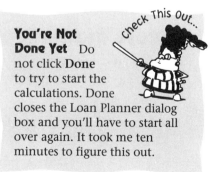

**You're Not Done Yet** Do not click **Done** to try to start the calculations. Done closes the Loan Planner dialog box and you'll have to start all over again. It took me ten minutes to figure this out.

10. You can continue changing the numbers until you get the answer you want or until you've exhausted the possibilities. Then you can either see a payment schedule or click **Done**.

## Hypothetical Payment Schedules

When you've calculated the payment or loan amount, you can see an estimated payment schedule for the length of the loan. Click **Schedule** to see a payment schedule that lists the principal, interest payment, and remaining balance that you would have for each payment. (See the following figure.) Notice the window says approximate; don't try taking this to a bank as proof that your payment should be less. If you want to keep a record of the schedule, click **Print**.

*See an estimated schedule of your hypothetical loan.*

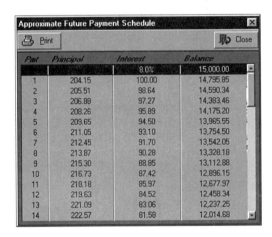

| Pmt | Principal | Interest | Balance |
| --- | --- | --- | --- |
| | | 8.0% | 15,000.00 |
| 1 | 204.15 | 100.00 | 14,795.85 |
| 2 | 205.51 | 98.64 | 14,590.34 |
| 3 | 206.88 | 97.27 | 14,383.46 |
| 4 | 208.26 | 95.89 | 14,175.20 |
| 5 | 209.65 | 94.50 | 13,965.55 |
| 6 | 211.05 | 93.10 | 13,754.50 |
| 7 | 212.45 | 91.70 | 13,542.05 |
| 8 | 213.87 | 90.28 | 13,328.18 |
| 9 | 215.30 | 88.85 | 13,112.88 |
| 10 | 216.73 | 87.42 | 12,896.15 |
| 11 | 218.18 | 85.97 | 12,677.97 |
| 12 | 219.63 | 84.52 | 12,458.34 |
| 13 | 221.09 | 83.06 | 12,237.25 |
| 14 | 222.57 | 81.58 | 12,014.68 |

When you're done looking at the payment schedule, click **Close** to return to the Loan Planner. You can continue trying out different rates and amounts, or click **Done**.

## The Least You Need to Know

Loans are an ugly fact of life today; they've become as American and as common as apple pie. No matter how many loans you have, Quicken's loan accounts and Loan Planner help make sense of it all.

➤ When you set up a loan, Quicken creates an asset or liability account for the loan to track payments.

➤ You can see instant payment schedules and a graph of the principal and interest over the life of the loan.

➤ If the terms of the loan change, Quicken automatically updates the payment information.

➤ You can make loan payments with memorized transactions, scheduled transactions, or repeating online payments.

➤ The Loan Planner lets you try out various payments, interest rates, and loan lengths before you go into debt.

# Madame Zerbina Forecasts Your Budget

In the next chapter I'm going to talk about using Quicken to plan for college and retirement, create savings goals, and other responsible behavior. But before we get to the long-term goals we need to deal with the here-and-now and the immediate future. So come along with Madame Zerbina as she polishes her crystal ball and takes you on a mystical journey through budgets and forecasts.

# Video Rental, Cat Food, and Diapers

The basis for any planning is a realistic budget, with the emphasis on realistic. We all know what kind of income we'd like to have, and what we'd like to spend it on, but we're dealing with the real world here. Take the title of this section as an example. In our little family, we don't get out much (videos), our cats eat like lions (cat food), and I'm beginning to wonder if we'll ever see the end of potty training (diapers). It ain't glamorous, but it's life.

To get to Quicken's budget planner, click on the **Plan** menu, then select **Budgeting**. The following figure shows an empty budget, just waiting for you to complete it.

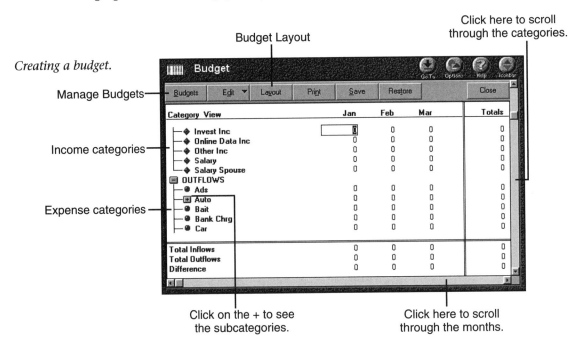

*Creating a budget.*

Quicken budgets amounts based on the category list. So before you start entering numbers, make sure the categories are as you want them. If you want to budget $100 per month for antique gumball machines, you'll need a Gumball category. Chapter 5 talks about categories and how to add and delete them.

There are two ways to create your first budget: from scratch, with you supplying all the numbers for the appropriate categories, or you can let Quicken complete the budget with information from your account registers. We'll talk about the latter option, called Autocreate, first.

## Which Way Should I Create a Budget?

If you've just set up your accounts and don't have much information in them, using Autocreate may not be helpful; Quicken won't have enough data to create a decent budget. However, if you don't have a clue where to begin, you can use Autocreate as a start and then go back and fill in the blanks in the budget.

# Autocreate Your Budget

To have Quicken start your budget for you:

1. Click the **Edit** button in the Budget window and select **Autocreate** from the menu. The following figure shows the Automatically Create Budget dialog box.

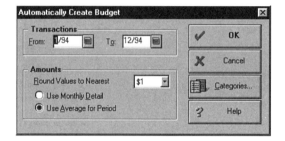

*Let Quicken create your budget.*

2. Quicken assumes you want to use transactions from last year. If you want to use a different time period, type in the dates or click on the Calendar button and use the calendar to enter the beginning date in the **From:** field and the ending date in the **To:** field.

3. From the Round Values to Nearest drop-down list, select whether you want Quicken to round numbers to the nearest $1, $10, or $100.

4. When **Use Average for Period** is selected, Quicken will budget the average amount spent on or received from each category. If you want Quicken to insert the exact amounts spent each month, click **Use Monthly Detail**.

5. If you only want to budget for specific categories, click the **Categories** button. All the categories are selected; click on the ones you don't want to deselect, then click **OK**.

6. Click **OK**. Quicken draws from your account registers to create your budget.

If you want to enter more information or change the budget, keep reading.

## Your Budget from Scratch

Creating a budget from scratch, or filling in the blanks from Autocreate, entails clicking and typing. As an example, I'll tell you how to budget an income of $3,000 per month; $400 per month for groceries; and $10 per month on leeches, $20 per month for minnows, for a total of $30 per month for bait.

1. In the January (Jan) column in the Budget window, click next to Salary.

2. Type **3000**.

3. To fill in the rest of the months of the year without typing 3000 twelve times, click on the **Edit** button and select **Fill Row Right** from the menu.

4. Quicken will ask you to confirm it. Click **Yes**. Quicken enters 3000 for every month. Notice the Totals columns shows 36,000.

5. Scroll down to the Groceries category and type **400** in the January column. Quicken enters it as -400 in red. Quicken shows all amounts for expense categories as negative numbers, because they're subtracted from your income.

6. Click **Edit**, select **Fill Row Right**, and click **Yes**.

7. Scroll up to the Bait category. Instead of a red circle, it has a + button. Click the + button, and Quicken displays Bait's subcategories and changes the + to a -.

8. Next to Leeches, type **10**, click **Edit**, select **Fill Row Right**, and click **Yes**.

9. Next to Minnows, type **20**, click **Edit**, select **Fill Row Right**, and click **Yes**.

10. To see the total amount budgeted to Bait, click the - button. Quicken hides the subcategories and shows a total of $30 per month for Bait, with an annual total of $360.

11. To save the budget, click the **Save** button.

### What If I Don't Spend the Same Amount Every Month?

If you need to budget a different amount for different months, you can either type the amount in each month's column, or fill the row as described in the steps, and then change the amount in the months that vary. Press **Tab** to move to the appropriate month's column, then type the new amount.

## Changing the Budget's Layout

You can change what appears in the budget's columns and rows. Instead of months, you can budget per quarter or year. You can also include supercategories and transfers in the budget, and hide the categories for which you don't enter an amount.

1.  Click the **Layout** button. The following figure shows the Layout Budgets dialog box.

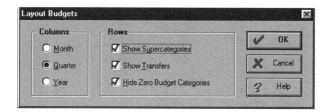

*Changing the budget's layout.*

2.  Select **Month**, **Quarter**, or **Year** for the budget's columns.

3.  You can choose one, two, or all three of the following options:

    ➤ If you read Chapter 5, you'll remember that supercategories are a way to group categories under a broader heading. Click **Show Supercategories** to include them in your budget.

    ➤ Likewise, click **Show Transfers** to include transfers between accounts. This is useful to budget credit card and loan payments.

    ➤ If you don't want to budget for every category, click **Hide Zero Budget Categories** and the budget won't show categories for which you don't enter an amount.

4.  Click **OK** to give the budget its new look.

## Creating Another Budget

You can have more than one budget. You can set up one for household expenses and another for business. Or you can set up a budget for something specific, like a renovation project or a trip around the world. (Can I come? Please?)

1.  Click the **Budgets** button.

2.  Click **Create**. The following figure shows the Create Budget dialog box.

3.  In the **Name:** field, Quicken calls it Budget 2. You can come up with something better than that. Press **Tab**.

*Creating another budget.*

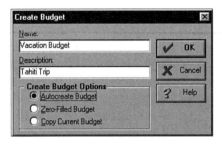

4. Type in a description (optional).

5. Tell Quicken how you want to create it:

   ➤ To have Quicken pull the information from your account registers, click **Autocreate Budget**.

   ➤ To start from scratch, click **Zero-Filled Budget**.

   ➤ If this budget is similar to your first, click **Copy Current Budget**. Quicken will copy the first budget, rename it, and you can make the changes you need.

6. Click **OK**.

7. Enter the budget information as described earlier in this chapter. Click the **Budgets** button again to open, rename, and delete budgets.

## Change the Budget, and Change It Back

You can play out some hypothetical budget situations without creating and saving a new budget. For instance, you want to see how making higher payments on your credit cards or starting a collection of Elvis memorabilia would affect your budget. If you have to, create a new Elvis category. Then enter or change the relevant amounts. Yow! Those velvet paintings are pricey! When you're done, click the **Restore** button and Quicken restores the original budget.

## Other Edit Options

The menu in the **Edit** button has other options to help you manage your budgets.

   ➤ **2-Week**   Lets you budget for a certain category every two weeks instead of monthly. If you get paid every two weeks, you may want to budget the Salary category this way.

1. Click on an amount in the category you want in the budget.

2. Click **Edit** and select **2-Week**.

3. Type in the amount to be budgeted for each two-week period.

4. Use the calendar to enter a starting date.

5. Click **OK**.

➤ **Copy All**  Copies the budget to the Windows Clipboard. You can then paste the budget into a spreadsheet program. (If you don't know what a spreadsheet is, never mind. You'll never have to use this option. But don't you feel better knowing it's there?)

➤ **Clear Row**  Erases all the amounts in the selected row.

➤ **Clear All**  Erases all the amounts in the entire budget.

➤ **Fill Columns**  Copies the amounts in the selected column to all the columns to its right. For example, if you select an amount in the June column and choose **Fill Columns**, Quicken copies the June amounts to the columns from July through December.

➤ **Supercategories**  Displays the Manage Supercategories dialog box. See Chapter 5 for details.

# I See in Your Future a Long-Range Forecast

Behold Madame Zerbina as she magically foretells your financial future! Oh, never mind. You can do it yourself.

Quicken's forecasting feature lets you see what your finances will look like in the near future. Use it to see when you'll be able to spring for a long-awaited luxury, map out your spending and savings, experiment with various category amounts to determine how the changes will affect your finances, and compare different outcomes with multiple forecasts.

Quicken creates the forecast from scheduled transactions, transactions that appear regularly in your account registers, and estimated items, which are average amounts spread out over a period of time. Quicken retrieves the estimated items from your budget and account registers.

To see your forecast, go to the **Plan** menu and select **Forecasting**. Quicken displays the Automatically Create Forecast dialog box, shown in the following figure.

*Enter the dates for your forecast.*

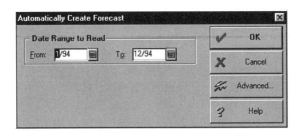

Quicken assumes you want to use transactions from last year. If you want to use a different time period, type in the dates or click on the calendar buttons and use the calendar to enter the beginning date in the **From:** field and the ending date in the **To:** field.

Click **OK**, and Quicken displays your forecast in the Forecasting - Base Scenario window, shown in the following figure.

*Quicken's psychic friend.*

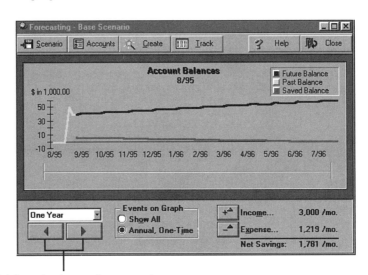

Click here to change the amount
of time of the forecast.

➤ Quicken shows the forecast over one year. You can also forecast for one month, six months, or two years from the drop-down list in the bottom left corner. Click the arrows to move forward and backward in time.

➤ **Events on Graph** determines what events are included in the forecast. **Show All** displays all your regular and scheduled transactions. **Annual, One-Time** shows only those that are annual or one-time. Show All gives more detail, but it can get crowded in there.

In the bottom right corner you can see your total income, expenses, and net savings.

# When Can I Afford That Range Rover?

By adding income and expense items to your forecast, you can see how your bonus for nailing the Treehugger account or payments on a Range Rover will affect your financial wherewithal. The process for both is the same.

1. Click the + button next to **Income** or the - button next to **Expense** to see the Forecast Items dialog box.

2. Click **New**. The following figure shows the Create New Income Item dialog box.

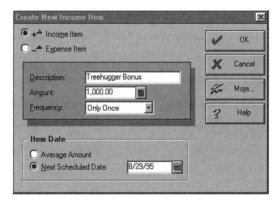

*Adding a new item to the forecast.*

3. Type a description of the income or expense in the Description text box and press **Tab**.

4. Enter the amount.

5. From the Frequency: drop-down list, select how often you'll see the income or expense item. For example, for the bonus, you'd choose **Only Once**. For payments on a Range Rover, choose **Monthly**.

6. Under Item Date, click **Average Amount** to enter the item as an estimated amount, spread out over the entire period. Click **Next Scheduled Date** to enter it as a scheduled amount on the date you specify.

7. If you want to include the income or expense in a category, click the **More** button.

8. Select a category from the drop-down list.

9. If you know you'll make a certain number of payments, such as for a loan, enter the number. (This option won't be available if you chose Only Once as the frequency.)

10. Click **OK** (twice). If you want, add another income or expense item.

11. Click **Done**. Quicken updates your forecast to include the new income or expense.

**177**

You can also edit (such as changing an amount) and delete an income or expense item by selecting it from the list in the Forecast Items dialog box and clicking **Edit** or **Delete**.

## Selecting Accounts for the Forecast

Quicken automatically uses all your accounts to create a forecast. Another way of altering what you see is to include specific accounts in the forecast. Quicken will create the forecast based on the scheduled and regularly occurring transactions in those accounts.

1. Click the **Accounts** button in the iconbar.

2. Click on the yellow checkmark to remove the account from the forecast.

3. To remove all of them, click **Clear All**. Then click on the accounts you want included.

4. Click **OK**. Quicken will recreate the forecast with only the selected accounts.

## Creating a New Forecast

In a minute I'll talk about how you can compare two forecasts. But before you can compare two, you have to have two. To create a new forecast:

1. Click **Create** in the iconbar.

2. In the From: field, enter a starting date for the forecast.

3. In the To: field, enter an ending date for the forecast.

4. If you only need to set dates for the forecast, click **OK**. But wait! There's more!

5. Click **Advanced**. The following figure shows the Advanced AutoCreate dialog box.

*Creating another forecast.*

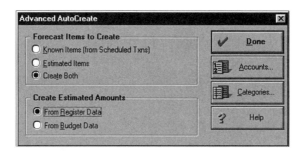

6. Under Forecast Items to Create, select whether you want the forecast to include only known items from scheduled transactions, estimated items from the account registers, or both.

7. Under **Create Estimated Amounts**, select whether you want Quicken to get the forecast amounts from your account registers or from a budget.

8. Click **Accounts** to select specific accounts to include in the forecast.

9. Click **Categories** to include certain categories in the forecast.

10. Click **Done** and **OK**. Quicken creates your new forecast.

# Managing Forecast Scenarios

Now you can save the new forecast and compare it with others. Click on the **Scenario** button in the iconbar and this is what you'll see:

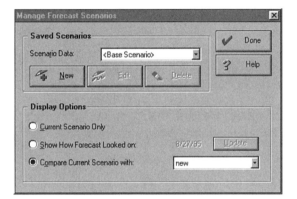

*The Manage Forecast Scenarios dialog box.*

The forecast that Quicken created automatically when you chose Forecasting from the menu is called the Base Scenario. You can compare your new forecast to this one, or create several new forecasts to compare.

To save your new forecast, click **New**, type a name for the forecast, and click **OK**. The new forecast is listed in the Scenario Data: drop-down list.

Under Display Options, you can control what shows in the Forecasting dialog box.

➤ **Current Scenario Only** displays the forecast you choose from the Scenario Data: drop-down list.

➤ **Show How Forecast Looked on:** lets you look at the forecast for today's date. Click **Update** to update the forecast for today's date.

➤ **Compare Current Scenario with:** compares the forecast in the Scenario Data: field with the forecast you select from this drop-down list.

When you click **Done**, Quicken changes or updates the forecast shown. If you chose to compare forecasts, Quicken shows the base scenario in green with the new forecast in blue and yellow.

## Create a Budget Based on Your Forecast

I mentioned how Quicken can create a forecast based on your budget. But Madame Zerbina's cosmic powers make the reverse true as well: you can create a budget based on your forecast.

### Before You Try This at Home

Creating a budget from a forecast will overwrite your current budget. Delete, erase, kaput, kaplooie. Even Madame Zerbina's cosmic powers cannot change this fact. So watch it.

To create a budget from your forecast, click **Track**. Quicken will warn you that you are about to overwrite your current budget. There's no shame in backing out now. To go through with it, click **OK**, then admire your handiwork.

# The Least You Need to Know

Madame Zerbina took you on a magical mystical tour of budgets and forecasts. Some of the wonders we encountered along the way:

➤ You can have Quicken create your budget, or do the heavy lifting yourself.

➤ Not only can you have more than one budget, you can change the columns and rows.

➤ How will that trip to Graceland affect your budget? Check it out, change it back.

➤ Forecasts let you glimpse into your financial future.

➤ Create, contrast, and compare different forecasts; maybe you'll come out richer in the end.

O.K., LET'S ROCK 'N' ROLL...

# Chapter 16

# Plan for That Long Journey Called Life

## In This Chapter

➤ Planning for college and retirement

➤ Deciding whether to refinance your mortage

➤ Savings goals

A couple of years ago my husband and I met with a financial planner. It was an informative meeting, until we learned they wanted $500 to tell us whether we could afford their services. We were faced with a decision: pay the rent next month, or pay some overpriced propeller-head $500 to tell us we're broke.

That was the era B.Q. (Before Quicken). Now we've got an electronic propeller-head to help us plan for the kids' college and our retirement, tell us whether we should refinance the mortgage, and create specific savings goals. If we play our cards right, maybe we'll actually be able to afford a vacation before the turn of the century.

## Planning for College (Pizza and Beer Not Included)

I've heard that sending my kids to college will cost upwards of 200 grand each. Yipes. I helped finance my college education by flipping burgers, washing dishes, and cashiering at a discount store, and I expect my daughters will do the same. But $200,000 is a lot of burgers. How much are we going to have to save to give them a fighting chance at getting through four years of higher education?

With the College Planner, you can calculate the annual amount it will cost to send your child to college; your current savings toward college, if any; and the amount you have to save every year. Quicken's calculations assume that you'll keep saving throughout your child's college career.

Like the Loan Planner discussed in Chapter 14, the College Planner is designed to let you try out hypothetical situations. When you're done, you can print a schedule of the savings deposits you'll need to make, but Quicken does not save the calculations. The College Planner does not affect any of your Quicken accounts.

## Calculating College Costs, Current Savings, and Annual Contributions

To use the College Planner:

1. Go to the **Plan** menu and select **Financial Planners**, then **College**. The following figure shows the College Planner dialog box.

*Use the College Planner to see why you can't afford your children.*

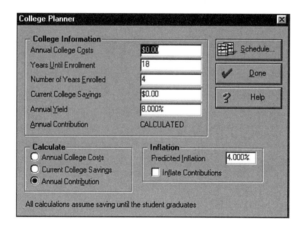

2. Under the Calculate area, the **Annual Contribution** option is selected, so Quicken will calculate the amount you need to save each year. Click **Annual College Costs** to calculate the estimated annual tuition, or click **Current College Savings** to calculate how much you've already saved toward college.

3. If you chose **Annual Contribution** or **Current College Savings**, type in your estimate of today's annual college costs in the Annual College Costs text box. This can vary widely, depending on whether you plan to send your kid to Harvard or Monsieur Mike's School of Hairdressing. Press **Tab**.

4. In the Years Until Enrollment text box, type the number of years until your child starts college and press **Tab**.

5. In the Number of Years Enrolled text box, type the number of years he or she will spend in college and press **Tab**. Hopefully your child will not be a professional student.

6. If you chose **Annual Contribution** or **Annual College Costs**, type the amount of your current savings toward college, if any, in the Current College Savings text box and press **Tab**.

7. Type the annual yield you expect to get from your savings as either a whole number (8) or a decimal (9.25) in the Annual Yield text box and press **Tab**.

8. If you chose **Annual College Costs** or **Current College Savings**, type your estimated yearly contribution to your college savings.

9. Under Inflation, Quicken predicts an annual inflation rate of 4%. If you think that's too optimistic, enter another rate.

10. Click **Inflate Contributions** if you want to increase your contribution every year to counteract inflation. Quicken will increase your annual contribution by the amount in **Predicted Inflation**.

11. You can continue changing the numbers and performing the different calculations. Then you can either see a savings deposit schedule, which tells you the amount you need to save each year, or click **Done**.

### Always Calculating!

As you enter data in every field, Quicken calculates the selected amount and updates it when you change any of the fields.

## Savings Deposit Schedules

For all the calculations, click the **Schedule** button to see a savings deposit schedule that lists the deposits you'll need to make each year and the savings balance. For the college years, it includes the amount you're shelling out in tuition. If you have a weak heart, you might not want to look. To keep a record of the schedule, click **Print**.

# A Comfortable Retirement

Besides college, you'd better start socking it away for those halcyon days of retirement—or they won't be so halcyon.

Use the Retirement Planner to calculate your current retirement savings, the annual amount you need to save, or your annual retirement income after taxes.

Like the other planners, the Retirement Planner lets you print out savings schedules but otherwise does not save the calculations or affect your Quicken accounts.

## Retirement Calculations

To use the Retirement Planner:

1. Go to the **Plan** menu and select **Financial Planners**, then **Retirement**. The following figure shows the Retirement Planner dialog box.

*Planning for the Golden Years.*

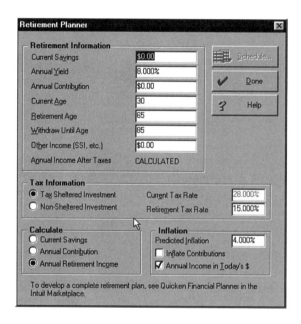

2. Under the Calculate section, the **Annual Retirement Income** option is selected, so Quicken will calculate your income after taxes. Click **Annual Contribution** to calculate how much you'll need to save each year, or click **Current Savings** to calculate your current retirement savings.

3. If you chose **Annual Contribution** or **Annual Retirement Income**, type your current savings toward retirement, if any, in the Current Savings text box and press **Tab**.

4. In the Annual Yield text box, type the annual yield you expect to get from your savings as either a whole number (8) or a decimal (9.25) and press **Tab**.

5. If you chose **Annual Retirement Income** or **Current Savings**, type your annual contribution to savings in the Annual Contribution text box, and press **Tab**.

6. In the Current Age text box, enter your current age (resist lying about your age) and press **Tab**.

7. In the Retirement Age text box, enter the age you expect to retire and press **Tab**. I'd like to retire at age 40, but let's get real.

8. In the Withdraw Until Age text box, type the age you expect to be when you stop withdrawing from your retirement account. To be blunt, when you expect to die. If you expect to live to be 110, more power to you, but you're going to need a lot more cash.

9. If you'll have other retirement income, such as a pension, include it in **Other Income** and press **Tab**. The way things are going, I wouldn't hold my breath waiting for a Social Security check.

10. If you chose **Current Savings** or **Annual Contribution**, enter your desired annual retirement income after taxes in the Annual Income After Taxes text box, and press **Tab**.

11. Under Tax Information, select whether you're saving in a tax-sheltered investment account, such as an IRA, or a taxable account. Press **Tab** and enter the account's taxable rate, if it's different than what's shown.

12. Under Inflation, Quicken predicts an annual inflation rate of 4%. Enter another rate to show what will happen if inflation goes through the roof.

13. Click **Inflate Contributions** if you want to increase your contribution every year to counteract inflation. Quicken will increase your annual contribution by the amount in **Predicted Inflation**.

**Quicken Figures It for You** As you press **Tab**, Quicken calculates the selected amount and updates it when you change any of the fields.

14. Click **Annual Income in Today's $** to show your retirement income accounting for 4% inflation.

15. You can continue changing the numbers and performing the different calculations. Then you can either see a savings deposit schedule or click **Done**.

## Savings Deposit Schedules

For all the calculations, click **Schedule** to see a savings deposit schedule that lists the deposits you'll need to make each year and the savings balance. For the retirement years, it shows your income in future, pre-tax dollars. To keep a record of the schedule, click **Print**.

# Should You Refinance Your Mortgage?

With interest rates jumping around, there's been a lot of talk about refinancing mortgages to take advantage of a lower interest rate. But there's more than interest to consider; closing costs and points can make a great deal not so great. Use the Refinance Planner to see whether you'll still come out ahead.

Techno Talk

**When My Banker Mentioned Points, I Just Smiled and Nodded** *Points* are another way for the mortgage lender to squeeze blood from a turnip, with you playing the part of the turnip. For every point charged, you pay 1% of the mortgage amount to the lender.

There is no schedule for the Refinance Planner, but you can print the Refinance Planner calculations page to keep a record of it or take it with you to shop for a new mortgage. Again, the planner will not affect your Quicken accounts.

To use the Refinance Planner:

1. Go to the **Plan** menu and select **Financial Planners**, then **Refinance**. The following figure shows the Refinance Planner dialog box.

2. In the Current payment text box, enter your current mortgage payment and press **Tab**.

3. If your mortgage payment includes other costs, such as property taxes and homeowner's insurance, enter the total amount of these costs in the Impound/escrow amount text box and press **Tab**. Quicken deducts this amount from the mortgage payment and shows the monthly principal and interest.

4. In the Principal amount text box, type the principal remaining on your mortgage and press **Tab**.

5. In the Years text box, type the number of years remaining on your mortgage and press **Tab**.

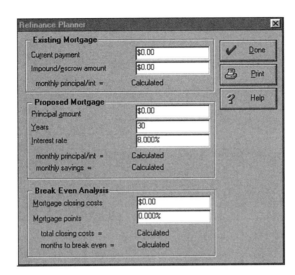

*Figure out whether to refinance your mortgage.*

6. In the Interest rate text box, type the interest rate you'll have if you refinance as either a whole number (8) or a decimal (9.25) and press **Tab**. Quicken recalculates your monthly principal and interest payment based on the new interest rate and shows it in the monthly principal/int= field. It also shows your net savings in the monthly savings= field.

7. Now you'll see if it's still worth it after paying closing costs and points. In the Mortgage closing costs text box, enter the closing costs you'd have to pay and press **Tab**.

8. In the Mortgage points text box, type the number of points charged as either a whole number (8) or a decimal (9.25) and press **Tab**. Quicken calculates the total closing costs, including what you'd pay on points. It also displays the number of months until you'd break even with the savings on the principal and interest. If it's a negative number; forget it. If it's a positive number, refinancing may be a good idea.

9. You can continue changing the numbers to see how various interest rates, closing costs, and points affect the equation. Then click **Print** to print a copy of the Refinance Mortgage calculations sheet or click **Done**.

## Stashing It Away for That Caribbean Vacation

Remember when you were a kid and your folks said you could have a new bike if you saved enough to pay for part of it? That was your parents' way of teaching you financial responsibility. Welcome to the grown-up version.

187

You can set up savings goals for vacations, a down payment on a home, or that sterling silver garden trowel you saw at Neiman-Marcus. Quicken will chart your progress toward your goal, which you can see either from the Savings Goals window, a snapshot, or a report.

To start saving, select **Savings Goals** from the **Plan** menu. The following figure shows the Savings Goals window.

*Stashing it away for that Caribbean vacation.*

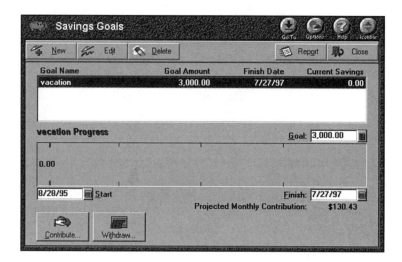

## Creating a New Goal

To create a new savings goal:

1. Click the **New** button in the iconbar.

2. Under Goal Name, type a name for the goal; go for the obvious, like vacation, house, or garden trowel. Press **Tab**.

3. Under Goal Amount, type or use the calculator to enter the amount you want to save. Press **Tab**.

4. Under Finish Date, use the calendar to enter the date when you want to splurge for your goal. Quicken uses the date to calculate the monthly amount you'll need to save between now and then.

5. Click **OK**. Quicken inserts the goal in the Savings Goals window, enters the goal amount and ending date, and shows your projected monthly contribution (see the preceding figure for an example).

If you look at the monthly contribution and realize it's way beyond your means, you can change the goal amount or extend the finish date to give yourself some breathing room.

You can create as many savings goals as you want. To see a different goal, just click it in the Goal Name list.

## Contributions and Withdrawals

When you contribute to your savings goal, Quicken will chart your progress. To make a contribution:

1. Click **Contribute**. The following figure shows the Contribute to Goal: dialog box.

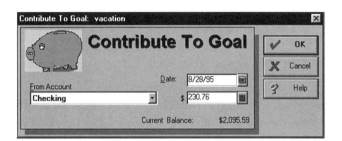

*Contributing to a savings goal.*

2. In the From Account drop-down list, select the account from which you want to make the contribution. Quicken shows the account's current balance in the lower right corner so you know if you have enough.

3. Quicken assumes you want to make the projected monthly contribution on today's date. Click on the calendar to enter a different date, and press **Tab** to type a new contribution amount.

4. Click **OK**. A green bar under Progress shows your contribution amount.

When you reach your goal, or if you need the money for something else, click **Withdraw** and follow the same procedures as contributing to put the money back in your account. The progress bar regresses to show the amount withdrawn from the savings goal.

## How Does the Savings Goal Affect My Bank Account?

When you make a contribution to your goal, Quicken deducts the amount from your account register. The money doesn't really go anywhere; it's still in your account but you just can't see it. If you can't see it, you won't spend it.

Quicken keeps track of both your actual account balance (including contributions to savings goals) and the balance without the money you socked away. Once you've contributed to a savings goal, your account register will have a checkbox called **Hide Sav. Goal**. When it's checked, you'll see your actual account balance without the savings goal contributions.

## Savings Goal Reports

Click the **Report** button in the Savings Goals window iconbar to see a report on your savings goal that shows each contribution to and withdrawal from the saving goal, subtotals for each, and the net balance. See Chapter 12 for more information on working with reports. You can also include your savings goal in the Snapshots window (see Chapter 13).

# The Least You Need to Know

As if it weren't enough keeping up with the monthly bills, college and retirement have long-term financial consequences. Maybe refinancing your mortgage would help. But there's the consolation that you can save to reward yourself with something frivolous and ridiculously expensive.

➤ Use the College Planner to calculate the annual amount it will cost to send your child to college; your current savings toward college; and the amount you have to save every year. Then lean back and fantasize about having the house to yourself.

➤ The Retirement Planner calculates your current retirement savings, the annual amount you need to save, and your annual retirement income after taxes. Then practice your putting.

➤ The Refinance Planner tells you if refinancing your mortgage saves as much as you think.

➤ Create savings goals to plan for big-time purchases. Quicken hides the money saved from your account so you won't spend it.

# Chapter 17

# Mollify the Infernal Revenue Service

## In This Chapter

➤ Linking Quicken's categories to tax schedules

➤ Use the Tax Planner to see the size of Uncle Sam's bite

➤ Tax reports wrap it up

The only certain things in life are death and taxes. While Quicken can't do anything about the former, it can make the latter a little more bearable.

There are three ways Quicken helps organize your taxes: assigning tax schedule line items to categories, figuring out what you owe with the Tax Planner, and creating tax reports.

If you want to take full advantage of Quicken's tax functions, you should invest in an income tax software package such as Turbo Tax. I've used income tax software, and I can assure you that it's perfect for financial idiots like us, and it's almost like having an accountant take up residence in your home.

Income tax software has computerized income tax forms that look just like the real thing. The software tells you what to enter where, copies information between forms, and performs all the calculations. When you set up tax information on Quicken, it transfers that information directly to the tax schedules in the income tax software. You can then print the forms or send them to the IRS through your modem. No more scrambling for receipts, endless number-crunching, and midnight dashes to the post office. And you'll save a small fortune on accountant's fees to boot.

While you can use Quicken's tax functions without it, Quicken is designed to work with Turbo Tax, which, as it happens, is also made by Intuit. (No, they're not paying me for this promo.) You can also use your Quicken data with another brand of tax software. In Chapter 18 I'll describe how to transfer your Quicken data to tax software.

# Assigning Line Items to Categories

When you set up your accounts, Quicken gave you the option of assigning tax schedules to the accounts (see Chapter 3). You can also assign specific schedule line items to categories. For example, you can tell Quicken to transfer alimony income to the Alimony Received line on your 1040, and medical expenses to Schedule A.

You assign line items to categories in the Category & Transfer List, shown in the following figure. Select **Category & Transfer** from the **Lists** menu to see the Category & Transfer List.

*Use the Category & Transfer List to link categories to tax schedules.*

## Reassign Predefined Categories

Quicken has already assigned line items to its predefined categories that have Tax next to the description. The Tax Link button lets you see which line items are assigned to which category and lets you reassign the line items yourself if necessary.

Click **Tax Link** and you'll see the Tax Link Assistant window, shown in the following figure.

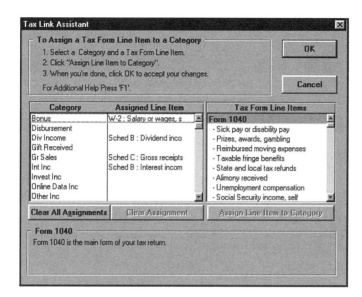

*The Tax Link Assistant window lets you reassign tax schedule line items to categories.*

Scroll through the categories to see how Quicken has assigned the line items. To reassign a schedule line item to a category:

1. Click on the category in the Category list on the left.

2. Find the new schedule line item you want by scrolling through the Tax Form Line Items list and click on it. After you scroll through the line items for Form 1040, you'll find the other forms and schedules.

3. Click **Assign Line Item to Category**.

4. Repeat steps 1-3 for any other categories you want reassigned.

## Why Is Salary Assigned to a W-2 Instead of the 1040?

Your income tax software creates an electronic W-2 for your salary and withholding information. It will transfer the information to the appropriate places on the 1040.

5. If you don't want tax schedules assigned to any of the categories, click **Clear All Assignments**. This probably isn't a good idea. Even if you don't have tax software now, you might someday, and then you'll just have created a lot of work for yourself.

6. Click **Clear Assignment** to remove a line item assignment from one category if you don't want the category included on the tax schedules.

**193**

7. Click **OK** and Quicken saves the changes.

## Assign New Categories

You can assign a line item to a new category when you create the category.

1. In the Category & Transfer List, click **New**.

2. Type a name for the category in the Name field.

3. If you want, type the category's description in the Description field.

4. Click the **Income** or **Expense** check box.

5. Click the **Tax-related** check box.

6. Select the tax schedule line item for the category from the Form: drop-down list.

7. Click **OK**. Quicken adds the category to the Category & Transfer List with a Tax designation.

# Tax Planner

The past several years I've had a mild stroke when I saw how much we owed in taxes. We should just send our paychecks directly to the government and save a lot of paperwork.

Quicken's Tax Planner lets you anticipate how far Uncle Sam will dip into your pocket. If you find you owe a lot, Quicken will help you determine how much you should increase your withholding so you won't get gouged on April 15. Then start brainstorming ways to blow your refund.

To get to the Tax Planner, shown in the following figure, select **Tax Planner** from the Plan menu. Tax Planner is designed to help you calculate your 1995 and 1996 taxes.

If you have a year's worth of transactions in your Quicken accounts, you can complete the Tax Planner the easy way: click **Quicken Data** and Quicken imports the relevant information from your accounts and inserts it in the Tax Planner. You can then update the information as described in the following steps.

If there isn't much in your Quicken accounts, you'll need to start from scratch. Dig out last year's income tax returns to help you complete the Tax Planner. As you enter information, press **Tab** to move from field to field or click in the appropriate field.

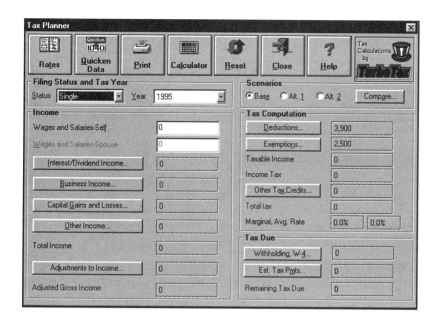

*Tax Planner reduces the incidence of shock on April 15.*

1. From the Status drop-down list, select your filing status (single, married filing jointly, and so on).

2. From the Year drop-down list, choose the year for which you want to estimate your taxes.

3. Type your annual salary in the Wages and Salaries-Self text box. As you enter income in the following steps, Quicken will calculate your total gross income.

4. If you're married and filing jointly, enter your spouse's salary in the Wages and Salaries-Spouse text box.

5. If you have taxable interest or dividend income, click **Interest/Dividend Income** to enter it and have Quicken calculate the total.

6. If you have income from a business you own, click **Business Income**. Here you'll enter your total business revenue and deductible expenses. Quicken will calculate your profit or loss.

7. If you expect any capital gains or losses, click **Capital Gains and Losses** to include them.

8. If you have other income to include, such as alimony, rents, royalties, farm income, or Social Security benefits, click **Other Income**.

9. If there are any adjustments to your income (IRA deductions, alimony paid, moving expenses, and so on), click **Adjustments to Income** and enter the appropriate amounts. If you entered income from a business or a farm, Quicken automatically deducts one-half of your self-employment tax. Click **OK** and Quicken calculates your adjusted gross income.

10. Quicken automatically includes the standard deduction for your filing status. To enter itemized deductions, click **Deductions**.

11. Click **Exemptions** to claim your dependents (you knew the little rugrats were good for something).

12. Quicken shows your total taxable income and the total tax you owe, not including withholding or estimated payments you've made. (We'll get into that in a minute.) If you need to include other taxes or credits, click **Other Tax, Credits**.

## So How Much Is My Refund?

To see your refund or how much you'll owe, you need to include your withholding and any estimated payments you make. We'll start with withholding.

1. Click **Withholding, W-4**. The following figure shows the Withholding and W-4 Allowances dialog box.

*Use the Tax Planner to calculate your withholding.*

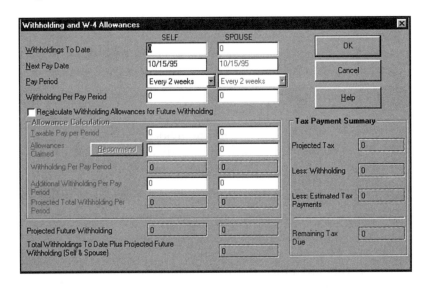

2. For yourself and your spouse, enter the total withheld to date in the Withholdings To Date text boxes.

3. From the Pay Period drop-down list, select how often you and your spouse get paid.

4. Enter the amount withheld each pay period. As you enter amounts, Quicken updates the Tax Payment Summary so you can see how much you will owe or get back. If you're not withholding enough, you can have Quicken estimate how much additional withholding you'll need to pay all your taxes.

5. Click the **Recalculate Withholding Allowances for Future Withholding** check box.

6. Click the **Recommend** button.

7. Quicken will ask if you want it to calculate additional withholding for you. Click **Yes** and Quicken displays its estimate in **Additional Withholding Per Pay Period**. This is the additional amount you should have withheld from each check to cover your taxes.

8. Click **OK** to return to the Tax Planner. Quicken updates the remaining tax due or shows your refund.

If you make estimated payments or applied last year's refund to this year's taxes:

1. In the Tax Planner window, click the **Est. Tax Pmts** button.

2. Enter the amount of the estimated payments you've made to date in the Estimated Taxes (1040-ES) Paid to Date text box.

3. Enter the amount of the estimated payments you will make in the Projected Future Estimated Tax Payments text box.

4. If you applied last year's refund to this year's taxes, enter the amount in the Refund Applied from Prior Year Federal Tax Return text box. Quicken calculates your total estimated tax payments and refund applied.

5. Click **OK** to return to the Tax Planner. Quicken updates the remaining tax due or shows your refund.

# Alternative Scenarios

If you'll receive a big year-end bonus or a raise, or you want to see how different deductions and exemptions affect your taxes, you can create a second and even a third tax scenario and compare them. Maybe there's a real benefit to having a sixth child.

Quicken uses the first Tax Planner scenario you created as the base scenario. To create a second:

1. Under Scenarios, click **Alt. 1**.

2. Quicken asks if you want to copy the current scenario. If you're only changing a few items, click **Yes**. If you want to start again from scratch (my, you are a glutton for punishment), click **No**.

3. Enter the new information in the scenario.

4. To compare scenarios, click **Compare**. Quicken shows your two scenarios side-by-side, with your filing status, tax year, adjusted gross income, deductions and expenses, taxable income, total tax, and tax rates.

## Other Tax Planner Options

The Tax Planner has some other options (the buttons at the top of the window) that come in handy.

➤ Click **Rates** to see a tax rate schedule, so you'll know if that raise will put you in a higher tax bracket.

➤ Click **Print** to print the Tax Planner window.

➤ The **Calculator** button displays the calculator.

➤ The **Reset** button resets the amounts in one or all of your scenarios to zero. Quicken will warn you before erasing all your hard work.

➤ Click **Close** to close the Tax Planner window.

## Tax Reports

I talked about Quicken's reports in Chapter 12, but I want to take this opportunity to highlight the tax reports. There are three of them, and I'll describe each of them briefly.

To refresh your memory, click **Reports** in the main iconbar to see the Create Reports dialog box. The tax reports are easy to spot; they're the ones with the Uncle Sam hat icon.

The first tax report is an EasyAnswers report that lets you see the tax-related transactions that occurred during a specified time period. Just select the time period you want and click **Create**.

The other two are listed with Home reports. The Tax Summary report lists transactions with tax-designated categories from all your taxable accounts. Tax-deferred accounts such as IRAs won't be included. The report shows the date, account, description, category, and amount of each transaction. It calculates your total tax-related income and expenses and the net income/expense.

The Tax Schedule report lists transactions with tax-designated categories and subtotals them according to tax schedule. This is an easy way to see itemized and business deductions.

You can customize, memorize, and print each of these reports as described in Chapter 12.

# The Least You Need to Know

No matter who's in office or what political "revolutions" we endure, Uncle Sam will always get his share. But you can save yourself some serious migraines if you learn your way around Quicken's tax functions.

➤ When you assign tax schedule line items to categories, Quicken can transfer the totals for those categories directly to tax schedules in Turbo Tax. Estimated time to complete your 1040: 30 seconds.

➤ With the Tax Planner, you can estimate your taxes for this year or next; see how different incomes, deductions, and exemptions affect your taxes; and estimate your withholding.

➤ Quicken provides three reports so you can see your tax-related transactions any time.

# Chapter 18

# Imports and Exports

## In This Chapter

➤ Importing accounts registers from a Macintosh version of Quicken

➤ Importing data from a spreadsheet to Quicken

➤ Exporting to tax software

➤ Copying a budget to a spreadsheet

➤ Exporting to another Quicken file

➤ Exporting registers and reports to a spreadsheet or word processing program

Now you're going to be introduced to the import and export business. *Importing* means to transfer data from another Quicken file or another software program into your Quicken 5 file. *Exporting* is the reverse; transferring your Quicken 5 data to another Quicken file or software program.

Why would you want to do such a thing? It probably won't be a daily occurrence, but you may encounter situations where you wish to do the following:

➤ If you have data from Quicken for Macintosh, you can import that data to Quicken 5 for Windows.

➤ You can import data from a spreadsheet to Quicken 5.

➤ You can also export Quicken 5 data to a spreadsheet.

### Techno Talk

### What's a Spreadsheet?

A *spreadsheet* is a software program that works like a chart, where you enter information in columns and rows. It can perform various numerical calculations. For example, I use a spreadsheet to keep track of my business expenses. I record the date, a description, and the amount of the expense, and calculate the total. Lotus 1-2-3 is a popular spreadsheet as is Microsoft Excel. Software packages such as Microsoft Works include a spreadsheet.

➤ You can export data from your current Quicken 5 file to a new Quicken file.

➤ In Chapter 17 I talked about how Quicken's tax preparation functions are designed to work with income tax software. In this chapter I'll tell you how to export your Quicken tax information to your income tax software.

# Importing Data to Quicken 5

As I mentioned, you can import data from Quicken for Macintosh and from a spreadsheet into Quicken 5. First I'll tell you some special considerations for working with Mac and spreadsheet data; the actual import process in Quicken 5 is the same for each.

## Importing from a Mac

I have a confession to make. Although I'm writing a book for Windows, I'm writing it on a Mac. I used Macintosh exclusively for five years, and treated IBM compatibles with thinly disguised contempt. Now that Windows dominates the computer universe, I'm finding my Mac increasingly useless professionally, but I hold onto it for sentimental reasons. Call it rooting for the underdog.

I have a three-year-old version of Quicken on my Mac, so as I tell you how to import data from a Mac version of Quicken, I'm also going to do it in real life.

Quicken 5 will import the information from your Quicken for Mac account registers. If you want to import the category and class lists, you'll have to do that separately. Quicken 5 will not import the Memorized Transaction List, reports, and QuickBillPay or CheckFree merchants.

## Your Mac and PC Have to Talk to Each Other

Macs and PCs are inherently incompatible; what works on one won't work on the other. A PC will **not** recognize a floppy disk formatted for a Macintosh. It spits it out and laughs at you with a maniacal cackle. To import data from a Mac, you need to have a program such as PC Exchange on your Mac that will allow you to copy your Quicken files onto a floppy disk formatted for a PC. The new Macintosh Power PCs are an exception; they will recognize both types of disks and software.

To import Quicken data from a Mac to Quicken 5 for Windows:

1. Open Quicken on your Mac and select the register that you want to import to Quicken 5.

2. From the File menu, choose **Export Transactions**.

3. Type the dates of the transactions that you want to export to Quicken 5. If your register covers several years, I suggest importing only those from the current year, or it will take forever. Click **OK**.

4. You're going to copy the register to a temporary file that you'll import to Quicken 5. Type a name for the temporary file, ending it with **.qif**. QIF stands for Quicken Interchange Format. An example: checking.qif.

5. Select the floppy disk to save the temporary file to and click **OK**. It may take a few minutes for Quicken to copy the register.

6. Repeat steps 1–5 for the other registers you want to import. Quicken 5 will import each register to a separate account, so you should save each one to a new temporary file (savings.qif, credit.qif, and so on).

7. To export the Category & Transfer List, open it and select **Export Categories** from the File menu. Then repeat steps 4 and 5.

# Importing from a Spreadsheet

I can't possibly tell you how every spreadsheet in existence works. The important thing is to save the data as a .qif (Quicken Interchange Format) file so Quicken 5 can read it. You're going to have to do some research on your own to see how your spreadsheet exports data. The computer maxim RTFM (Read The Fine Manual) applies here.

# The Quicken 5 Import Process

Once you've got your files ready, importing them into Quicken is the proverbial piece of cake. Ready? Here goes:

1. If you saved the data to import on a floppy disk, insert it in the disk drive. (If you're importing from a Windows spreadsheet, you probably saved the files on your hard drive.)

2. Open Quicken 5 for Windows.

3. From the File menu, select **Import**. The following figure shows the QIF Import dialog box.

*Importing data to Quicken 5.*

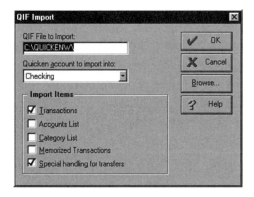

4. Under QIF File to Import:, type the letter of the drive and the name of the file where you saved your import data; for example, **a:\checking.qif**. You can also click the **Browse** button to select your file from the Directories list.

5. From the Quicken account to import into: drop-down list, select the account where you want to import the data.

6. Under Import Items, select the items you're importing. For example, if you're importing a register from the Mac, click **Transactions**. If you're importing transfers or QuickBillPay or CheckFree information, click **Special handling for transfers**. Click **Accounts List**, **Category List**, or **Memorized Transactions** if you're importing those lists.

7. Click **OK**.

8. If Quicken encounters categories or classes that you haven't set up in Quicken 5, Quicken will ask if you want it to create them. Click **Yes**.

9. When it's done, it will tell you it successfully imported x number of items. Click **OK**. Your account registers on Quicken 5 will include the imported transactions.

# Exporting Data from Quicken 5

While there's one basic process for importing data into Quicken 5, how to export depends on what you're exporting. You'll learn different Technonerd techniques for exporting to tax software, copying a budget to a spreadsheet, exporting to another Quicken file, and exporting to another software application.

## Exporting to Tax Software

For this export, you're going to save the Tax Schedule report as a file that your income tax software can use. The Tax Schedule report lists all your tax-related transactions by the tax schedule assigned to them. If you need a refresher course on Quicken's tax preparation functions, see Chapter 17.

### If You Use Turbo Tax

Because Turbo Tax and Quicken are designed to work together, you don't need to export your Quicken data. Turbo Tax will import what it needs from Quicken without any work on your part. This is another way Intuit encourages you to continue buying their products.

1. Click the **Reports** icon in the main iconbar.

2. In the Create Reports dialog box, click the **Home tab**, then **Tax Schedule report**, and finally the **Create** button.

3. The Tax Schedule report has an additional button in the iconbar: Export. Click it. The following figure shows the Create Tax Export File dialog box.

4. Under File Name: type a name for the Tax Schedule report file; for example, **taxes**.

5. Under Directories:, select the directory where you want to save the new file.

6. Click **OK**. You'll have to check your tax software documentation to see how to import the Quicken data.

*Exporting to tax software.*

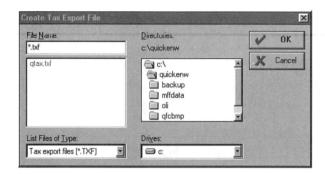

## Copying a Budget to a Spreadsheet

When you create a budget on Quicken, you can copy it directly to a spreadsheet and work with it there. It's very simple:

1. From the Plan menu, select **Budgeting**.

2. If you have more than one budget, open the one you want with the **Manage Budgets** button in the iconbar.

3. Click the **Edit** button in the iconbar and select **Copy All**. Quicken copies the budget to the Windows clipboard.

4. Open your spreadsheet and use the Paste command to paste the budget into the spreadsheet. That's all there is to it.

## Exporting to Another Quicken File

If you create another Quicken 5 file to use for your business accounts or some other purpose, you can copy registers; category, class, and memorized transactions lists; and reports to the new file. Chapter 3 talks about creating another file. To export data from one Quicken file to another:

1. Open the register, list, or report that you want to export.

2. From the File menu, select **File Operations**, then **Copy**. The following figure shows the Copy File dialog box.

3. Type the name of your new Quicken file in the Name field.

4. Quicken assumes the new file is located in the QuickenW directory in your c: drive (C:\QUICKENW\). If the file is in another directory, enter it in the Location: text box.

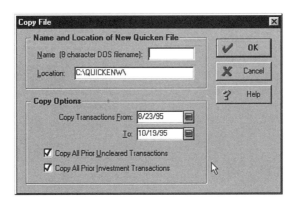

*Exporting data to another Quicken file.*

5. For registers and reports, Quicken automatically copies all transactions. If you want to copy a narrower date range, use the calendar buttons to enter the new dates in the Copy Transactions From: and To: fields.

6. The Copy All Prior Uncleared Transactions check box is selected. Quicken will include all transactions dated prior to the From: date that have not yet been cleared in your register. You need to include these to reconcile your accounts.

7. If your current Quicken file has an investment account, the **Copy All Prior Investment Transactions** check box is selected. Quicken will include all investment transactions dated prior to the From: date. You need to include these transactions if you want your new investment account to reflect the prior performance of your investments.

8. Click **OK**. Quicken copies the information to the new Quicken file. You'll have to repeat this process for each register, list, and report you want to export.

## Exporting to Another Software Application

We talked about importing data from a spreadsheet; you can export Quicken registers and reports to a spreadsheet as well. You can also export to a word processing program if you want to include a register or report with a text document. Let's say you create an accounts receivable report on Quicken and your boss demands a memo about it. You can export the report and make it part of the memo.

1. Open the register or report that you want to export.

2. For reports, click **Print**. For registers, select **Print Register** from the File menu, then click **Print**. Wait a gosh-darned minute. Did you say print? Yes, I did. Stay with me. Instead of printing to a piece of paper, Quicken will "print" the register or report to your spreadsheet or word processing file. The following figure shows the Print Report dialog box (it's the same for reports and registers).

*"Printing" to files.*

3. Under Print to:, select the format in which Quicken should save the report or register:

   ➤ **ASCII Disk File**   Click this if you want to save to a word processing program.

   ➤ **Tab-delimited Disk File**   Click this to save to a spreadsheet other than Lotus 1-2-3. Each column in the register or report will be inserted into a separate column in the spreadsheet.

   ➤ **1-2-3(.PRN) Disk File**   Click this to save to a Lotus 1-2-3 spreadsheet.

**What's an ASCII?**

ASCII (pronounced ASS-key) is an acronym for American Standard Code for Information Interchange. Basically, it's a universal computer format that just about any computer and software program can read and understand. It looks like gibberish to you and me, but your computer knows what it is.

4. Click **OK**. The Create Disk File dialog box appears.

5. In the File Name: text box, type the name of your word processing or spreadsheet file.

6. From the Directories: list, select the directory where the file is located.

7. Click **OK**. Quicken copies the report or register to the new file. You can then edit it with your word processing or spreadsheet program.

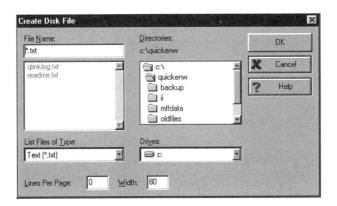

*Creating a file to export Quicken data.*

Now that wasn't so bad, was it? See how easy it is to achieve Technonerd status? To receive your Official Embossed Technonerd Certificate, send $10 and five floppy disk box tops to the International Society of Technonerds, Bill Gates, President.

# The Least You Need to Know

Every once in a while you may find it would be really helpful to transfer information from another program into Quicken 5, or vice versa. Here's what you can do:

➤ Import account registers from Quicken for Macintosh to Quicken 5.

➤ Import data from a spreadsheet to Quicken 5.

➤ Export Quicken's Tax Schedule report to income tax software.

➤ Copy a Quicken budget directly to a spreadsheet.

➤ Export Quicken 5 data to another Quicken file.

➤ Export registers and reports to word processing documents or spreadsheet.

# Chapter 19

# The Personal Touch: Customizing Quicken

## In This Chapter

➤ Customizing Quicken's general options

➤ QuickFill options

➤ The way checks print

➤ How your account registers look

➤ And the features in the iconbar

When you installed Quicken, it came with certain preset options, such as window colors and drop-down lists, that determine how Quicken looks and acts. Everything works just peachy. But just because it's set that way doesn't mean you can't imbue Quicken with your own personal style. This is America, after all, where individualism is practically the national religion.

The Options button in the window border lets you work your magic on general options, checks, registers, reports, reminders, and the iconbar. The following figure shows the Options dialog box.

*Leave your personal imprint.*

To see what kinds of options are available, click on the **Options** button on the iconbar and then click on the appropriate button in the Options dialog box. A few options will require you to make a selection from a drop-down list or type a number. But for most of them, click on each option to check it and make it functional or if it's already checked, click to turn it off. I'll explain what each option does when it's functional.

### Why You Won't See Reports and Reminders in This Chapter

The report options here are exactly the same as those in the Options button of the Reports window, which you'll find in Chapter 12. The reminder options are the same as those in the **Options** button of the Quicken Reminders window, which I talk about in Chapter 10. I don't want anyone accusing me of repeating myself.

# General Options

The general options are, well, general. They affect Quicken's windows and commands and miscellaneous features. The following figure shows the General Options dialog box.

Here are the options you have to choose from:

➤ **Show HomeBase on Top at Startup** When you start Quicken, HomeBase will always be the top window, no matter what other windows you had open when you last quit Quicken.

➤ **Confirm Investment Transactions from Forms** Quicken asks you to confirm a transaction you've entered on an investment form before Quicken records it in the investment account register.

➤ **Use Tax Schedules with Categories** This option allows you to assign tax schedule line items to categories (see Chapter 17).

➤ **Use Bold Text in Dialogs** All the text in Quicken's windows and dialog boxes will be bold.

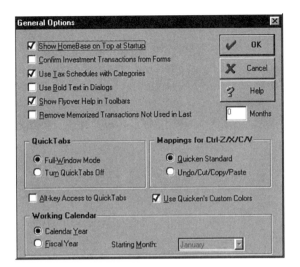

*Customizing the general options.*

➤ **Show Flyover Help in Toolbars**  Flyover help displays a short description of each button's function when you move your mouse over an icon in an iconbar.

➤ **Remove Memorized Transactions Not Used in Last _ Months**  Select this option if you want Quicken to automatically delete memorized transactions from the Memorized Transaction List if you haven't used them in the number of months you enter in the Months text box. Quicken will delete them from the Memorized Transaction List, not from the account registers.

# QuickTabs

QuickTabs are the little tabs along the left of your screen that allow you to switch from window to window. Click one of these options to control how you work with Quicken's windows.

➤ **Full-Window Mode**  Quicken displays one window at a time with the QuickTabs on the left.

➤ **Turn QuickTabs Off**  Displays the windows without QuickTabs.

➤ **Alt-key Access to QuickTabs**  If you select this option, each QuickTab will have a number on it next to the QuickTab's name. You can then press the **Alt** key and the appropriate number to select the QuickTab instead of clicking on it. I guess this is for people who have a mouse aversion.

➤ **Use Quicken's Custom Colors**  When this option is on, Quicken's windows have a gray background. If you turn it off, you can use the color scheme you set up using the Windows control panel.

## Mappings for Ctrl+Z/X/C/V

This option determines the commands for Ctrl+key combinations; in other words, what happens when you press **Ctrl** and another key at the same time. Here you can choose between the Quicken standard and the Windows standard.

The Quicken standard is to press **Ctrl+X** to Go to Transfer (an Edit menu command), **Ctrl+C** to bring up the Category & Transfer List (Lists menu), **Ctrl+V** to void a transaction (Edit menu), and **Ctrl+Z** doesn't do anything.

These same Ctrl+key combinations perform different commands in Windows and most other Windows software: **Ctrl+X** for cut, **Ctrl+C** for copy, **Ctrl+V** for paste, and **Ctrl+Z** for undo. If you keep pressing **Ctrl+Z** and wonder why Quicken doesn't undo anything, it's because Quicken is using its own standard. To switch to the Windows standard, click **Undo/Cut/Copy/Paste**.

## Working Calendar

This option determines whether Quicken uses a standard calendar (January-December) or a fiscal year calendar you designate. To use a fiscal year calendar, click the **Fiscal Year** option button and select its starting month from the Starting Month drop-down list.

When you've set all the general options, click **OK**.

## Checks

With the checks options, you can customize how your printed checks will look, and how you fill out the check. The Checks Options dialog box, shown in the following figure, are divided into three tabs: Checks, Miscellaneous, and QuickFill.

*Customize the way you write and print checks.*

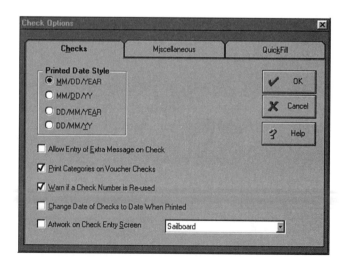

214

# Checks Tab

The dialog box options in the Checks tab determine how your printed checks will look.

➤ **Printed Date Style**   Select how you want Quicken to print the date on the check: MM/DD/YEAR (12/31/1995), MM/DD/YY (12/31/95), DD/MM/YEAR (31/12/1995), or DD/MM/YY (31/12/95).

➤ **Allow Entry of Extra Message on Check**   Quicken includes an extra message line on the check, in addition to the memo line.

➤ **Print Categories on Voucher Checks**   If you use voucher checks (checks with an A/P or payroll voucher attached), this option will print the check's categories on the voucher.

➤ **Warn if a Check Number is Re-used**   Quicken will warn you if you enter the same check number twice.

➤ **Change Date of Checks to Date When Printed**   If you print checks on a different day than when you wrote them in the Write Checks window, this option will change the date on the check to the day when you print them.

➤ **Artwork on Check Entry Screen**   Quicken provides some clever little pictures you can include in the Write Checks window by selecting one from the drop-down list. Quicken will **not** print the picture on the check. Bummer.

# Miscellaneous Tab

The miscellaneous options, shown in the following figure, deal with warnings and confirmations, among other things. These same options are also available for the account registers.

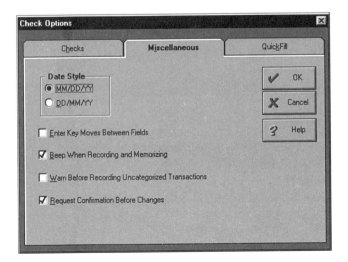

*Changing the miscellaneous checks options.*

➤ **Date Style** Select how you want the date displayed in the Write Checks window (or the register): MM/DD/YY (12/31/95) or DD/MM/YY (31/12/95).

➤ **Enter Key Moves Between Fields** This option lets you use the **Enter** key as well as the **Tab** key to move from one field to the next.

➤ **Beep When Recording and Memorizing** Your computer will beep at you when Quicken records and memorizes a transaction.

➤ **Warn Before Recording Uncategorized Transactions** If you want every transaction to include a category, Quicken will warn you if you try to record one that doesn't.

➤ **Request Confirmation Before Changes** If you make changes to a check or transaction and don't record them, Quicken will warn you when you go on to another transaction or window.

## QuickFill Tab

*QuickFill* is the collective name for the features on Quicken that make entering information easier: drop-down lists, automatic memorization of transactions, filling in a name after you type the first few letters, and so on. The QuickFill options, shown in the following figure, let you choose which QuickFill features to use. These same options are also available for account registers.

*Choosing the QuickFill options.*

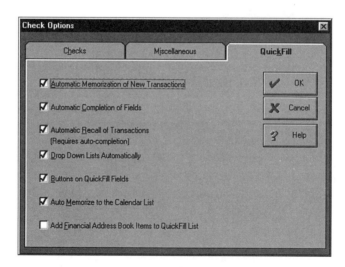

➤ **Automatic Memorization of New Transactions** Quicken automatically memorizes a new transaction when you enter it and adds it to the Memorized Transaction List. Turn it off if you only want to memorize selected transactions.

➤ **Automatic Completion of Fields**   Quicken completes a field after you enter the first few characters, if it matches a memorized transaction. If you turn this option off, Automatic Recall of Transactions will not be available.

➤ **Automatic Recall of Transactions**   When you enter a payee in the check or register and press **Tab**, Quicken automatically inserts the amount and category for the payee's memorized transaction.

➤ **Drop Down Lists Automatically**   Quicken opens a field's drop-down list when you tab to the field.

➤ **Buttons on QuickFill Fields**   In the Payee field of the account register and Write Checks window, this option includes an arrow button in the field so you can select from the list, even if you turn off the option to drop down lists automatically. When this option is off, there's no arrow button in the Payee field.

➤ **Auto Memorize to the Calendar List**   Adds automatically memorized transactions to the transaction list on the Financial Calendar. This option won't work if you turn off automatic memorization of new transactions.

➤ **Add Financial Address Book Items to QuickFill List**   Adds names and addresses from the Financial Address Book to the Memorized Transaction List, if the names and payees match.

When you've set your check options, click **OK**.

# Registers

Like the check options, the register options are divided into three tabs: Display, Miscellaneous, and QuickFill (see the following figure). The display options let you customize how the registers look. The Miscellaneous and QuickFill tabs contain exactly the same options as the Miscellaneous and QuickFill tabs for checks (see the previous section), so I'm not going to repeat them here.

When you change the display options, the changes will affect all of your account registers.

➤ **Show Account Selector**   The account selector displays all of your accounts along the bottom of the register so you can switch account registers by clicking on the account name.

➤ **Show Description Bar**   The description bar labels each field in the register (Date, Num, Payee, and so on).

➤ **Date In First Column**   If this option is on, the date is in the first column of the register. If it's off, the check number field is in the first column.

*Customizing the account register options.*

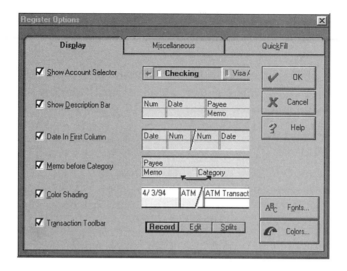

➤ **Memo before Category**   If this option is on, the memo field comes before the category field. Turn it off to reverse them.

➤ **Color Shading**   Shades the second line of each transaction in the register. This makes it easier to scan for items in a register.

➤ **Transaction Toolbar**   Displays the transaction toolbar (the Record, Edit, and Splits buttons) with every transaction.

If you get bored looking at the same thing day after day, you can give your account registers a make-over with new fonts and colors.

## Changing Fonts

You can choose a new font, or type style, for your registers. All the text in the registers will appear in the font you choose. To change the font:

1. Click the **Fonts** button in the Display tab in the Register Options dialog box.

2. Select a font from the Font: drop-down list. When you select a font, Sample Text shows you what the font looks like. Try them out until you find one you like.

3. Select a size from the Size: drop-down list. Different sizes may be available for different fonts. Again, the Sample Text will show you what it looks like.

4. If you change your mind and want to go back to the preset font, click **Reset**.

5. Click **OK**. When you open your registers, you'll see the new font.

### Fun with Fonts

The fonts you see in the dialog box will vary according to what fonts you have installed on your computer. There are certain standard fonts that come with Windows. There are also thousands upon thousands of different kinds of fonts available, from the elegant to the bizarre. I have a thing for fonts; I currently have about 50 of them on my computer and I'm always on the lookout for more. They're an easy way to liven up an otherwise prosaic computer file.

## Changing Colors

You may have noticed that each account register is in a different color. You can change that, too. The colors available will depend on the type of monitor you have; some monitors display more colors than others.

1. Click the **Colors** button in the Display tab of the Register Options dialog box.

2. Each of your account registers is listed next to a drop-down list that contains various color options. Select the color you want for each register from the drop-down list.

3. If you want to go back to the preset colors, click **Reset**.

4. Click **OK**. When you open your registers, you'll see their new look.

## Iconbar

These options control the way the main iconbar looks. If you frequently use a function that's not on the iconbar, you can add it. If you rarely use a function that's there, you can delete it. The following figure shows the Customize Iconbar dialog box:

The top part of the window shows the iconbar as it currently appears. Click on the arrows under the icons to see all of the icons.

*Customize the
iconbar for the way
you work.*

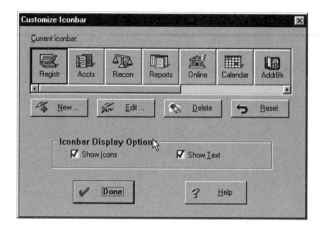

# Adding an Icon

When you add an icon to the iconbar, you can also select the graphic and text, and enter
a key combination to use instead of clicking the icon. For example, as Quicken is now,
you can either click on the **Accts** icon in the iconbar or press **Ctrl+A** to bring up the
Account List. Ctrl+A is called a speed key.

To add an icon to the iconbar:

1. Click the **New** button. Quicken displays the Add Action to Iconbar dialog box,
   shown in the following figure.

*Adding a new icon to
the iconbar.*

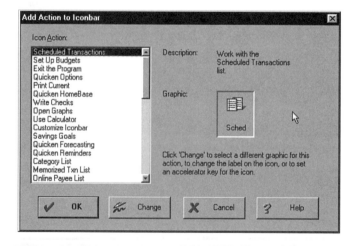

2. The Icon Action list shows all the available functions you can put on the iconbar. When you click on a function in the list, Quicken gives you a description of it and shows how the icon would look.

   If that's all you want to do, click **OK**. The following four steps are purely optional.

3. To give the icon a different picture, label, or key combination, click **Change**.

4. Select a new picture for the icon from the Graphic: list.

5. In the Icon Label: field, type a new label.

6. You can also assign a speed key to the function. In the **Speed Key:** text box, type the letter, number, or character to press, along with the **Alt** and **Shift** keys, to use the function. For example, for the Exit function, enter **E** in the **Speed Key:** field and you'll be able to press **Alt+Shift+E** to exit Quicken.

7. Click **OK**. You can continue adding icons or click **OK** again to return to the Customize Iconbar dialog box.

# Other Iconbar Options

In the Customize Iconbar dialog box, you can also edit an icon in the current iconbar, delete an icon, reset the iconbar to the way it was before you changed it, and specify whether the iconbar displays text, icons, or both.

➤ **Editing an Icon**   For each icon on the iconbar, you can change the graphic, label, and add or change the speed key. To edit an icon, click on it under Current iconbar: in the Customize Iconbar dialog box and click **Edit**. The Edit Action on Iconbar dialog box is exactly the same as the Add Action to Iconbar dialog box. Edit any of the options you want. See the previous steps for help.

➤ **Deleting an Icon**   Although Quicken included the most common functions in the iconbar, you may find you don't use some of them very often. If you add new icons, the iconbar may become unwieldy. To delete an icon from the iconbar, click on the icon in the Current iconbar and click **Delete**. Quicken will ask if you're sure; click **OK** and the icon disappears.

➤ **Reset the Iconbar**   If you want to change the iconbar back to the way it was when you first installed Quicken, click **Reset**. Whatever changes you made adding, editing, or deleting are gone and the iconbar returns to its preset state.

➤ **Iconbar Display Options**   These options set how the iconbar looks. It can show just the icon (or picture), just the text (or label), or both. If neither option is on, you won't see the iconbar.

221

# The Least You Need to Know

The Options button lets you customize Quicken to fit the way you work. You can also change the way some of the features look if you need to spice up your life a little; it's easier than re-arranging the furniture.

➤ In General Options, customize how you work with Quicken's windows and how they look.

➤ QuickFill makes entering data in the checks and registers easier, but you can turn off the QuickFill options that you don't find helpful.

➤ You can change the way checks print and account registers look.

➤ In the iconbar, you can add icons for the functions you use frequently, and delete icons for the ones you don't.

# Troubleshooting

Quicken is a fine program, and I'm sure Intuit's Technonerds worked their little hearts out to make it as idiot-proof and trouble-free as possible.

But no matter how good a software program is, or how computer-literate you are, things are going to go wrong. Inevitably, they will go wrong when you least expect it and can least afford to spend the time figuring out how to fix it. This chapter will give you solutions to some common problems you may encounter.

So instead of banging your head against a wall, scan the headings to find your problem and the solution. Oftentimes, I'll refer you to the chapter that explains the feature where you encounter your problem.

If you don't get an answer here, Quicken Help goes into a lot more depth. To use Help to shoot your troubles, perform the following steps:

1. Click **Help** in the iconbar.

2. Click **Search**.

3. Type **troubleshooting**.

4. Click **Display**. Help lists all the troubleshooting topics, as shown in the following figure.

*Use Quicken's online help to shoot your troubles away.*

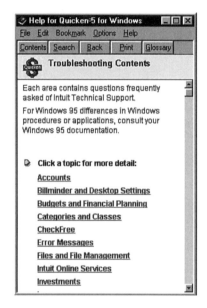

5. Click on the topic you want.

If all else fails, you can always call Quicken's Technical Support and have the real Technonerds help you out.

## The Department of Duh

The first thing to do when you encounter a problem is to check the obvious. To give my own bone-headed example: recently I put a CD-ROM in my disk drive, but I could not get the darn thing to run. My computer kept telling me it couldn't read the drive. I was getting increasingly frustrated, thinking I'd just spent a month's salary on a lemon. Finally, I popped open the drive and discovered I'd put the CD-ROM in upside-down. Duh.

➤ Make sure any devices you're trying to use (printer, modem, speakers, and so on) are turned on.

➤ Check the tangle of cables behind your computer to make sure none of the connections is loose.

➤ If you're using a floppy disk or CD-ROM, make sure you have the right disk and you're telling Quicken to read the correct drive.

> **Which Drive Is Which?**
> Windows gives letter designations to each drive, followed by a colon and a backslash. Generally, your hard drive is the c:\ drive. The floppy disk drive is the a:\ drive. If you have two floppy disk drives, the second one is the b:\ drive. The CD-ROM drive is the d:\ drive.

# My Accounts Aren't Accounting

If you're having trouble with your accounts, check that they're set up the way you want them. You can add, edit, and delete accounts from the Account List (see Chapter 4).

## I can't get my account to balance.

If your account doesn't balance, here are a few things to try:

➤ If this is the first time you've reconciled the account, the first thing to check is whether the opening balance in the account register matches the opening balance in your bank statement. If it doesn't, click **Recon** again and change the opening balance to match your statement.

➤ Make sure that you've entered all the transactions that have not yet cleared the bank. Then scroll through the list of transactions in the Reconcile window and check that they match your statement. You may have:

  ➤ Missed marking a transaction. In the list of transactions, click in the **Clr** column to mark it.

  ➤ Forgotten to record a transaction. To add a transaction to the register, click the **New** button.

  ➤ Missed entering a service charge.

  ➤ Entered a service charge twice. Remember that you entered a service charge in the Reconcile window; make sure you didn't also record a separate transaction for it.

  ➤ Mistakenly marked an item as cleared. Click the yellow checkmark in the list of transactions to unmark it.

➤ Entered a deposit as a payment or a payment as a deposit.

➤ Entered the wrong amount for a transaction. To edit a transaction from the Reconcile window, select the transaction from the list and click the **Edit** button. Quicken will switch to the account register. When you're done editing the transaction, click **Recon** to continue reconciling the account.

Chapter 8 describes reconciling accounts in detail.

## When I set up an account, Quicken tells me, "Name Already in Use."

Each account has to have a name that's different from all your other accounts *and* from the categories. Quicken won't let you use the same name twice. You'll have to come up with another one.

# BillMinder Isn't Reminding Me

If BillMinder isn't reminding you, or is reminding you when you don't want it to, or is reminding you too far in advance, check the **Reminders** settings in the **Options** button (see Chapter 10).

# My Budgets Aren't Budgeting

## Autocreate won't create a budget.

Check the date range for Autocreate. You have to have transactions in that date range or there won't be any information to put in the budget. Clear the report, change the date range, and try again.

## The amounts in the budget are different from the actual amounts.

Check the Autocreate settings:

If **Use Average for Period** is checked, Quicken will average the amounts over the course of the date range. For example, if you have a single $200 transaction, Autocreate budgets $17 per month for that transaction, for a yearly average of $204.

If **Round Values to Nearest $** is checked, Quicken will round the amounts either up or down. $23 will be rounded to $20; $27 will be rounded to $30.

Chapter 15 gives the details on working with budgets.

# My Files Aren't Filing

## I can't find my file.

When you choose **Open** from the **File** menu, Quicken files have a .qdb suffix, such as qdata.qdb. Open all the files with this suffix to see if one of them is the one you want.

Quicken automatically saves its files in the QUICKENW directory. If your file isn't there, try looking in another directory. You can search for .qdb files with Windows Explorer:

1. Click **Start** in the Windows taskbar.

2. Select **Programs**, then **Windows Explorer**.

3. In the Tools menu, select **Find** and then **Files or Folders**.

4. Type **\*.qdb** and click **Find Now**. Windows will list all the files with a .qdb suffix, as shown in the following figure.

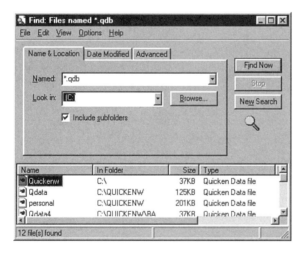

*Finding a file in Windows Explorer.*

In the Open Quicken File dialog box, open the folder where you found your file by clicking on it in the Directories: list. Your file will be listed in the File Name: list. Click on your file name, and click **OK**.

## I deleted a file. Can I get it back?

If you deleted a file, you can restore a backup copy, either from a floppy, if you backed up to one, or from the QUICKENW/BACKUP directory. Every seven days, Quicken backs up your file to this directory. When you restore a file from the QUICKENW/BACKUP directory, Quicken will restore the latest backup copy. So if you've made changes to the file in between the last backup and the time you deleted the file, you'll lose those changes. Chapter 3 talks about backing up and restoring files.

### I can't restore my file.

Again, check the obvious. Make sure you're using the correct directory or disk drive that has the backed-up file.

Quicken will warn you if it is about to overwrite an existing file. If you click **Yes**, Quicken will replace the existing file with the backup copy. If the backup is older than the existing file, you're going to have to replace the information you created in the meantime.

# General Protection Faults—AACK!

General Protection Faults (GPFs) are Windows error messages that are not unique to Quicken. I mention them here because they are the bane of every Windows user's existence.

If you get a GPF, basically you're hosed. Quicken and any other programs you're using will shut down and there's nothing you can do about it. You will lose any data that has not been saved. The thing to remember is to restart your computer. A GPF can cause all kinds of wacky problems and restarting will clear the computer chips of its nasty presence. If your screen freezes (you can't use the mouse or keyboard), press **Ctrl+Alt+Delete** to restart your computer. If that doesn't work, take a deep breath and turn the computer power off.

If you consistently get a GPF, write down exactly what the error message says (it won't mean squat to you) and what you were doing when you got it, and call Technical Support. Only genuine Technonerds can deal with this one.

# Loans

### I deleted a loan and want to create another loan with the same name.

When you delete a loan from the View Loans window, Quicken saves its associated liability account unless you tell it not to. The liability account has the same name as the loan you deleted. You cannot give another loan the same name unless you rename the first liability account or delete it.

# The loan schedule is wrong.

If you delete or edit a loan transaction from an account register, you need to reset the loan schedule from the View Loans window. To reset the schedule:

1. Click the **Edit Payment** button in the View Loans window. The following figure shows the Edit Loan Payment dialog box.

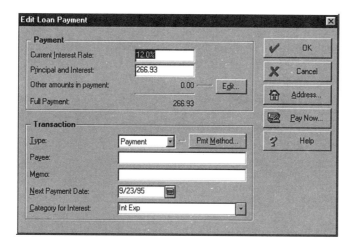

*Edit the loan payment to reset the loan schedule.*

2. If you deleted a transaction, enter the date of your next regular payment in the Next Payment Date field.

3. If you made a different payment amount, enter the amount in the Principal and Interest text box and the date paid in the Next Payment Date field.

4. Click **OK** and Quicken will reset the loan schedule.

# The memorized loan transaction is wrong.

Quicken may have inadvertently replaced the loan transaction in the Memorized Transaction List with another transaction to the same payee.

This isn't supposed to happen. When you set up a loan, Quicken should add a locked loan transaction to the Memorized Transaction List, which means it can't be overwritten by another transaction.

But, as we all know, stuff happens. To fix it, open the Memorized Transaction List and make sure the transaction is **unlocked**. Then make a loan payment from the View Loans window. Go back and check the Memorized Transaction List; Quicken should put the loan transaction back on the Memorized Transaction List as a locked transaction.

If Quicken is being particularly stubborn about this, select the loan transaction in the Memorized Transaction List and click the **Lock** icon. That should do it.

# My Printer Won't Print

Printers hate me. I can be working merrily along without a care in the world, but when I try to print, something always goes wrong. The paper jams or goes in crooked, the printer prints garbage, or the ink smears. If it's not one thing, it's another.

If the suggestions here don't solve your problem, your printer manual may have the solution, or you could try calling the printer manufacturer's technical support.

## General Printing Headaches

First, know how to use your printer: how to load the paper, clear paper jams, get it to stop if it prints 50 pages of a five-page document. (This actually happened to me. Three times.) Troubleshooting for other printing problems follows:

### The print-out is faded or illegible.

Try changing the toner cartridge.

### Nothing prints.

Try printing from another software application. If you can't print from there either, first check the printer setup in Windows 95 to make sure your printer is selected.

1. Click **Start** in the Windows 95 taskbar.

2. Select **Settings**, then **Printers**. The following figure shows the Printers window.

3. Click on the name of your printer. If your printer isn't listed, you will have to install the printer driver. Your printer manual will tell you how to do this.

4. From the **File** menu, select **Set As Default**.

*Select your printer from the Printers window in the Windows 95 settings.*

5. Close the Printers window and try printing again.

If your printer was already set as the default, look in your printer manual for a possible cause.

If you can print from another application, the problem is with Quicken. Restart your computer and Quicken and check the printer driver.

1. In the **File** menu, select **Printer Setup**, then **Report/Graph Printer Setup** or **Check Printer Setup**, depending on what you're trying to print.

2. Check the Printer: drop-down list. It should give the name of your printer.

3. If it doesn't, look for your printer in the drop-down list.

4. If your printer isn't listed, you will have to install the printer driver. Your printer manual will tell you how to do this.

## It prints gibberish.

Check your printer's emulation mode. Many printers can emulate other printers; that is, they pretend to be something they're not. Check your printer manual to see how to deal with this.

You may have selected a symbol font (some font styles, such as Wingdings, use symbols instead of letters and numbers) or a font your printer can't handle. Try changing to a standard font, such as Arial or Times New Roman.

1. In Printer Setup, click **Head Font** to change the font style for headings and **Body Font** for the main text.

2. Select **Times New Roman** from the Font: drop-down list.

3. In the Size: drop-down list, choose a small size for the font. Try 10 or 12.

4. Click **OK**.

## The edges of my report or graph are cut off.

Increase the margins by following these steps:

1. In the File menu, select **Printer Setup**, then **Report/Graph Printer Setup**.

2. All four margins are set at one-half inch. Highlight the margin you want to change and type in the new margin. Try 0.75 or 1.0.

3. Click **OK**.

## Check Printing Problems

These are problems you may encounter specifically when printing checks.

### The check alignment is off.

Adjust the Fine Alignment:

1. In the File menu, select **Printer Setup**, then **Check Printer Setup**.

2. Click **Align**.

3. Click the button that matches the number of checks you have on a page.

4. Click the arrows to adjust the vertical and horizontal alignment.

5. Click **Print Sample** and use a blank piece of paper. Hold the paper up to a page of checks to see if the alignment is correct.

6. Repeat steps 4 and 5 until the checks are aligned.

### The payee address isn't printing on the check.

There are two things to try.

To print an address on a check, you have to write the check in the Write Checks window. Entering the transaction in your checking account register won't work because the register doesn't include an address field.

In the Memorized Transaction List, check the transaction type. It has to be a Chk (print check) to print an address on the actual check. Click **Edit** to change the transaction type.

### I click the Print icon in the Write Checks window and nothing happens.

First, make sure you have checks to print. Open the **Account List**, and the Chks column shows the accounts that have checks to print.

If you have checks to print, the **Print** icon in the Write Checks window may have another account assigned to it. Quicken Help can give you specific ways to solve this problem.

## QuickBillPay Isn't Paying My Bills Quickly

Before you can use QuickBillPay or QuickBanking with an account, you have to tell Quicken you want it that way. See Chapter 8 to learn how to set up an account for QuickBillPay and QuickBanking.

Quicken automatically sets up your modem for use with Intuit Online Services. If you're using another service, such as CheckFree, check the Help menu under Troubleshooting - CheckFree to see how to set up your modem, or call Intuit Technical Support.

# Registers and Transactions

## I entered a transaction in my account register and now I can't find it.

Quicken automatically and immediately sorts transactions by date. Scroll through the register until you find the transaction. Or if you know its exact date, click **Edit** and select **Go to A Specific Date**.

## Quicken is putting a split in a transaction and I don't want it there.

When you first entered the transaction, Quicken memorized it as a split. To fix it:

1. Open the **Memorized Transaction List**.
2. Select the transaction and click **Edit**.
3. Click **Splits**.
4. Click **Clear All** and **OK**.

## I imported transactions and now I have duplicate transactions in my register.

You imported transfers. When you import transactions that have transfers, be sure to click **Special handling for transfers** in the QIF Import dialog box. See Chapter 18 for details.

# My Reports Aren't Reporting

## The report isn't showing all my data, or it just plain looks wrong.

Click **Customize** in the report window and check that Quicken is including the dates, accounts, and categories you want. Chapter 12 deals with customizing reports.

# My Taxes Are Taxing

## Quicken didn't export everything to my tax software.

First, make sure that all the categories you want exported have been assigned a tax schedule line item. Chapter 17 describes how to do this.

Quicken will not export to line items that require a tax table or calculations. You can use a Tax Summary report to see the total amounts for these line items, but you'll have to perform the calculations yourself, or check your income tax software for details.

Quicken also won't export transactions from tax-deferred accounts, such as an IRA.

## The tax withheld is too high in the Tax Planner.

You may have categorized a tax payment in the same category you use for taxes withheld. Create a new category, such as "Tax paid," for tax payments. Do not make it tax-related.

# The Least You Need to Know

Computers are wonderful devices, until they don't work right. Then they can be the most evil, sadistic instruments of torture ever created.

➤ Don't panic. Computer problems happen to everyone, even to the people who invented them.

➤ Remember the Department of Duh: check the obvious. Everything's hooked up, turned on, and your toddler didn't put peanut butter in the disk drive.

➤ Don't be afraid to call Technical Support, especially if you're intimidated by a problem. That's what they're there for.

# Part 3
# Quicken Makes House Calls

*Just what, exactly, do you own? Where is it? What is it worth? If you needed to squeeze a payment out of your insurance company, would you have what you need to back up your claim?*

*With Quicken Home Inventory, you can record each of your worldly possessions, where it is, what you paid for it, and how much it's worth now. You can enter the details about your insurance policies and what possessions are covered by which policy. When you make an insurance claim, you'll have a record of that, too—everything all together in one easy package.*

*Quicken and Quicken Home Inventory work together so the value of your possessions is included in your net worth in Quicken. And when you buy something new, Quicken adds it to your home inventory.*

THE PLEASURE OF A HOME OFFICE.

# Chapter 21

# Eight Easy Steps to Your Home Inventory

## In This Chapter

➤ Keep track of your stuff with Quicken Home Inventory

➤ Choosing locations and categories

➤ Adding, copying, and editing items

➤ Creating reports

➤ Finding and moving items

Quicken Home Inventory does for your home what an inventory does for a business: records what possessions you have, how many you have, and how much they're worth.

Why? If you were to suffer a major catastrophe, your insurance company is going to want proof of what you owned before your home was wiped out and how much it was worth. If you're planning a move, Home Inventory is a good way to see what you have and whether you want to move it all. Or you might just want to see how much stuff you have.

This chapter will take you through the basic steps of creating a home inventory. As an example, I'll inventory the items in an imaginary living room. The next chapter explains how Home Inventory works with Quicken.

Home Inventory also enables you to keep track of your insurance policies and will help you decide if you're adequately covered, which we'll get into in Chapter 23.

# Step 1: Open Home Inventory

Although Home Inventory interacts with your Quicken file, it's saved separately from your accounts. You can open Home Inventory either from the Windows desktop or from your Quicken file.

To open Home Inventory from the desktop, click on the **Start** menu in the Windows taskbar. Select **Programs**, then **Quicken**, and finally **Quicken Home Inventory**.

If you've already opened Quicken, select **Quicken Home Inventory** from the **Add-Ons** menu, or click on the **Inventory** icon in the iconbar. The following figure shows the Home Inventory window.

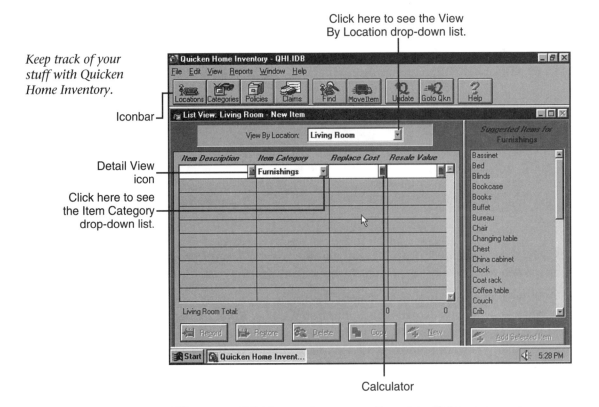

Click here to see the View By Location drop-down list.

*Keep track of your stuff with Quicken Home Inventory.*

Iconbar

Detail View icon

Click here to see the Item Category drop-down list.

Calculator

# Step 2: Choose a Location

Home Inventory organizes your possessions by location—rooms, garage, closets, patio or deck, and even safe-deposit box or special collection (for all of you people out there who collect Precious Moments, Hummels, and miniature village houses). Click the **View By Location:** drop-down list to see all of the locations available for Home Inventory.

The first step to creating an inventory is to decide which location you want to inventory first. To follow along with my example, click on the **View By Location:** drop-down list and select **Living Room**. When you want to enter items for another location, just select one from the list.

## Adding, Editing, and Deleting Locations

The locations listed in the menu are adequate for most standard homes, but maybe your mansion includes a five-lane bowling alley and private screen room. To add a location:

1. Click the **Locations** button in the iconbar to see the Locations list.

2. Click **New**.

3. Type a name for the location, such as "bowling alley," and click **OK**.

When you click on a location in the list and click **Edit**, the only thing you can change is the location's name. If the list is too cumbersome for you, select a location and click **Delete**.

# Step 3: Choose an Item Category

Item categories group your possessions: furnishings, appliances, electronics, that kind of thing. They have nothing to do with the categories in your Quicken accounts.

We're going to inventory the furnishings in our imaginary living room, so click on the **down arrow** in the Item Category column and select **Furnishings** from the drop-down list. You can include as many different categories in each location as you want.

## Adding, Editing, and Deleting Categories

Again, the preset list of item categories is not sacrosanct. To add a category:

1. Click the **Categories** button in the iconbar to see the Categories list.

2. Click **New**.

3. Type a name for the category, such as "bowling pins," and click **OK**.

Select a category and click **Edit** to change the category's name. To get rid of a category, select it and click **Delete**.

# Step 4: Enter Items from Memory

Instead of lugging your computer from room to room, the way to proceed is to enter as many items as you can from memory. Then in the next step, you'll create a report of your mental inventory and lug that from room to room. To enter an item:

1. Click in the **Item Description** column.

2. On the right of your screen, Home Inventory gives a list of suggested items for the category you chose in Step 3; in our case, items for the category Furnishings. Double-click **Couch**.

3. Home Inventory puts Couch in the Item Description column, along with its suggested replacement cost (600) and resale value (300) in their respective columns.

4. The replacement cost is highlighted; to change it, just type in a new value. You can also click on the calculator icon in the Replace Cost field to use the calculator.

5. When you enter a new replacement cost, Home Inventory automatically puts half the replacement cost in the resale value column. If you don't think you could get that much for it, type a new value.

6. If you change the replacement and resale values, click **Record** to save the changes. If you don't change the values, Home Inventory automatically saves the item as is. The following figure shows the Couch item for our living room example.

*Entering items for a location.*

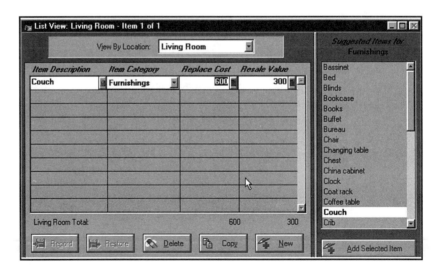

7. Click on the next line to add another item. Continue adding items until you've inventoried all the items in that location.

8. Select another location from the View By Location drop-down list and add items for that location.

## Adding an Item That's Not in the List

If you want to add an item that's not listed in the suggested items, the procedure is slightly different, but far from complicated.

1. Click in the Item Description column.

2. Type the name of your item; say, **Jukebox**.

3. Tab to or click on the **Replace Cost** and **Resale Value** columns and enter the jukebox's values.

4. Click **Record**.

## Copying Items

If you have more than one of the same item in a location, you can copy the item. Just click on the item in the list and click the **Copy** button. Home Inventory adds the copied item to the bottom of the list. You can then edit the item description to differentiate between them.

## Editing an Item Description

Our imaginary living room has two chairs, but we want to differentiate the blue wing chair from the pink swivel chair.

1. Double-click on **Chair** in the suggested items.

2. Click **Copy**.

3. In the Item Description column for the first chair, click so the cursor is after "Chair." You don't want to highlight Chair or you'll type over it.

4. Type **blue wing**.

5. For the second chair, click and type **pink swivel**.

6. Click **Record** to save the changes.

## Alphabetizing the List

Home Inventory initially lists the items in the order you enter them. When you switch to another location or category, or quit Home Inventory, it automatically alphabetizes the list. If you want it alphabetized as you work with the list, select **Alphabetize Register** from the Edit menu.

The following figure shows a completed inventory for our example.

*Items entered for our imaginary living room. Lava lamp is actually listed in the suggested items!*

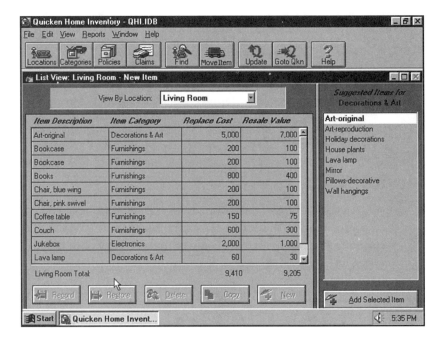

## The Detail View

When you click on an item in the Item Description column, there's an icon that looks like a blue piece of paper on the right side of the column. Click on it to bring up the Detail View window, where you can enter details about the item, such as the make and model, purchase date, and original purchase price.

The following figure shows details about the original art piece in our living room: a glass carp sculpture by the renowned artist Ima Fish, purchased on August 8, 1994 at the U Can't Afford It Gallery for $3,500. The replacement cost and resale value are higher because such fine art appreciates.

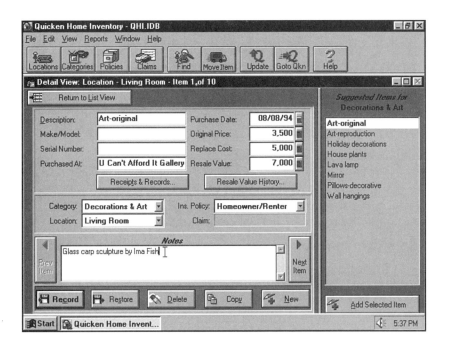

*Adding details about an item in your home inventory.*

1. The Description field is automatically filled in with the Item Description from List view. Tab to the Make/Model: field and type the item's make and model. Press **Tab**.

2. Type the item's serial number in the Serial Number: text box and press **Tab**.

3. Type the store where you bought it in the Purchased At: text box and press **Tab**.

> **A Little or a Lot** You can enter as little or as much information as you want in the Detail View window for each item.

4. In the Purchase Date: field, type or use the calendar icon to enter the date when you bought it and press **Tab**.

5. In the Original Price: field, type or use the calculator to enter the item's original purchase price.

6. If you want to adjust the replacement cost or resale value, tab to the Replace Cost: and Resale Value: fields, respectively, and enter a new value.

7. Click **Receipts & Records**. The following figure shows the Receipts and Records dialog box.

*Keep track of your receipts and records for an item.*

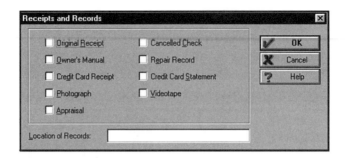

8. Click on the fields that describe the receipt and/or records that you have for this item. Original Receipt and Cancelled Check are examples of receipts; Photograph and Appraisal are examples of records. Click as many as apply to the item.

9. In Location of Records:, type where you keep the records and receipts for the item. Click **OK**.

10. If the resale value of the item changes over time, you can keep a record of the values. For example, our fine carp sculpture will appreciate. Click **Resale Value History**.

11. Click **New**.

12. Type or use the calendar to enter the date of the resale value change.

13. Type or use the calculator to enter the new resale value effective on that date. Click **OK** and **Close** to return to the Detail View.

14. Click in the **Notes** field to type a more complete description of the item, or whatever you want to remember about it.

15. Click **Record** to save the details.

16. To go to the Detail View of the next item on your list, click **Next Item** on the bottom right of the window. To return to the list of items, click **Return to List View** at the top left of the window.

## Step 5: Create a Report or Two

Once you have entered your items from memory, you can create a summary and a detail report about the items that you'll then take on a tour of your home to check against what you actually own.

The summary report includes the item description, and replacement, resale, and purchase values. To create a summary report:

1. From the **Reports** menu, choose **Inventory Value Summary**. Home Inventory automatically creates a summary report of the items for all locations, as shown in the following figure.

| Inventory Value Summary Report<br>Oct 19, 1995 05:38 PM | | | | |
|---|---|---|---|---|
| Category   Description | Replace Cost | Resale Value | Purchase Date | Purchase Price |
| **Decorations & Art** | | | | |
| Art-original | $5,000 | $7,000 | 08/08/94 | $3,500 |
| Lava lamp | $60 | $30 | | |
| **Total Decorations & Art** | $5,060 | $7,030 | | |
| **Electronics** | | | | |
| Jukebox | $2,000 | $1,000 | | |
| **Total Electronics** | $2,000 | $1,000 | | |
| **Furnishings** | | | | |
| Bookcase | $200 | $100 | | |
| Bookcase | $200 | $100 | | |
| Books | $800 | $400 | | |
| Chair, blue wing | $200 | $100 | | |
| Chair, pink swivel | $200 | $100 | | |
| Coffee table | $150 | $75 | | |
| Couch | $600 | $300 | | |

*A summary report of our sample living room.*

2. The summary report lists the items by category. If you want to list the items by location, which would make it easier to see what you have in each room, select **By Location** from the View: drop-down list.

3. Click **Preview** to see how your report will look before you print it.

4. Click **Print** to print your summary report. Click **Close** to return to the item list.

For some items, such as electronics, you'll want to record serial numbers and make and model as you walk around the house. For these items, create a detail report that you can then use to fill in the blanks. Here's how:

1. From the Reports menu, select **Inventory Detail**. Home Inventory automatically creates a detail report for your items.

2. To list the items by location, select **By Location** from the View: drop-down list.

3. You probably don't need to see the details for every item on the list. Click **Select Items**.

4. All items are in bold, which means they'll all be included in the report. Click **Clear All**.

5. Click on the items you want included in the report and click **OK**.

6. Click **Preview** to see how your report will look before you print it.

7. Click **Print** to print your detail report. Click **Close** to return to the item list.

# Step 6: Take the Reports on a Tour of Your Home

Take the reports around your house, checking off items that are OK, adding details and items that you missed, changing what needs to be changed. It's up to you to decide what's important enough to include; you probably don't need to inventory the contents of the junk drawer in your kitchen, unless there's a Picasso buried under the balls of string and scraps of tin foil.

# Step 7: Fix It Up

Now go back to the item list and update your inventory. To edit an item, just click on the field in either List View or Detail View and enter the changes. To delete an item, click on it in List View and click the **Delete** button.

## Finding an Item in Your Inventory

When you've got dozens of items for each location, scrolling through the lists to find one item can cause serious eye strain. Instead, use the Find feature.

1. Click **Find** in the iconbar.

2. Type the name of the item you want to find.

3. Home Inventory automatically searches both the item description and the notes in Detail View. To search in only one or the other, click on the one you don't want to deselect it.

4. Click **Find All**. Home Inventory lists all the items with that name and their location.

5. Click **View** and Home Inventory brings up the Detail View for the selected item, or click **Find** to search for another item.

## Moving Items

When you rearrange furniture or banish that atrocious lamp from Aunt Gertrude to the attic, you can move the items in your inventory from one location to another.

1. Click **Move Item** in the iconbar. The following figure shows the Move Item dialog box.

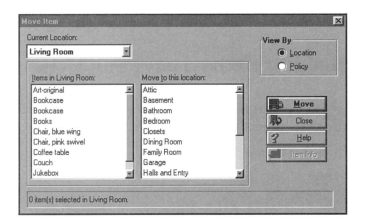

*Moving items between locations.*

2. Current Location: shows the location you had in the List View when you selected **Move Item**. If the items you want to move are in another location, select it from the drop-down list.

3. Under Items in Living Room: (or whatever the location), click on the item(s) you want to move. Hold down the Shift key to select a range of items, or hold down the Ctrl key to select several non-consecutive items.

4. Under Move to this location:, click on the item's new location.

5. Click **Move**.

6. Continue moving items or click **Close** to return to the List View.

# Step 8: Back Up Your File and Give the Reports a New Home

Whenever you update your inventory, back it up on a floppy disk so you don't lose all your hard work.

1. Put a floppy disk in the disk drive.

2. From the File menu, select **Backup**.

3. If the floppy is in a disk drive other than a:, select the drive from the drop-down list.

4. Click **OK**.

When you update the inventory, you should also print out new detail and summary reports. At least one reason why you created a home inventory is to satisfy the insurance company if your home is wiped out by some disaster. Therefore, it is not a good idea to store the reports in your home. Keep them in a safety-deposit box or some other place outside of your property.

# The Least You Need to Know

Quicken's Home Inventory lets you keep track of furniture, electronics, fish sculptures, and other valuable items throughout your home. Use it for insurance purposes, preparing a move, or give it to your heirs to fight over when you prepare your will.

Creating a home inventory involves eight easy steps:

➤ Open **Home Inventory**.

➤ Choose a location to inventory.

➤ Choose a category for your possessions.

➤ Enter items from memory.

➤ Create summary and detail reports for the inventory.

➤ Carry the reports from room to room and write down additions and changes.

➤ Update your inventory.

➤ Back up your file, and store the updated reports outside your home.

# Chapter 22

# Home Inventory and Quicken on a Bicycle Built for Two

## In This Chapter

➤ Tying up Home Inventory loose ends

➤ Sending the value of your home inventory to Quicken

➤ Using reports and graphs to see it

➤ Sending a transaction from Quicken to Home Inventory

In the last chapter we talked about how you can use Home Inventory to keep track of your possessions, where they are, and how much they're worth. Although Quicken saves your Home Inventory in a different file than your Quicken accounts, they work together like two people riding a tandem.

**Techno Talk**

## How Can I Tell Which File Is Which?

Quicken automatically names your accounts file qdata.qdb (which stands for Quicken **data**.Quicken **database**) and saves it in the QUICKENW folder. It names your home inventory file qhi.idb (Quicken **H**ome **I**nventory.**i**nventory **d**ata**b**ase) and also saves it in the QUICKENW folder.

You can send the value of your home inventory to Quicken, where it's saved in a special asset account. When you create a Net Worth report or graph, Quicken includes the value of your inventory so you can get a full accounting of your worth. So, at least on paper, you're wealthier than you think you are. When you buy something new and record the transaction in a Quicken account, you can transfer it from Quicken to your inventory.

But before we get into how Home Inventory and Quicken share information, we're going to tie up some loose ends on working with Home Inventory that didn't get covered in Chapter 21.

# Home Inventory Miscellany That Didn't Fit with the 8 Steps

I thought the "8 Easy Steps to a Home Inventory" concept was a pretty good one, but it didn't quite cover everything. So stuck in this chapter are: how to create a new Home Inventory file; set up a password; change Home Inventory's options; and restore a vanished Home Inventory file.

## Creating a New Home Inventory File

If you have two homes, or summer in Kennebunkport, you may want to have two Home Inventory files to record a second inventory of your other house. To create a new Home Inventory file:

1. Open Home Inventory.

2. From the File menu, choose **New**. The following figure shows the New Home Inventory File window.

*Creating a new Home Inventory file.*

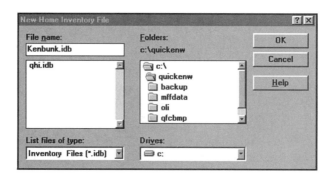

3. In the File name: text box, type a name for the new file; for example, **Kenbunk**.

4. If you want to save the file in a folder other than QUICKENW, select it from the **Folders:** list.

5. Click **OK**.

# Setting Up a Password

If you don't want your nosy brother-in-law sneaking a peek at how much your stuff's worth, you can set up a password for your home inventory. Because they're saved separately, the password you set up for your Quicken accounts won't apply to your Home Inventory files.

1. From the File menu, choose **Password**.

2. Type the password. You'll only see an asterisk (*) for each character you type, so anyone hanging over your shoulder can't read it. Press **Tab**.

3. Retype the password exactly as you did the first time to confirm it.

4. Click **OK**. The next time you open Home Inventory, it will ask you to enter your password.

# Changing Home Inventory Options

The Home Inventory options let you select how Home Inventory reacts when you enter items. For each option, a checkmark shows whether it's active. Click on the option to select or deselect it.

To see the options, choose **Options** from the **Edit** menu. The Options dialog box, shown in the following figure, is divided into three tabs: Suggested Item List, Display, and General. I'll give you a rundown on what each item does.

*Changing Home Inventory Suggested Item List options.*

In the Suggested Item List tab:

➤ **Use suggested values for new inventory items** inserts Home Inventory's suggested values in the Replace Cost and Resale Value fields.

➤ **Automatically set Resale Value to 50% of Replacement Cost** does what it says. You can either turn this option off entirely or type in a new percentage.

In the Display tab (shown in the following figure):

*Changing the Home Inventory Display options.*

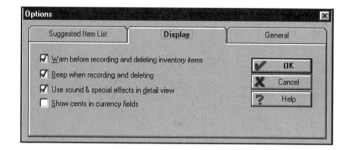

➤ The first two options tell Home Inventory to warn and beep at you when you record and delete items.

➤ When you click **Next Item** or **Prev Item** in the Detail View, **Use sound & special effects in detail view** makes a sound like a whoopee cushion and supposedly "simulates a page turning," but you have to look hard to catch it.

➤ **Show cents in currency fields** displays the actual amount in the cost and value fields. If this option is off, Home Inventory rounds the amounts to the nearest dollar.

In the General tab (shown in the following figure):

*Changing the Home Inventory General options.*

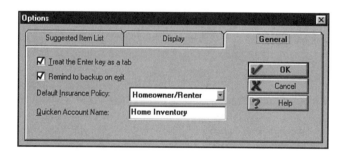

➤ **Treat the Enter key as a tab** lets you press **Enter** as well as **Tab** to move from field to field.

➤ **Remind to backup on exit** reminds you to backup your file whenever you quit.

We'll deal with the Default Insurance Policy option in Chapter 23, and the Quicken Account Name option later in this chapter.

## Retrieving a Backup Home Inventory File

At the end of Chapter 21, I talked about backing up your home inventory file so if something nasty happens to it, you have a copy. Well, something nasty did happen, and now you want to retrieve your backup. Here's how:

1. Put the floppy with the backup copy of your file in the disk drive.

2. From the File menu, choose **Restore**.

3. From the Drives: menu, select **a:** or the drive you are using.

4. The list under File name: shows what's on the floppy disk. Click on the name of your backup file.

5. Click **OK**.

If you made any changes to your home inventory since the last time you backed up the file, you'll have to make them again. But at least you won't have to start completely from scratch.

## Sending Home Inventory Info to Quicken

When you transfer your Home Inventory to Quicken, Quicken creates a new asset account called Home Inventory. The Home Inventory asset account works differently from a regular asset account, which I'll explain in a minute.

Home Inventory only transfers the total resale value of all the items in your inventory to Quicken. The resale value is what you could get if you sold everything you own; hence it's the value of your home inventory assets.

1. Open Home Inventory, if you haven't already (you don't need to open Quicken, too). See Chapter 21 for instructions if you need a refresher.

2. Click the **Update** button in the iconbar. You'll see the following confirmation window:

*When you transfer your home inventory, Quicken asks you to confirm the asset account it's transferring to.*

3. Click **Yes**. Home Inventory transfers the resale values to the Home Inventory account in Quicken.

Your Home Inventory asset account will not have a register like other accounts. Quicken includes the total value of the Home Inventory account in your net worth, but does not create transactions or a register for the account.

All right, that's a little confusing. At least, I'm confused. Bear with me while I figure this out.

In Home Inventory, click **Goto Qkn** in the iconbar and Quicken opens all by itself. Open the Account List and you'll see the Home Inventory account listed, as shown in the following figure.

*The new Home Inventory asset account appears in the Account List.*

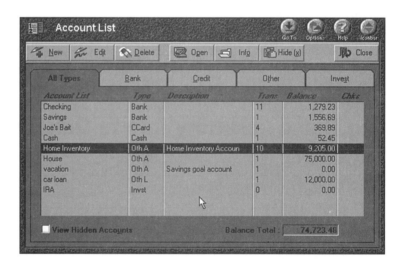

Click **Open** in the Account List and whaddya know, you're back in Home Inventory. So the Home Inventory asset account isn't like other accounts, with payments and deposits and transactions. It's more like a place marker, a place to park the total value of your stuff so Quicken doesn't forget to include it in your net worth. Capiche?

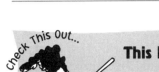

### This Is Not a One-Time Fling

Whenever you update your home inventory, update your Home Inventory asset account, too, to keep your net worth current. Just click **Update** in the Home Inventory iconbar, and Quicken replaces the old inventory account value with the new.

## Sending Home Inventory to Another Asset Account

You can also have Quicken create a second asset account where you can send your inventory. For those of you summering in Kennebunkport, you'd want to do this to create a second asset account for your second home inventory.

1. Open Home Inventory.

2. In the Edit menu, choose **Options**.

3. Click the **General** tab in the Options window.

4. Tab to Quicken Account Name: and type a name for the new asset account.

5. Click **OK**.

6. Home Inventory will ask you to confirm that the new name is not the same as an existing Quicken account. Click **OK**.

7. Click **Update** in the iconbar and your inventory is transferred to the new asset account.

### Can I Transfer My Inventory to an Existing Asset Account?

In a word, no, and for two reasons. Home Inventory asset accounts are special cases, and do not have transactions and registers and all that other stuff you're used to having in accounts. Quicken will only transfer the total Home Inventory resale value to a Home Inventory asset account. Secondly, whenever you click **Update** in the Home Inventory iconbar, Quicken completely erases the previous value of the account and replaces it with the new. It won't tack on the value of your inventory to the value of a regular asset account. They are completely separate entities.

# Viewing Your Home Inventory in Quicken

You already saw how you can check out the total value of your home inventory in the Account List. You can also see it using Net Worth reports and graphs.

When you create a Net Worth report (see Chapter 12), Quicken includes the resale value of your home inventory with your total assets and factors it into the net worth balance.

With a Net Worth graph, you can also see an asset comparison of every item in your home inventory. Here's how it works:

1. Create a Net Worth graph (see Chapter 13).

2. Double-click on the yellow bar that shows your assets. Quicken creates an asset comparison pie graph, with Home Inventory shown in brown.

3. Double-click on the brown pie slice. Quicken creates an asset comparison of the items in your home inventory, as shown in the following figure.

*A Home Inventory asset comparison.*

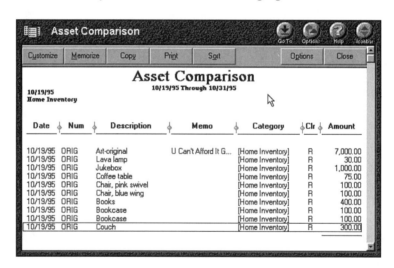

So even though the Home Inventory asset account is an oddity that Quicken keeps in the background, it does play a part in your complete financial picture. It's kind of like the weird uncle no one talks about, but who skews the family dynamics.

# Sending a Transaction from Quicken

When you buy something new for your home, or purchase a new car, boat, or hot air balloon, you can enter the transaction in Quicken and transfer it to your Home Inventory, so you don't have to record it twice. You need to enter the transaction in a checking, cash, or credit card account.

1. Enter the transaction in your account register, keeping in mind that the fields in the register will correspond to fields in Home Inventory:

   ➤ Transaction date is entered in Purchase Date.

   ➤ Payee is entered in Purchased At.

   ➤ Payment amount is entered in Original Price, Replace Cost, and Resale Value.

   ➤ Memo is entered in Item Description. If you leave the memo blank, Home Inventory will put "Quicken item" in the Item Description.

   After you record the transaction, make sure you click on it again to select it.

2. Click on the **Inventry** button in the iconbar.

3. Home Inventory opens and asks if you want to add the transaction to the inventory. Click **Yes**.

4. Home Inventory adds the transaction as a new item and shows you its Detail View, where you can edit the item and add information about it.

5. Home Inventory put the item in an "Unassigned" category in an "Unassigned" location. Put it in its rightful place by selecting a category and location from the respective menus.

# The Least You Need to Know

Quicken and Home Inventory are separate electronic entities, but they can share information.

➤ When you transfer your home inventory to Quicken, Quicken records the total resale value of your inventory in a special asset account.

➤ The Home Inventory asset account is Quicken's funny uncle; you can't record transactions and work with it like a normal Quicken account. However, Quicken does include the inventory value when calculating your net worth.

➤ Use Net Worth reports and graphs to see the value of your home inventory.

➤ When you buy something new, you can transfer the transaction from Quicken to Home Inventory.

# Chapter 23

# Fire, Floods, and Things That Go Bump in the Night

**In This Chapter**

➤ Using Home Inventory to record your insurance policies

➤ Creating policy reports

➤ Submitting a claim

Modern science has done wonders, but thus far no one has figured out a way to stop hurricanes, tornadoes, floods, and fire from wreaking havoc on our carefully ordered lives. So we do the only thing we can do—shell out hundreds of dollars a year on insurance that we hope we'll never need. In fact, most states require you to have auto insurance, and most mortgage companies require you to have property insurance. So, unless you take a vow of poverty, there's no escaping the insurance industry.

In Quicken Home Inventory, you can record the information for your various insurance policies and then keep track of which policies cover which possessions. Then, if the unfortunate does befall you, you can use it to record your insurance claims.

# Entering Your Policy Information

The first thing to do is to enter the information for each insurance policy you have. To start, open Home Inventory and click **Policies** in the iconbar. The following figure shows the Policies window.

*Use Home Inventory to keep of track your insurance.*

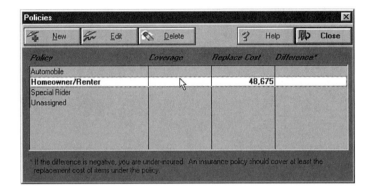

Home Inventory has policies for auto insurance, homeowner's or renter's insurance, and policy riders for things like jewelry and antiques. First I'll tell you how to enter your information for these policies, then I'll tell you how to add a policy to the list.

In the Replace Cost column for homeowner's insurance, Home Inventory entered the total replacement cost of your home inventory. After you enter the value of your insurance, Home Inventory will calculate the difference between your insurance coverage and the replacement value so you can see if you're adequately insured.

1. Click on the policy in the list for which you want to add details.

2. Click **Edit**, and you'll see the Edit Policy dialog box shown in the following figure.

*Adding policy information.*

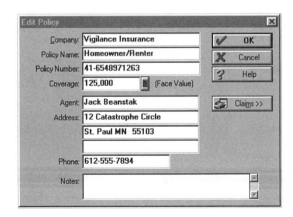

3. In the Company: field, type the name of your insurance company.

4. In the Policy Number: field, type your policy number.

5. In the Coverage: field, type or use the calculator to enter the face value of your policy.

6. In the Agent:, Address:, and Phone: fields, type your insurance agent's name, address, and phone number.

7. You can type anything else you want to remember about the policy in the Notes field.

8. If you want to include information about the claims adjuster for the policy, click the **Claims>>** button. The Edit Policy dialog box drops down to include fields for the claims adjuster's name, address, and telephone number. Type the appropriate information in these fields.

9. Click **OK**.

In the Policies window, Home Inventory enters the value of your insurance policy in the Coverage column and gives the difference between the coverage and replacement cost in the Difference column. If the number is negative, you may be underinsured.

### Actually, the Difference Seems Rather High

Your homeowner's policy probably includes the cost of replacing your house as well as its contents. The Replace Cost column just shows the cost of replacing your stuff, not the house itself. You can either add the cost of your home as an item in your inventory, which would then be included in the Replace Cost. Or you can enter only the amount insurance would cover for your belongings. For example, if your insurance includes $100,000 for your home and $50,000 for your belongings, enter $50,000 for the value of the policy.

If your insurance changes—you add more coverage, change agents, or whatever—click **Edit** and use the Edit Policy window to record the changes.

## Adding a New Policy

If you have additional insurance besides homeowner's and auto, you can add those policies to the list. Click **New**, and the New Policy window looks exactly the same as the Edit Policy window. Enter your information, click **OK**, and Home Inventory adds the policy to the list.

# Assigning Items to Policies

When you entered items in your inventory, Home Inventory automatically assigned everything to the homeowner's/renter's insurance policy. If you included your car or things covered by a policy rider in your inventory, you'll want to change the policy for those items. There are two ways to do it:

1. In the List View, click on the item whose policy you want to change.

2. Click the **Detail View** icon in the Item Description field.

3. Select the new policy from the Ins. Policy: drop-down list and click **Record**.

If you have several items to assign to another policy, you can do all of them at once.

1. Click **Move Item** in the iconbar.

2. Under View By, click **Policy**.

3. In the Items in Homeowner/Rental: list, click on the items you want to assign to the new policy. Hold down the **Shift** key to select a range of items, or hold down the **Ctrl** key to select several noncontiguous items.

4. In the Assign to this policy: list, click on the policy you want to assign the items to.

5. Click **Move**. Home Inventory assigns all the selected items to the new policy.

6. Click **Close** to return to Detail View.

# Changing the Default Policy

As I mentioned, Home Inventory automatically assigns the items you enter to the homeowner's/renter's policy. If you want new items assigned to a different policy when you enter them, you can change the default policy in Home Inventory's options. For example, if you want new items assigned to a new policy, you can choose the new policy as the default.

1. From the Edit menu, choose **Options**.

2. Click the **General** tab.

3. From the Default Insurance Policy drop-down list, select the policy you want Home Inventory to assign to new items.

4. Click **OK**. Whenever you enter a new item to your inventory, it will automatically be assigned to this policy.

# Creating Reports About Your Coverage

You can create two instant reports about your insurance coverage: a summary report and a detail report.

The Insurance Coverage Summary report lists the replacement cost and resale value of every item in your inventory, and subtotals the values by category. It also gives the total replacement cost and resale value of your entire inventory, and compares them to your policy coverage. It also shows the details of your policy: account number, agent, address, and all that.

To create an Insurance Coverage Summary report:

1. From the Reports menu, select **Insurance Coverage Summary**. Home Inventory creates the report for the default insurance policy (which is homeowner's/renter's, unless you changed it in the Options window). The following figure shows a sample Insurance Coverage Summary report.

| Insurance Coverage Summary Report<br>Oct 19, 1995 06:03 PM | | | | |
|---|---|---|---|---|
| Category  Description | Replace Cost | Resale Value | Purchase Date | Purchase Price |
| Safe | $300 | $150 | | |
| Stationery | $100 | $50 | | |
| Typewriter | $200 | $100 | | |
| **Total Office Equipment** | **$9,000** | **$4,500** | | |
| **Total for Homeowner/Renter Policy** | **$48,675** | **$28,913** | | |

The coverage amount of your Homeowner/Renter policy ($125,000) is more than the replacement cost of yo
($48,675).

\*Homeowner/Renter Policy from: Vigilance Insurance
Account #41-654-8971263
Which provides $125,000 worth of coverage.
Agent:    Jack Beanstak          Claims Adjuster:
Phone:    612-555-7894           Phone:
Address:  12 Catastrophe Circle  Address:
          St. Paul, MN 55103

Notes:

*The Insurance Coverage Summary report.*

2. If you want to see a summary report for another policy, select it from the Policies: drop-down list.

3. If you want to see subtotals for locations instead of categories, select **Location** from the Sort by: drop-down list.

4. Click **Print** to print the report.

5. Click **Close** to return to the List View.

263

The Insurance Coverage Detail report lists, by policy, everything you entered in the Detail View for each item in your inventory. You can narrow it down by selecting certain items to include. That way, if your son the future scientist blows up your workshop while creating his science fair project, you can create a detail report for just the things he destroyed. Handing a detail report to your insurance company when you make a claim will impress the pants off them, and, who knows, maybe they'll give you more money (don't count on it).

To create an Insurance Coverage Detail report:

1. From the Reports menu, select **Insurance Coverage Detail**. Home Inventory creates the report for the default insurance policy. The following figure shows a sample Insurance Coverage Detail report.

*The Insurance Coverage Detail report.*

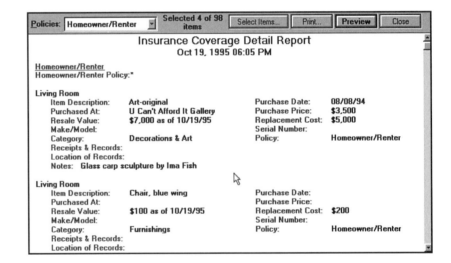

2. If you want to see a detail report for another policy, select it from the Policies: drop-down list.

3. To include only certain items in the report, click **Select Items**.

4. Home Inventory displays the Inventory List with every item in bold, which means they'll all be included in the report. Click **Clear All**, then click on the items you want included. Hold down the **Shift** key to select a range of items, or the **Ctrl** key to select several noncontiguous items.

5. Click **OK**. Home Inventory re-creates the report with just the items you selected.

6. Click **Print** to print the report.

7. Click **Close** to return to the List View.

# When the Unthinkable Happens: Making an Insurance Claim

I have been fortunate enough never to have suffered a major calamity. I do remember once in high school, though, my father and I decided to make microwave popcorn...using regular popcorn in a brown paper bag. After we extinguished the ensuing fire, the inside of the microwave looked (and smelled) like Chernobyl. At least my dad was in on it, too, so he couldn't punish me for it. And then there was the time my mother nuked the coleslaw... Well, let's just say my family shouldn't be trusted around sharp objects or electrical appliances.

When you do need to make an insurance claim, use the information you've set up on Home Inventory to make it go smoothly. If you've had a run of bad luck, Home Inventory can track multiple claims.

## Setting Up a Claim

When you make a claim to your insurance company:

1. Click the **Claims** button in the iconbar and Home Inventory brings up the Insurance Claims dialog box.

2. Click **New**. Quicken tells you how to create a new claim. Click **OK** to see the New Claim window, shown in the following figure.

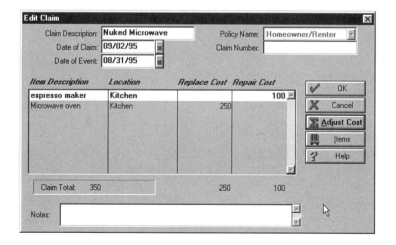

*Making a claim.*

3. In the Claim Description: field, type a description of the claim. To use the example of the ill-fated popcorn adventure, Nuked Microwave.

4. In Date of Claim:, use the calendar to enter the date you made the claim.

5. In Date of Event: use the calendar to enter the date of the disaster.

6. From the Policy Name: drop-down list, select the insurance policy that covers this claim.

7. In Claim Number, type the number of your claim (your insurance agent will tell you).

8. Next you want to select the items that your insurance is paying to repair or replace. Click the Items button.

9. Home Inventory lists all the items in your inventory. If you were completely wiped out (in which case your computer would be toast, but why quibble), click **Select All**. Otherwise, click on the items for the claim (hold down the **Shift** key to select a range; hold down the **Ctrl** key to select noncontiguous items) and click **OK**. Home Inventory lists them in the New Claim window, along with their location and replacement cost.

10. If your insurance company will pay to repair the item, not replace it, you can enter the cost of repair. Select the item from the list and click the **Adjust Cost** button.

11. Under Claimed Value, click **Use Repair Cost** and enter the amount of the repair. Click **OK**, and Home Inventory lists the repair cost instead of the replacement cost in the New Claim window.

12. Click **OK** to return to the Insurance Claims window. Quicken asks if you want to create a report for the claim; we'll talk about reports in the next section. Click **No**.

When you select a claim in the Insurance Claims window and click **Edit**, the Edit Claim window looks exactly like the New Claims window we just discussed. You can add more items, change the replacement or repair costs, or make any other adjustments you need.

The **Delete** button in the Insurance Claims window deletes a claim entirely. There's a separate process to closing the claim when your insurance company pays up, which we'll talk about at the end of the chapter.

Click **Close** to close the Insurance Claims window.

# Creating Claim Reports

There are two ways of seeing your claim: with an Insurance Claim Summary or an Insurance Claim Detail report.

The Insurance Claim Summary report is similar to the Insurance Coverage Summary report. For the items in your claim, it lists their description, location, repair and replacement costs, and gives the total of your claim, along with the other information you entered when you set up your claim. The report also includes your insurance policy information.

To create an Insurance Claim Summary report, select **Insurance Claim Summary** from the Reports menu. The following figure shows the summary report for our sample claim.

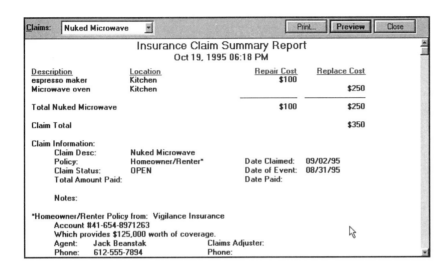

*An Insurance Claim Summary report for the ill-fated popcorn adventure.*

If you have more than one claim, you can see a summary report for another claim by selecting it from the Claims: drop-down list. Click **Print** to print the report. Click **Close** to return to the List View.

The Insurance Claim Detail report is also similar to the Insurance Coverage Detail report. It lists the information you entered in the Detail View for each item, along with the claim and policy information.

To create an Insurance Claim Detail report, select **Insurance Claim Detail** from the Reports menu. Click **Print** to print the report. Click **Close** to return to the List View.

# Closing the Claim

When your insurance company pays up, you should close the claim. Home Inventory will maintain a record of the claim so you can view it later if you need to.

1. Click Claims in the iconbar.

2. If you have more than one claim in claims list, select the one you want to close and click **Paid**.

3. In Date Paid:, use the calendar to enter the date when the insurance company paid the claim.

4. In Amount, enter how much your insurance paid for the claim.

5. Click **OK**.

6. Home Inventory asks if you want to see a claim report. If you click **Yes**, it will bring up an Insurance Claim Summary report.

When you close a claim, two things happen. First, Home Inventory shows the amount and date paid in the Insurance Claims window. Because this claim is closed, you can no longer edit it. The only way to see it is to create a summary or detail report for the claim.

Second, any items that were destroyed in the disaster for which you entered a replacement cost in the claim, are deleted from your inventory. If you entered a repair cost, it keeps the item in the inventory.

For example, for the Nuked Microwave claim, the microwave was totaled and I entered a replacement cost of $250. When I closed the claim, Home Inventory deleted the microwave from the kitchen inventory list. When I replace the microwave, I'll have to add it to the inventory. I also put in a claim for the espresso maker, which was an innocent bystander caught in the crossfire. But instead of replacing it, the insurance company paid $100 to repair it. So the espresso maker remains in the inventory.

# The Least You Need to Know

Coping with a disaster is bad enough, but trying to get your insurance to cough up the cash to recover from it only adds insult to injury. (My rantings about the inherent unfairness of the insurance industry are censored, lest a horde of lawyers descend and slap me with a libel suit.) Home Inventory's insurance features make it easier to cut through the bureaucracy. Let's just hope your computer isn't destroyed along with the rest of your worldly possessions.

➤ Record all the important information about your insurance policies.

➤ Home Inventory will compare the amount of your coverage to what it would cost to replace your possessions so you can see if you're under- or overinsured.

➤ You can assign each item in your inventory to a specific policy.

➤ When you make a claim, you can record the reason for the claim, the amount, and the date your insurance paid up.

➤ Create summary and detail reports about your policies and claims.

# Part 4
# Rolling Down Easy Street

*Even though you know you should invest in something more lucrative than a CD at your local bank, do your eyes glaze over when you encounter the stock quotes in the newspaper? All that talk about stocks, bonds, and mutual funds is about as interesting as reading the instruction manual that came with your computer.*

*Mutual Fund Finder helps you, the novice investor, decide what you need in a mutual fund and shows you a list of funds that suit you. When you're ready to dabble, use Investor Insight to create portfolios and keep them updated with the latest news, price information, and stock quotes straight from Wall Street.*

*Ready to be a high roller? Come on, then; baby needs a new pair of shoes…*

# Chapter 24

# Stash Your Cash with Mutual Fund Finder

**In This Chapter**

➤ Mutual Fund Finder: the investment dating service

➤ Tell it what you're looking for in a fund

➤ Read about what the fund can do for you

➤ Check out its 8 × 10 glossy

In earlier chapters we talked about how Quicken can help you plan for retirement, your kids' college education, and other goals that require a hefty stash of cash. To save that kind of money, you're going to have to invest in something beyond the standard bank CD with 5% interest.

Mutual funds are a relatively safe, stable investment that you can buy directly from mutual fund companies or through a broker. Quicken's Mutual Fund Finder helps you decide which funds are right for you. You can tell Mutual Fund Finder what your investment criteria are and Quicken creates a list of funds that meet them. Then you can see a detailed history of the fund's performance. Morningstar provides the history and information on the mutual funds.

If the only thing you know about Wall Street is that Michael Douglas was in the movie, don't worry. Mutual Fund Finder will ask you specific questions about what you need and will lead you through every step. Repeat after me: "Greed is good."

# Starting Mutual Fund Finder

Mutual Fund Finder is completely separate from your Quicken accounts and the other features such as Home Inventory. You can start Mutual Fund Finder from either Quicken or from the Windows desktop. To open Mutual Fund Finder from Quicken, click on the **MutualF** icon in the main iconbar. To open Mutual Fund Finder from the Windows desktop:

1. Click the **Start** button in the Windows taskbar.

2. Select **Programs**, then **Quicken**, then **Mutual Fund Finder**.

# Creating a List of Funds

When you first start Mutual Fund Finder, it will take you through an EasyStep process to create a list of funds. The following figure shows the Mutual Fund Finder EasyStep window.

*Use EasyStep to get started with Mutual Fund Finder.*

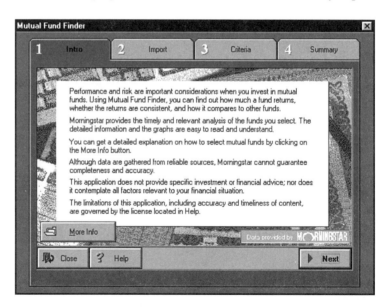

As you go through EasyStep, you'll select the criteria for the funds you want to find. In every EasyStep window, clicking **More Info** brings up Mutual Fund Finder Help, so you can learn more about the terms and features in the window. Also, in each window,

Mutual Fund Finder has already selected a common option for the search criteria. If you're not sure what to do, you can leave it as is.

1. To start EasyStep, click **Next**.

2. If you already have a mutual fund investment account set up in Quicken, you can include it in Mutual Fund Finder. Click **Import**, then **Next**. If you don't have a mutual fund investment account, just click **Next**.

3. Mutual Fund Finder divides its funds into two asset classes: basic and extended. Under Asset Class Type, click **Basic Asset Classes** or **Extended Asset Classes**.

## What's Basic and What's Extended?

*Basic asset classes* are broad groups of funds, such as domestic stocks. *Extended asset classes* let you look for a fund with a specific objective, like asset allocation or aggressive growth. If you're not sure, just wing it. You can always search for a different asset class later.

4. Each asset class includes types of funds, such as domestic and international stocks, as shown in the following figure. Select one or more asset class types from the list. All the types of funds are selected; click **Clear All** if you want to select just a few. To select types of funds, click **Include All** to include all of them, hold down the **Shift** key to select a range, or hold down the **Ctrl** key to select noncontiguous items. Click **Next**.

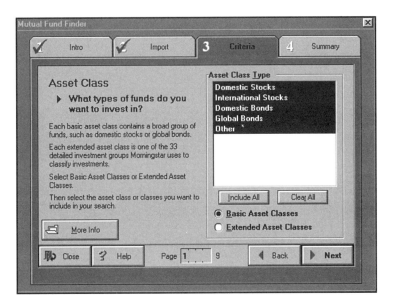

*Select the asset class and types of mutual funds you want to look for.*

5. EasyStep asks you if you want to limit the front load you are willing to pay. *Front load* is the commission you pay when you invest in a mutual fund. Brokers charge commissions, from 1% to 8.5%; mutual fund companies don't. If you want to limit your front load, select the limit from the drop-down list. Click **Next**.

6. The next window asks about *star ratings*. Morningstar gives funds a star rating based on their historical profitability and risk. Funds with more stars have higher profitability, less risk, or both. Select a star rating from the drop-down list and click **Next**.

7. Next it wants to know how much risk you're willing to take on a mutual fund. The *risk rating* (low, medium-low, medium, and medium-high) uses the fund's past performance to determine the likelihood that you'll take a bath if you invest in it. High-risk funds are for the Donald Trumps of the world. Select a risk rating from the drop-down list and click **Next**.

8. If you buy a fund because of its past performance, you may want to know if the current manager of the fund is the one who's built its track record. *Manager tenure* is the length of time the current manager has managed the fund; the longer the tenure, the less likely it's a fly-by-night fund. Select a manager tenure from the drop-down list and click **Next**.

9. Mutual funds require a minimum investment; some require hundreds and others thousands of dollars before they'll even return your phone calls. Select the minimum investment you can make from the drop-down list (as shown in the following figure) and click **Next**.

*Select the minimum investment you can afford.*

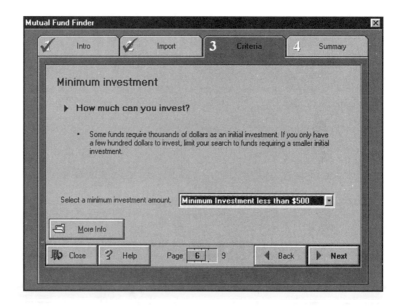

10. *Expense ratio* is a fund's overhead, expressed as the percentage of assets deducted for operating expenses. The higher the ratio, the less the profit and the lower your return. Select an expense ratio from the drop-down list and click **Next**.

11. Next you'll need to choose what dividend yield you expect from the fund. In growth funds, the dividend doesn't mean much; you make your money when the share price goes up. Income and bond funds pay a certain dividend percentage to the investor. Select a dividend yield from the drop-down list and click **Next**.

12. The five-year *performance* averages a fund's return over the past five years. For example, if you select a five-year performance of 10%, you'll limit your search to funds that have paid an average return of at least 10% over the past five years. Select a five-year performance from the drop-down lists and click **Next**.

13. EasyStep gives you a summary of the asset class you choose and the criteria you selected. If you want to change any of the criteria, you can select a different option from the drop-down lists. Click **Search**.

Mutual Fund Finder lists all the funds that meet your criteria, as shown in the following figure. It shows the fund's name; class; its year-to-date, one, three, five, and ten-year performance; its dividend yield; and its star rating.

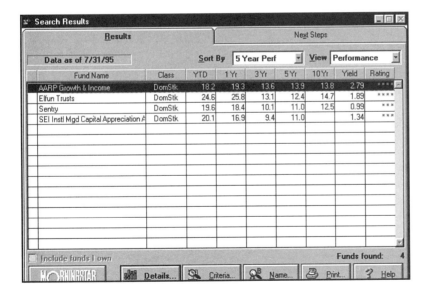

*The results of an EasyStep search.*

If you want to create a different list of funds, click **Criteria** in the Search Results window to return to the EasyStep Summary window. There you can choose a new asset class and select different criteria from the menus. Click **Search** and Mutual Fund Finder shows the results of your new search.

# Working with a List of Funds

Once you have a list of funds in the Search Results window, you can narrow the list, get ideas and suggestions for choosing a fund, sort the list, and view different information about the funds.

## Narrowing the List

If Mutual Fund Finder listed so many possible funds that it makes your head spin, you'll want to do another search using stricter criteria. Click **Criteria** in the Search Results window to return to the EasyStep Summary window. There, use the menus to select stricter criteria; you might try choosing a lower expense ratio or a higher five-year performance. Click **Search** and Mutual Fund Finder will recreate your list with the new criteria.

## Ideas and Suggestions for Choosing a Fund

The investment professionals at Callan Associates, Inc. have provided ideas and suggestions for choosing a mutual fund. (To be brutally honest, I have no idea who Callan Associates are, but I'm sure they're top-notch.)

In the Search Results window, click the **Next Steps** tab, shown in the following figure.

*Get advice from the experts.*

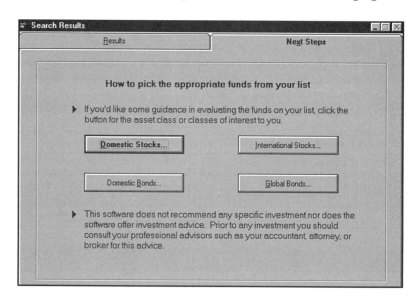

The suggestions cover four basic asset class types: domestic stocks, international stocks, domestic bonds, and global bonds. Click on the appropriate button and the Mutual Fund

Finder Help window appears with what Callan has to say on the subject. Close the Help window to return to Mutual Fund Finder. Click the **Results** tab to see your list again.

**Caveat Emptor** Notice the "don't sue us if you lose your shirt" language in this window. Before you throw your life savings into any investment, get some advice from your own experts—your attorney, accountant, or broker.

# Sorting the List

When it first creates the list, Mutual Fund Finder sorts the funds by name. The Sort By drop-down list in the Search Results window offers other ways of sorting the funds:

➤ Select 1, 3, 5, or 10 Year Performance to sort the funds by best performance (best to worst) over the time period.

➤ Select Expense Ratio to see which funds deducted the smallest percentage for operating expenses.

➤ Yield sorts the funds by their income return on capital investment for the past 12 months.

# Viewing Different Information in the List

For the list you created, Mutual Fund Finder showed you the funds' performance information: their year performances, yields, and star ratings. The View drop-down list lets you see different information for the funds in the list.

➤ Select **Fees** to see a breakdown of the fees each fund charges.

➤ **Rating** highlights each fund's star and risk ratings.

➤ **Criteria** gives the criteria you selected for your search and how each fund meets them.

You can combine the View and Sort By options to get a clearer picture of the funds. For example, to see the funds based on performance, sort by 5 Year Perf and view by Performance. To see the funds based on expense ratio, sort by Expense Ratio and view by Fees.

## How Do I Save My List?

Well, you don't. When you quit and later restart Mutual Fund Finder, it remembers whatever window (Summary or Search Result) you were using when you quit. But the lists themselves are transitory; whenever you conduct a new search, the new list replaces the old. If you want to keep a copy of the list, click **Print** to print it out.

# Viewing Funds in Intimate Detail

You can see more detailed information for each fund. The Details window shows a fund's basic and extended asset class; yield; net assets; total returns; the fees and expenses charged; the fund company name, address, and telephone number; the manager of the fund; and its ratings and style.

To see the details for a fund, click on a fund in the list and click **Details**. The following figure shows the details for an AARP Growth & Income fund.

Click on the arrows to move to the next fund on the list.

*Grasping the details of a fund.*

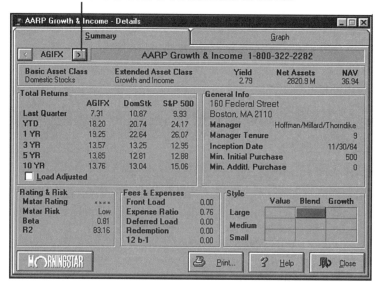

## A Graphic Version

You can also see bar and quartile graphs of the fund's performance by clicking on the Graph tab of the Details window, shown in the following figure.

The bar graph compares the fund's annual percentage return with other funds in its extended asset class and with another index (the S&P 500 for stocks and Lehman Brothers for bonds).

Select **Cumulative** from the Type drop-down list, and you'll see a line graph comparing your fund's performance in dollars with other funds and the S&P 500 or Lehman Brothers.

The quartile graph tells you whether the fund's performance ranked in the 25th, 50th, or 75th percentile for each year. The box on the graph shows where the fund ranked.

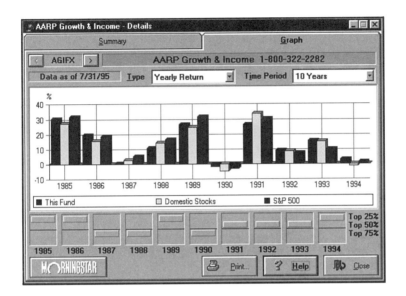

*A graphic account of the fund's performance.*

The graph automatically displays the fund's performance over the past ten years. You can see the fund's performance for the past one through nine years by selecting a different time period from the Time Period drop-down list.

# Searching for a Fund

If you want to get information about a fund that's not listed in the Search Results window, you can search for it by name or ticker symbol. (A ticker symbol is the abbreviation the stock market uses for the fund.)

1. In the Search Results window, click the **Name** button.

2. Type the name in the Fund Name text box, or the ticker symbol in the Symbol text box.

3. Click **Search**. Mutual Fund Finder displays a new Search Results window with the fund listed.

Find Fund by Criteria in the Find menu brings you back to the EasyStep Summary window.

# The Least You Need to Know

Enter the world of the rich and powerful with Mutual Fund Finder. Actually, anyone who needs to invest in something more lucrative than a savings account will find it helpful.

➤ Tell Mutual Fund Finder your criteria for an investment and it presents you with a list of funds that meet your criteria.

➤ You can get ideas and suggestions on investing from the experts.

➤ Sort and view your list by various criteria.

➤ You can see detailed information for each fund and graphs on each fund's performance.

# Chapter 25

# Adventures in Cyberspace: Setting Up Investor Insight

## In This Chapter

➤ Sam Stockenbond presents Investor Insight

➤ Setting up the Watch List

➤ Setting up simple and advanced portfolios

➤ Setting up custom indexes

In this exciting episode of Adventures in Cyberspace, we take you to the fast-paced world of stocks, mutual funds, and pork bellies. Our intrepid hero, Sam Stockenbond, uses Quicken's Investor Insight to be forever rid of the ink-stained hands that come from getting stock quotes from the newspaper. Maneuvering a mouse with surgical skill, he can instantly receive up-to-the-minute stock quotes, update his portfolio, and create reports and graphs worthy of Wall Street.

In this chapter, Sam takes you through the simple process of setting up Investor Insight to track the stocks and mutual funds that will lead you out of the drudgery of everyday investing. Then stay tuned for the sequel, "Adventures in Cyberspace II: Updating Your Investments Online," in Chapter 26.

# What You Need to Use Investor Insight

Of course, Sam Stockenbond has only the latest in computer technology. The rest of us mere mortals need to check our systems before we dive into Investor Insight. It is a memory hog; you need to have at least 6MB of RAM in your computer to run Investor Insight. You also need to have a Hayes-compatible modem that's 2400 bps or faster to receive investment news and stock quotes from Intuit. That's a lot of technonerd jargon to throw at you in two sentences. If you're not sure what you have, check your computer and modem manuals.

### Can You Repeat That in English?

Your *RAM*, or the amount of memory available to run software applications, is measured in megabytes (MB). The higher the number, the more memory you have and the faster applications can run. Most computers have either 4MB or 8MB.

Modem speeds are measured in *bits per second (bps)*. A 2400 bps modem can send and receive 2400 bits (another measurement term) per second; the higher the number, the faster the modem. Hayes-compatible is a modem standard, like an IBM-compatible computer.

And here's a tip for working with computers: you don't really have to know what the jargon means. Just check the numbers.

# Starting Investor Insight

Like Mutual Fund Finder, Investor Insight is separate from your Quicken accounts and other features. You can start Investor Insight either from the Windows desktop or from Quicken. To Open Inventory Insight from Quicken, click the **Investr** icon in the main iconbar. To open Investor Insight from the Windows desktop:

1. Click the **Start** button in the Windows taskbar.

2. Select **Programs**, then **Quicken**, then **Investor Insight**.

The first time you start Investor Insight, it will show you an Overview window, shown in the following figure.

Click on the icon that you want to learn more about, then click **Return** to get back to the Investor Insight Overview window. Click **Exit** to go into Investor Insight. If you want to see the overview again, choose **Overview** from the Help menu.

When you close the overview, Investor Insight will take you through an EasyStep introduction, as shown in the following figure.

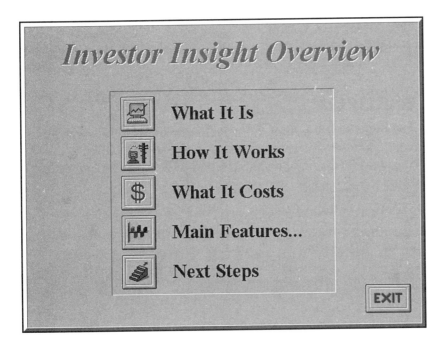

*An overview of Investor Insight.*

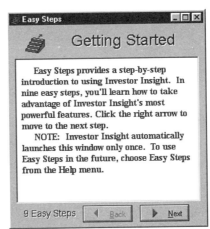

*Get an introduction to Investor Insight.*

Unlike other Easy Steps you've encountered in Quicken, this one doesn't ask you to enter anything. Instead, each of its nine windows gives you information about Investor Insight's features. You can close the window at any time.

If you want to return to the EasyStep windows later, select **Easy Steps** from the Help menu.

When you close Easy Steps, you see the Watch List and Portfolios windows. Investor Insight has sample data in these windows already. As you work with Investor Insight, you can delete what's in the windows and add your own.

## Setting Up the Watch List

The main thing you'll use in Investor Insight is the Watch List. You set up the Watch List to track the stocks and mutual funds you want to keep an eye on. Investor Insight uses the Watch List to download price information and news about the stocks and funds, and to create portfolios, custom indexes, charts, and reports.

To add a stock or a mutual fund to the Watch List:

1. Click the **Add** button in the Watch List window. The following figure shows the Add Securities to Watch List window.

*Adding to the Watch List.*

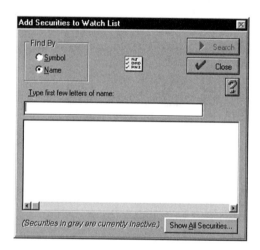

2. If you want to add stocks by their name, click **Name**. To add stocks by their ticker symbol (their stock market abbreviation), click **Symbol**.

3. Click **Show All Securities** to see a list of securities. The first time you do this, Investor Insight needs to build its database of stocks and funds. It can take a few minutes, but you only have to do it once. Click **Build Indexes**. (If you have the CD-ROM version of Quicken, the database is already built and you can skip this step.)

4. In the Add Securities to Watch List window, Investor Insight shows its list of securities, and the Search button becomes the Add button. You can scroll through the list, or type the first letters of a security's name or symbol to jump to it in the list. Click on the one you want and click **Add** (you can only select one at a time).

5. Continue adding securities, if you want, then click **Close**.

**284**

Whenever you add to your Watch List, a window pops up asking if you want to get news and quotes for the added securities. If you want to do it right away, click **Call Now**. Click **Call Later** to return to the Watch List. (I'll explain how all that calling works later in Chapter 26.)

To remove a security from the Watch List, click on it in the list and click **Remove**.

# Setting Up Portfolios

A *portfolio* is a group of stocks and/or mutual funds with a dollar value. You can set up a portfolio to include the investments you hold and ones you don't hold but want to track anyway. You can create three types of portfolios:

➤ Simple portfolios track gains and losses on a group of stocks and mutual funds based on the number of shares and the purchase price per share. Simple portfolios show changes in the total portfolio value and are the easiest to set up.

➤ Advanced portfolios track all of the transactions for each stock and mutual fund in your portfolio. Advanced portfolios calculate the true portfolio value on any given day and the stocks' and funds' performance for any time period. While they're more complicated to set up, you can record detailed information for every investment in the portfolio.

➤ Quicken portfolios import transactions from your Quicken investment accounts to Investor Insight. Investor Insight creates a separate Quicken portfolio for each investment account, and treats it as an advanced portfolio. We'll talk about Quicken portfolios in Chapter 26, in the section "Sharing Info with Quicken."

# Creating Simple Portfolios

To create a simple portfolio, click on the Portfolios window, shown in the following figure. (If the Portfolios window isn't visible, click **Portfolio** in the iconbar.)

"Burt's IRA" is a sample portfolio that came with Investor Insight. Assuming you're not Burt, you'll want to delete it. Click on it and click **Delete**.

1. Click **New** in the Portfolios window.

2. Type a name for the portfolio and click **OK**.

3. An Add to Portfolio window appears, showing the securities in your Watch List. Select a security and click **Add**.

4. Investor Insight displays the Enter Holdings window. In the Shares owned: text box, type the number of shares you own and press **Tab**.

5. In the Purchase Price per Share text box, type the purchase price per share and click **OK**.

*Create portfolios
with the Portfolios
window.*

6. Repeat steps 3-5 until you have added all the securities for this portfolio, then click **Close**. A Simple Portfolio window shows each security's symbol, the number of shares, and purchase price per share.

# Creating Advanced Portfolios

To create an advanced portfolio:

1. Click **New** in the Portfolios window.

2. Type a name for the portfolio.

3. Click **Advanced** and **OK**.

4. Next you'll need to enter a start date for the portfolio. Investor Insight uses the date as the start point for calculating the value and performance of the portfolio. You'll have to enter every transaction that has occurred between the start date and the present date, so the earlier the start date, the more transactions you'll have to enter. Click on the bottom arrow next to the date to go backward one day at a time; click the top arrow to advance the date. Click **OK**.

5. Type the total cash level for the portfolio as of your start date and click **OK**. The Advanced Portfolio window appears, shown in the following figure. You use this window to enter the transactions for the portfolio.

There are several different types of transactions you can record for the portfolio: buy, sell, contribution, withdrawal, income, split, and cash adjustment. We'll take one at a time.

## Buy

Use the **Buy** button to record transactions of when you bought shares.

1. Click **Buy** in the Advanced Portfolio window.

2. From the Security: drop-down list, select the security for which you bought shares.

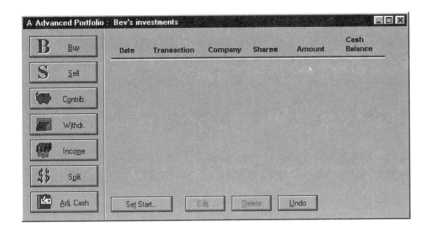

*The Advanced Portfolio window.*

3. Enter the date you bought the shares; click on the arrows to advance or turn back the date.

4. In the Shares: field, type the number of shares you bought.

5. In Price/Shr:, type the price per share. Type it as a decimal (6.54) and Investor Insight converts it to a fraction (6 1/2).

6. In Commission:, type the commission you paid on the transaction, if any.

7. In Total Cost:, type the total cost of buying the shares. (You can leave this blank and Quicken will calculate it for you.)

8. Click **Add** and Investor Insight adds the transaction to your advanced portfolio.

9. Repeat steps 2-8 to continue adding buy transactions, and then click **Close**.

## Sell

Use the **Sell** button to record transactions when you sold shares.

1. Click **Sell** in the Advanced Portfolio window.

2. From the Security: drop-down list, select the security for which you sold shares.

3. Enter the date you sold the shares; click on the arrows to advance or turn back the date.

4. In the Shares: field, type the number of shares you sold.

5. In Price/Shr:, type the price per share. Type it as a decimal (6.54) and Investor Insight converts it to a fraction (6 1/2).

6. In Commission:, type the commission you paid on the transaction, if any.

7. In Total Proceeds:, type the total proceeds from selling the shares. (You can skip this step and Quicken will calculate it for you.)

8. Click **Add** and Investor Insight adds the transaction to your advanced portfolio.

9. Repeat steps 2-8 to continue adding sell transactions, and then click **Close**.

## Contribution

Use this transaction for an investment account, such as an IRA, to which you make straight cash contributions.

1. Click **Contrib.** in the Advanced Portfolio window.

2. Enter the date you made the contribution; click on the arrows to advance or turn back the date.

3. In the Amount: field, type the amount of the contribution.

4. Click **Add** and Investor Insight adds the transaction to your advanced portfolio.

5. Repeat steps 2-4 to continue adding contribution transactions, and then click **Close**.

## Withdrawal

Use this transaction for an investment account from which you can take cash withdrawals.

1. Click **Withdr.** in the Advanced Portfolio window.

2. Enter the date you made the withdrawal; click on the arrows to advance or turn back the date.

3. In the Amount: field, type the amount of the withdrawal.

4. Click **Add** and Investor Insight adds the transaction to your advanced portfolio.

5. Repeat steps 2-4 to continue adding withdrawal transactions, and then click **Close**.

## Income

Use the Income transaction to record dividends, capital gains, and interest on your investments.

1. Click **Income** in the Advanced Portfolio window.

2. From the Security: drop-down list, select the security for which you received income.

3. Enter the date you received the income; click on the arrows to advance or turn back the date.

4. In the Amount: field, type the amount of the income.

5. Under Type, select whether the income is from a dividend, short-term capital gain, long-term capital gain, or interest.

6. Click **Add** and Investor Insight adds the transaction to your advanced portfolio.

7. Repeat steps 2-6 to continue adding income transactions, and then click **Close**.

## Split

The **Split** button lets you record transactions with a split ratio.

1. Click **Split** in the Advanced Portfolio window.

2. From the Security: drop-down list, select the security with a split ratio.

3. Enter the date of the transaction; click on the arrows to advance or turn back the date.

4. Under Split Ratio, type the split ratio.

5. Click **Add** and Investor Insight adds the transaction to your advanced portfolio.

6. Repeat steps 2-5 to continue adding split transactions, and then click **Close**.

## Cash Adjustment

If your Investor Insight portfolio balance doesn't match your investment statement, you can adjust the balance amount.

1. Click **Adj. Cash** in the Advanced Portfolio window.

2. Enter the date of the adjustment; click on the arrows to advance or turn back the date.

3. Balance is: shows your current portfolio balance. In the Change to: field, type the adjusted balance. Investor Insight will calculate the difference.

4. Under Record Adjustments As, select whether you want the adjustment recorded as a dividend, short-term capital gain, long-term capital gain, or interest.

5. Click **OK** and Investor Insight adds the transaction to your advanced portfolio.

6. Repeat steps 1-5 to continue adding adjustment transactions.

Whenever you start Investor Insight again, the Portfolios window will show the name of each of your portfolios, preceded by S for a simple portfolio and A for an advanced portfolio. To work with the portfolios, click on the name and click **Open**.

# Setting Up Custom Indexes

Like a portfolio, a *custom index* is a grouping of stocks and/or mutual funds that you want to analyze as a group. Unlike portfolios, however, custom indexes do not include number of shares and prices per share. Instead, they track price changes for the group of stocks and mutual funds as a whole. For example, you can set up a custom index for a specific industry, such as telecommunications or health care, and then track the price changes for that industry.

To create a custom index:

1. From the List menu, select **Custom Indexes**.

2. The Custom Indexes dialog box appears, shown in the following figure. Click **New**.

*The Custom Indexes window.*

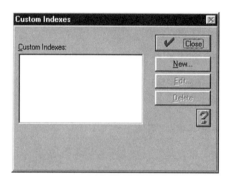

3. Type a name for the index.

4. The Contents: list shows the stocks and bonds in your Watch List. Click on the securities you want to include in the custom index (you don't need to hold down the **Shift** or **Ctrl** keys to select more than one).

5. Click **OK**. The custom index appears in the Custom Indexes window. If you want, repeat steps 2-5 to create more custom indexes.

If you want to add or delete securities within a custom index, select it in the Custom Index dialog box and click **Edit**. Then select or deselect securities from the Contents: list and click **OK**.

# The Least You Need to Know

Investor Insight brings investing to the 21st Century. In this chapter, you learned how to set up Investor Insight to track your stocks and mutual funds, portfolios, and custom indexes. Stay tuned for the sequel where the Sultan of Stocks, Sam Stockenbond, takes you through another Adventure in Cyberspace.

➤ To use Investor Insight, you need 8MB of RAM and a 2400 bps Hayes-compatible modem.

➤ Investor Insight uses your Watch List of stocks and bonds to create portfolios, custom indexes, reports, and charts.

➤ Simple portfolios let you track price changes for a group of stocks and funds.

➤ Advanced portfolios record detailed transactions for each stock and fund in the portfolio.

➤ Custom indexes let you follow the price changes for a group of stocks and funds as a whole.

# Chapter 26

# Adventures in Cyberspace II: Updating Your Investments Online

## In This Chapter

➤ Using Investor Insight to keep track of your investments

➤ Download price information, stock quotes, and news stories

➤ Create charts and reports about securities and companies

➤ Send e-mail to Intuit Customer Service

➤ Transfer your Quicken investment account to Investor Insight

➤ Send updates from Investor Insight to Quicken

In the last episode of Adventures in Cyberspace, our intrepid hero, Sam Stockenbond, introduced you to Investor Insight and got you started setting up the Watch List, portfolios, and custom indexes.

In this episode, Sam proves why he's the one-and-only Stockmeister by downloading news and price information, creating reports and graphs, dashing off electronic messages, and transferring information to and from Quicken with laser-like precision and ruthless efficiency.

# Registering with Intuit

Before you can receive the latest about the investment world, you need to register with Intuit so they know to whom they're sending their factoids.

1. If you haven't already, open Investor Insight.

2. Click the **Call** button in the iconbar. Investor Insight will configure your modem and tell you when it's done. Click **OK**.

3. The Set Up Modem window appears, showing the information about your modem. You don't need to change anything in this window, because Investor Insight sets it up for you. Click **OK**.

4. A pop-up window asks if you already have a user name and password registered with Investor Insight. I assume you don't or you wouldn't be reading this, so click **No**.

5. Investor Insight tells you about the subscription service and terms of agreement. Click **Accept**.

6. Now it wants to know everything about you except the name of your dog. Type in the information requested, as shown in the following figure, and click **Register Now**.

*Registering with Intuit.*

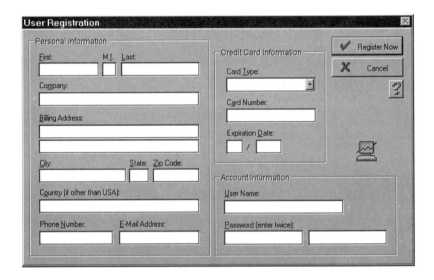

## Is a User Name Some Kind of Alias?

It can be. The *user name* is what Intuit uses to identify you whenever you call to download information. Investor Insight automatically inserts your first initial and last name in the User Name field, but you can change it to your full name, nickname, or initials. If you've always wanted to be known as Buck Naked, use that.

# Newsflash!

The first time you call Intuit from Investor Insight, it sends you price information on mutual funds for the past five years and news stories for the last 90 days, up to a maximum of 50 stories. Whenever you call again, it sends you the updated prices and news since the last time you called.

Once you've registered, Investor Insight displays the Download dialog box (shown in the following figure), which you'll also see whenever you click **Call** in the iconbar.

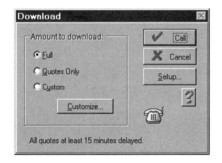

*Receiving news from Investor Insight.*

You can limit the amount of information you get by clicking on an option under Amount to download:

➤ **Full** sends all the latest news and price information.

➤ **Quotes Only** sends just price information for mutual funds.

➤ **Custom** downloads all the price information and news stories for selected companies in your Watch List. Click the **Customize** button, select the companies you want, and click **OK**.

**You Don't Have to Sit There and Watch It** When all the information has been sent, Investor Insight will automatically hang up and disconnect your modem. So go grab a snack.

When you're ready, click **Call** in the Download dialog box. It may take a few minutes to download everything.

A window pops up to tell you it's done; click **OK**.

# Reading News Stories

No, this isn't a plug for Hooked on Phonics. I'm going to explain the News window.

The news stories that Investor Insight downloads provide information about the companies and stocks in your Watch List, including stock price quotes. If a news story applies to more than one company, Investor Insight saves more than one copy of the story and associates them with each company.

Besides reading the articles and quotes, you can search for key words in an article and copy articles to the Windows Clipboard. That way you can paste the information from the Clipboard into another program like Microsoft Word or WordPerfect.

To read the news, click **News** in the iconbar. The following figure shows the News window.

*Reading the latest.*

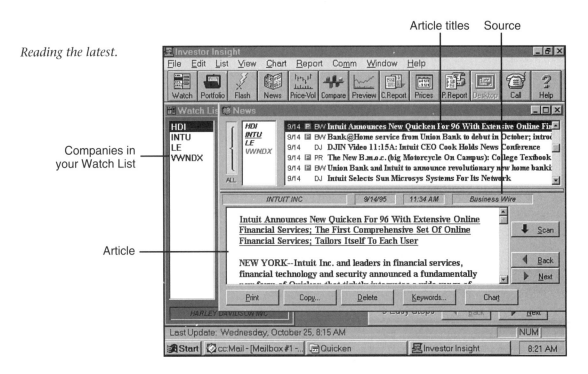

In the upper left corner of the window, click on the company you want to read about. Then click on an article title and the article appears in the bottom half of the window.

You can search for key words in the article:

1. Click on the **Keywords** button in the News window.

2. Type the key words you want to search for (up to three of them).

3. Click **OK**.

4. Click the **Scan** button in the **News** window. It highlights the key word in the article; click **Scan** again to keep looking.

If you want to copy an article to a word processing program, click **Copy**. A new window shows the text of the article. Click **Copy to Clipboard** and you can then paste the article into another program.

# Making Cents of It All

Investor Insight gives you a bevy of charts and reports to use to analyze your investments. There are way too many of them to go into detail here, but I will give you an overview of the charts and reports available.

## An Overview of Charts

There are five types of Investor Insight charts: price-volume, index, portfolio, comparative, and company preview. I'll tell you what each one shows and how to view it.

> **Learn More About It** This is going to be short and sweet; as I said, an overview. Your Quicken user's guide goes into excruciating detail about every chart and report.

## Price-Volume Charts

Price-volume charts display a line graph of the price and volume change for a stock. When you click on the **Price-Vol** icon in the iconbar, Investor Insight displays a miniature, or overview, price-volume chart for each security in your Watch List. Double-click on one of the overview charts to see a more detailed price-volume chart for that security.

## Index Charts

Index charts plot the high, low, and closing values over the past year for either the Dow Jones Industrial Average or Standard & Poor's 500 indexes. From the **Chart** menu, select **Index Charts**. Select either Dow Jones or S&P 500 and click **OK**.

## Portfolio Charts

**Portfolio** charts display information about your portfolios. There are four types of portfolio charts: holdings, relative value, portfolio value, and portfolio vs. Dow Jones.

➤ **Holdings** charts are pie charts that show how the total portfolio value is distributed among the stocks and mutual funds in the portfolio.

➤ **Relative Value** charts are bar charts that show the current value of each stock or mutual fund in the portfolio, sorted in descending order. Each bar has two segments: the full height of the bar shows the current value, and the black line shows what you paid for it. That way you can see if you've made or lost money on the security.

➤ **Portfolio Value** charts are bar charts that show how the total value of the portfolio has changed over time.

➤ **Portfolio vs. Dow Jones** charts are three-dimensional line charts that compare your portfolio's performance with the Dow Jones Industrial Average index.

To create a portfolio chart, select a portfolio in the Portfolios window. Click the **Chart** button in the Portfolios window, then click on the icon of the portfolio chart type you want.

## Comparative Charts

Comparative charts, true to their name, compare the performance of stocks, mutual funds, indexes, or any combination thereof. There are three types of comparative charts: percent change, abnormal volume, and burst.

➤ **Percent Change** charts are bar charts that show the percentage change in the value of each stock, fund, or index.

➤ **Abnormal Volume** charts are bar charts showing how the trading volume of each stock or fund compares with its normal trading volume over the past quarter.

➤ **Burst** charts are similar to percent change charts, except they're line charts instead of bar charts.

To create a comparative chart, click the **Compare** icon in the iconbar, then click on the icon of the comparative chart you want. Click the **Scope** button in the chart window to select which stocks, funds, and indexes you want included in the charts.

## Company Preview Charts

Company preview charts show a selected stock or fund's price information history for the past five years. You can see price information for any stock or mutual fund, whether it's included in your Watch List or not. However, Investor Insight updates the price information only if you add the stock or fund to your Watch List. Click the **Preview** icon in the iconbar, then click on a stock in the list to see its company preview chart.

# An Overview of Reports

Reports are another permutation of your Online Investment data. There are six of them: personal, flash, historical prices, current prices, portfolio, and company snapshot reports.

## Personal Reports

Personal reports are like a newsletter about your investments. They show summary tables, charts, and news stories about the companies in your Watch List, updated every time you download new information. To see it, click **P. Report** in the iconbar. Personal reports are difficult to read on your monitor; they're meant to be printed (click **Print** in the Personal Report window).

## Flash Reports

Flash reports present the day's most pressing news whenever you download information from Intuit. Investor Insight automatically displays a flash report every time you download. To see it again later, click **Flash** in the iconbar. Click on the arrows next to each line in the flash report to jump to related charts or news stories.

## Historical Prices Reports

Historical prices reports display a table of the high, low, and closing prices, and volume traded for a selected stock over the past month. Select **Historical Prices** from the Report menu. Select the stock or fund you want from the drop-down list at the top of the Historical Prices window.

## Current Prices Reports

Current prices reports show a table of the current price, point change, percent change, and value of specific stocks or funds. Select **Current Prices** from the Report menu.

## Portfolio Reports

Portfolio reports report on your portfolio, and there are four of them (reports, that is): value, performance, lot, and tax reports. All four types of portfolio reports are available for advanced portfolios; simple portfolios only display a value report.

➤ Portfolio value reports display a table of the portfolio's total value, as well as the value of each individual stock or fund in the portfolio.

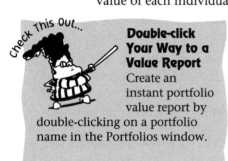

**Check This Out...**

**Double-click Your Way to a Value Report** Create an instant portfolio value report by double-clicking on a portfolio name in the Portfolios window.

➤ Portfolio performance reports show the return on your investment in your portfolio.

➤ Portfolio lot reports list all the sell and buy transactions in your portfolio.

➤ Portfolio tax reports display the taxable income your portfolio earned: interest, dividends, and short- and long-term capital gains.

To create a portfolio report, select a portfolio in the Portfolios window and click the **Report** button. Then click on the icon for the report you want.

## Company Snapshot Reports

Company snapshot reports include a price-volume chart, headlines, and recent news stories for a company or group of companies from your Watch List. To create a company snapshot report:

1. Choose **Company Snapshot** from the Report menu.

2. Click on the companies you want to include (you can choose more than one).

3. Select a time period from the drop-down list.

4. Under **Include**, select whether you want to include just headlines, complete news stories, or both.

5. Click the **Preview** button to see the snapshot. Click the **Print** button to print it.

# Hot Spots

Throughout Investor Insight, you'll find "hot spots" where you can click on an icon to jump to a related chart, report, or news story. You'll know a hot spot when you see it because when you move your cursor over a hot spot, the cursor changes shape.

As an example, the following figure shows a price-volume chart. Move the cursor over a colored point on the chart and the cursor turns into a newspaper. Double-click on the point, and a related news story pops up.

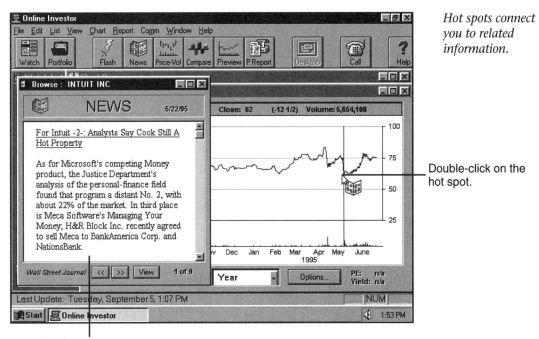

*Hot spots connect you to related information.*

Double-click on the hot spot.

Related news story

# Using E-Mail

*E-mail* is short for electronic mail—sending and receiving messages through your computer and modem. You type a message on your computer, send it with your modem, and someone else can read it on their computer immediately, whether they're down the block or in Singapore.

Investor Insight lets you exchange e-mail messages with Intuit Customer Service. To send a message:

1. From the Comm menu, select **Write E-mail**. The following figure shows the Write E-Mail dialog box.

2. In the Subject: field, type the subject of your message (this is like the Re: line of a memo).

3. In the Message: field, type your message.

4. Click **OK**.

*Sending e-mail to customer service.*

5. To send the e-mail message, click the **Call** icon in the iconbar. Investor Insight will send the message at the same time that it downloads price information and news stories.

Investor Insight also receives return messages during an online session. If you receive an e-mail message, Investor Insight will display it to you after it completes the online session. You can read it again by selecting **Inbox** from the Comm menu.

# Sharing Info with Quicken

If you have investment accounts set up in Quicken, you can import them to Investor Insight and analyze it with Investor Insight's features. Investor Insight creates a new portfolio for each Quicken account and lists them in the Portfolios window with a Q next to the name. Investor Insight treats Quicken portfolios like advanced portfolios, including each transaction in the portfolio. However, you can only add, edit, and delete transactions for the account when you're in Quicken.

When Investor Insight imports a Quicken investment account, each transaction in the account is converted to a corresponding advanced portfolio transaction. For this to work right, before you import the account into Investor Insight, you need to enter transactions in the investment account register using the **Action** button, shown in the following figure.

The options in the Action list correspond to advanced portfolio transactions in Investor Insight. When you select an option from the Action list, you'll need to enter the same information as you would for an advanced portfolio transaction, which we talked about in Chapter 24. For example, selecting Buy Shares in the Action list is the same as entering a buy transaction in an Investor Insight advanced portfolio.

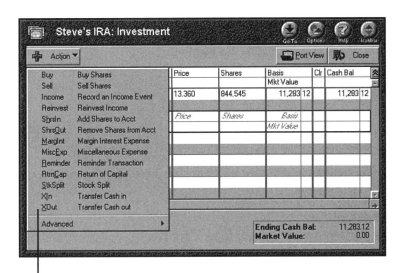

*Use the Action button in your Quicken investment account register to enter transactions that will be imported to Investor Insight.*

Action list

Using the Action list to record transactions in the Quicken investment account register lets you record actions on specific securities. When you import a Quicken account to Investor Insight, it adds each security in the account to the Watch List so you can update them.

To import an account from Quicken:

1. From the File menu in Investor Insight, choose **Get Quicken Investments**.

2. Select the account(s) to import.

3. Click **Get Data**. Investor Insight imports the account.

When you add, edit, or delete transactions in your Quicken investment account register, you need to import the new or changed transactions into Investor Insight. Repeat the steps above, and Investor Insight will import only the transactions that have been changed or added since the last import.

Whenever you download stock quotes and mutual fund prices in Investor Insight, it automatically updates your Quicken investment account the next time you open Quicken. If Quicken is running when you download, it updates immediately.

Now, isn't that slick? You'll always know the value of your investments. Sam Stockenbond would be proud.

# The Least You Need to Know

In this chapter, you learned how Investor Insight brings you up-to-the-minute news, quotes, and price information, and how it works with Quicken to keep your investment accounts current.

➤ Before you can download information, you need to register with Intuit.

➤ When you call Intuit, it sends you the latest price information for mutual funds, stock quotes, and news stories on companies in your Watch List.

➤ Use Investor Insight's charts and graphs to get a clearer picture of your investments, or any security you're interested in.

➤ Hot spots let you see related charts, reports, and news stories with a double-click.

➤ Exchange e-mail with Intuit customer service.

➤ When you import your Quicken investment account into Investor Insight, Investor Insight updates its value every time you download new information.

# Installation

You took the first step toward fiscal responsibility when you bought Quicken. You can set it on your shelf and admire the attractive packaging, but it won't actually do anything until you take the disks out of their shrinkwrap and install them on your computer.

*Installation* is a geek term for plugging software into a computer to make it run. It sounds like a long, involved process requiring a degree in computer science and an extensive collection of pocket protectors, but it's actually very simple and takes about five minutes.

## This Is As Tricky As It Gets

Okay, turn your computer on (bet you saw that one coming) and Windows 95 starts automatically.

Quicken comes on a numbered set of nine floppy disks. (If you bought the CD-ROM version, it's not even that complicated.) Put disk 1 or the CD into the appropriate drive in your computer, and follow the steps:

1. Click on the **Start** button on the bottom left corner of your screen.

2. Select **Run**.

3. Next to Open, type **a:setup**, as shown in the following figure. If you have the CD-ROM version, type **d:setup**.

*Type a:setup to start installing Quicken.*

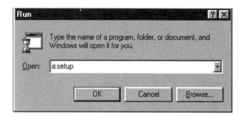

4. Click **OK** or press **Enter**.

### "Cannot find file a:setup"

If you get some kind of annoying error message, try one of two things. First, make sure disk 1 is in the disk drive. Second, if your computer has two disk drives, the one you're using may be the b: drive. Try typing **b:setup**.

## Pick and Choose Your Options

Your computer will chug and think things over for a few seconds, then the Quicken Deluxe Setup window will appear, as shown in the following figure:

The list of Quicken features is all highlighted in blue, which means that all of these features will be installed, unless you tell it not to.

You have two options when installing Quicken: install every feature or just the basics. Here's how to decide:

Look at the two numbers underneath the list of features. The first shows the amount of *memory* (computer storage space) your computer has. The second number shows the amount of memory Quicken needs to install all of its features.

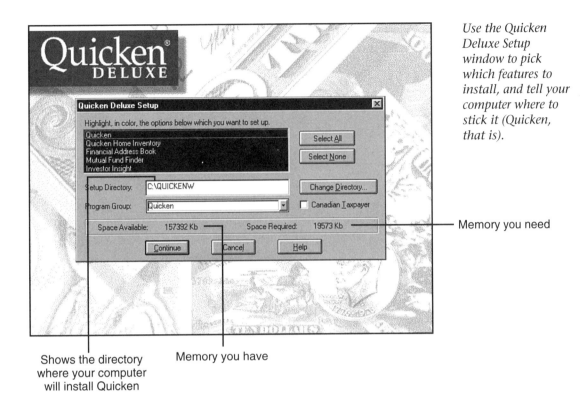

*Use the Quicken Deluxe Setup window to pick which features to install, and tell your computer where to stick it (Quicken, that is).*

Memory you need

Shows the directory where your computer will install Quicken

Memory you have

➤ If the first number is bigger than the second, you have enough memory to install everything.

➤ If the first number is smaller than the second, you won't be able to install some of Quicken's memory-chomping features, such as Mutual Fund Finder and Online Investor. To tell Quicken not to install these, click on the name to *deselect* it. The features are no longer highlighted and the second number drops precipitously.

But don't worry. You'll still be able to use the rest of Quicken's bells and whistles. You'll just have to check the morning paper for the stock report like everybody else.

The Quicken Deluxe Setup window also shows the setup directory and program group that tell you where your computer will stash Quicken. My advice: don't mess around with them. They're set up just the way they should be, and changing them would only complicate things.

Now, click **Continue** or press **Enter**, and catch up on a little light reading.

# Sit Back and Let Quicken Do Its Thing

A window will pop up with a bar showing how far along Quicken is in the installation. Another window extolling Quicken's many virtues gives you something to read if you don't have *Reader's Digest* handy.

When Quicken is done with the first disk, your computer will beep and a window will tell you to put in the next disk, as shown in the following figure. (If you're installing from a CD-ROM, you won't get a message asking you to switch disks.)

*Quicken lets you know where you are in the installation process.*

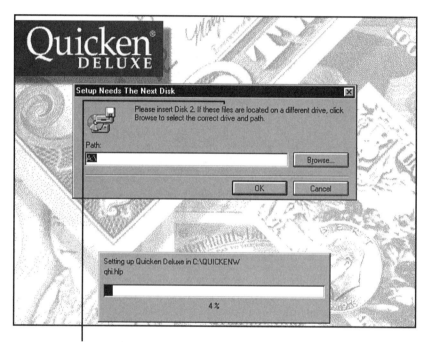

Tells you which disk to insert

This goes on until Quicken finishes the installation. More thinking, more chugging, then a window proclaims cheerfully, "Congratulations, Setup is done." Click **OK**.

Quicken tells you that before you can start Quicken, you need to finish the installation by restarting Windows. Click **OK** and Quicken restarts Windows for you. After Windows restarts, you'll see the new Quicken program window on the desktop. You're done with installation and ready to roll.

# The Least You Need to Know

Installing Quicken is idiot-proof. You couldn't screw it up if you tried. Just follow these steps:

➤ Start Windows.

➤ Put disk 1 or the CD-ROM in the drive.

➤ Click on the **Start** button and select **Run**.

➤ Type **a:setup** (or **d:setup** for a CD-ROM) and click **OK**.

➤ If you're low on memory, you may not be able to install a few of the fancy-schmancy options.

➤ When your computer beeps at you, put in the next disk.

# Speak Like a Geek: The Complete Archives

**account** In Quicken, accounts are where you keep track of your income and expenses. There are eight types of Quicken accounts: checking, savings, cash, credit card, money market, asset, liability, and investment.

**amortization** The division of a loan payment into principal and interest. As you pay the loan, the amount of each payment that goes to the interest decreases and the amount that goes to the principal increases.

**archive** A backup of your file, usually of historical data that you no longer use regularly.

**ASCII** Pronounced ASS-key, a universal computer format that just about any computer and software program can read and understand.

**backup** A copy of a file to use in case your original file is corrupted.

**balloon payment** A payment at the end of a loan that's much larger than the regular payments.

**basic asset class** A broad group of mutual funds, such as domestic stocks. See also *extended asset class*.

**bits per second (bps)** Modem speeds are measured in bits per second. A 2400 bps modem can send and receive 2400 bits (another measurement term) per second; the higher the number, the faster the modem.

**category** Lets you specify exactly what every transaction in your accounts is for; rent, groceries, utilities, or whatever. In Quicken Home Inventory, categories group the items in your inventory; for example, furnishings is a category in Home Inventory.

**class** A class groups categories under a broader heading that specifies where, to what, or to whom your categories apply.

**compounding period**   How often the interest on a loan is recalculated.

**custom index**   A grouping of stocks and/or mutual funds. A custom index tracks price changes for the group of stocks and mutual funds as a whole, rather than changes in individual stocks and funds (which is what a portfolio does).

**default**   An option that Quicken, or any other program, automatically uses when you perform a function. When you print, Quicken uses the default printer. There can be default type styles, margins, dates, and so on.

**dialog box**   When Quicken needs more information before it can perform a function, it presents a dialog box, where it asks you questions and you answer them.

**downloading**   The process of getting information from another location and sending it to your computer with a modem. See also *uploading*.

**drop-down list**   A menu that drops down when you click on a field or click on the arrow button on the right side of a field.

**e-mail**   Short for electronic mail, e-mail is the messages sent and received through your modem.

**expense ratio**   A mutual fund's overhead, expressed as the percentage of assets deducted for operating expenses.

**exporting**   Transferring your Quicken 5 data to another Quicken file or software program.

**extended asset class**   A group of mutual funds that meets a specific investment objective.

**file**   Where Quicken stores everything you create with Quicken. A file holds all your accounts and the transactions for those accounts, plus related creations such as reports and graphs. Quicken creates separate files for Financial Address Book, Home Inventory, and Investor Insight.

**file password**   Controls who has access to your Quicken file. Anyone opening Quicken must enter the file password.

**flyover help**   When you move your mouse pointer over an icon, Quicken displays a little box that tells you what the icon does.

**forecast**   A Quicken feature that uses scheduled and regularly occurring transactions to create a graph that shows what your finances will look like in the near future.

**front load**   The commission you pay when you invest in a mutual fund.

**icon**   A picture or graphic of a feature. Clicking on the icon launches the feature. Clicking an icon is an alternative to selecting a feature from a menu.

**iconbar**   In Quicken, a group of commonly used features located at the top of the screen (the main iconbar) or in specific windows (such as account registers).

**importing**   Transferring data from another Quicken file or another software program into your Quicken 5 file.

**income and expense filters**   When you select certain categories, classes, accounts, and securities to include in graphs and reports, Quicken calls them income and expense filters because they filter what information the reports and graphs use.

**installation**   The process of plugging software into a computer to make it run.

**locked transaction**   A memorized transaction that will not be overwritten if you change the amount of the payment. Unlocked transactions are updated every time you change the amount.

**manager tenure**   The length of time the current manager has managed a mutual fund. The longer the tenure, the less likely it's a fly-by-night fund.

**memorized transaction**   A transaction for which Quicken memorizes the payee, amount, and category so you can enter the transaction again without retyping it.

**menu**   A list of options and/or features.

**online help**   Essentially a how-to manual within a software program. Quicken's online help defines terms, explains what the various features do and how to use them, and it provides helpful hints.

**online repeating transaction**   A transaction that automatically makes deposits or payments through your online accounts.

**online services**   In very general terms, services you access with your modem. QuickBillPay, QuickBanking, and Investor Insight are all online services; they let you send and receive information to and from Quicken with your modem.

**performance**   How well a mutual fund does, averaged over a period of time. For example, a five-year performance averages the fund's profit and loss over the past five years.

**points**   When you buy a house or refinance your mortgage, mortgage lenders charge points. For every point charged, you pay 1% of the mortgage amount to the lender.

**portfolio**   A group of stocks and/or mutual funds with a dollar value. The price changes of each stock and fund is tracked individually to calculate the total portfolio value.

**printer driver**   A program that works as a go-between between your computer and printer. It tells your computer what kind of printer you have, and tells your printer when and how to print something.

**QuickFill** The collective name for the features on Quicken that make entering information easier: drop-down lists, automatic memorization of transactions, filling in a name after you type the first few letters, and so on.

**RAM** Stands for Random Access Memory. RAM is your computer's electronic memory, measured in megabytes (MB). The more RAM, the more memory, and the more stuff your computer can handle.

**register** What you use to record everything that happens in an account. Each account has a register that's similar to a checkbook register, where you can enter the date of a transaction, what it was for (a deposit or payment to someone), the amount, and its category.

**report** In Quicken, reports sort through your accounts, Home Inventory, or Investor Insight portfolios and display specified information in table form. For example, Cash Flow reports use your accounts to summarize your income and expenses by category.

**risk rating** The risk rating (low, medium-low, medium, and medium-high) uses a mutual fund's past performance to determine the likelihood that you'll take a bath if you invest in it.

**snapshots** Miniature graphs that provide an instant overview of your finances.

**split** You use splits to record more than one category for a single transaction.

**spreadsheet** A software program that works like a chart, where you enter information in columns and rows. It can perform various numerical calculations.

**star rating** Morningstar gives mutual funds a star rating based on their historical profitability and risk. Funds with more stars have higher profitability, less risk, or both.

**subcategory** Subcategories let you split hairs in your categories. For example, the Auto category contains subcategories for Fuel, Insurance, Loan, and Service—all expenses related to owning a car.

**submenu** A menu within a menu. Sometimes selecting a menu option brings up even more options; for example, in the File menu, File Operations has a submenu for the Copy, Delete, Rename, and Validate commands.

**supercategory** Another way to group categories under a broader heading. Unlike classes, however, you don't record supercategories in an account register. Supercategories are used only in budgets, budget reports, cash flow, and summary reports.

**transaction** A specific record in an account register; a deposit, withdrawal, payment, or anything that affects the account balance.

**transaction password** Controls who can change transactions in your accounts. Anyone can open your Quicken file (unless you also have a file password), but they have to enter the transaction password to enter or edit transactions.

**transfer**   Moving money from one account to another. In Quicken, a transfer also includes making payments on one account from another. For example, when you record a check for paying your credit card, Quicken records the amount as a withdrawal from your checking account and a deposit in your credit card account, so you only have to enter the transaction in one register.

**uploading**   The process of sending information from your computer to a computer in another location with a modem.

**user name**   The name by which an online service, such as Investor Insight, identifies you.

**validate**   The validate function checks your file for nasty things that might corrupt it, backs it up, and rebuilds it, minus the nasties.

# Index

# Complete and Return this Card
# for a *FREE* Computer Book Catalog

Thank you for purchasing this book! You have purchased a superior computer book written expressly for your needs. To continue to provide the kind of up-to-date, pertinent coverage you've come to expect from us, we need to hear from you. Please take a minute to complete and return this self-addressed, postage-paid form. In return, we'll send you a free catalog of all our computer books on topics ranging from word processing to programming and the Internet.

Mr. ☐   Mrs. ☐   Ms. ☐   Dr. ☐

Name (first) ☐☐☐☐☐☐☐☐☐☐☐ (M.I.) ☐ (last) ☐☐☐☐☐☐☐☐☐☐☐☐☐☐☐☐

Address ☐☐☐☐☐☐☐☐☐☐☐☐☐☐☐☐☐☐☐☐☐☐☐☐☐☐☐
☐☐☐☐☐☐☐☐☐☐☐☐☐☐☐☐☐☐☐☐☐☐☐☐☐☐☐

City ☐☐☐☐☐☐☐☐☐☐☐☐☐☐☐ State ☐☐ ZIP ☐☐☐☐☐ ☐☐☐☐

Phone ☐☐☐ ☐☐☐ ☐☐☐☐ Fax ☐☐☐ ☐☐☐ ☐☐☐☐

Company Name ☐☐☐☐☐☐☐☐☐☐☐☐☐☐☐☐☐☐☐☐☐☐☐☐☐

E-mail address ☐☐☐☐☐☐☐☐☐☐☐☐☐☐☐☐☐☐☐☐☐☐☐☐☐

## 1. Please check at least (3) influencing factors for purchasing this book.

Front or back cover information on book ☐
Special approach to the content ☐
Completeness of content ☐
Author's reputation ☐
Publisher's reputation ☐
Book cover design or layout ☐
Index or table of contents of book ☐
Price of book ☐
Special effects, graphics, illustrations ☐
Other (Please specify): _____ ☐

## 2. How did you first learn about this book?

Saw in Macmillan Computer Publishing catalog ☐
Recommended by store personnel ☐
Saw the book on bookshelf at store ☐
Recommended by a friend ☐
Received advertisement in the mail ☐
Saw an advertisement in: _____ ☐
Read book review in: _____ ☐
Other (Please specify): _____ ☐

## 3. How many computer books have you purchased in the last six months?

This book only ☐   3 to 5 books ☐
2 books ☐   More than 5 ☐

## 4. Where did you purchase this book?

Bookstore ☐
Computer Store ☐
Consumer Electronics Store ☐
Department Store ☐
Office Club ☐
Warehouse Club ☐
Mail Order ☐
Direct from Publisher ☐
Internet site ☐
Other (Please specify): _____ ☐

## 5. How long have you been using a computer?

☐ Less than 6 months   ☐ 6 months to a year
☐ 1 to 3 years   ☐ More than 3 years

## 6. What is your level of experience with personal computers and with the subject of this book?

| With PCs | | With subject of book | |
|---|---|---|---|
| New | ☐ | New | ☐ |
| Casual | ☐ | Casual | ☐ |
| Accomplished | ☐ | Accomplished | ☐ |
| Expert | ☐ | Expert | ☐ |

Source Code ISBN: 0-7897-0559-1

### 7. Which of the following best describes your job title?

- Administrative Assistant ☐
- Coordinator ☐
- Manager/Supervisor ☐
- Director ☐
- Vice President ☐
- President/CEO/COO ☐
- Lawyer/Doctor/Medical Professional ☐
- Teacher/Educator/Trainer ☐
- Engineer/Technician ☐
- Consultant ☐
- Not employed/Student/Retired ☐
- Other (Please specify): _____ ☐

### 8. Which of the following best describes the area of the company your job title falls under?

- Accounting ☐
- Engineering ☐
- Manufacturing ☐
- Operations ☐
- Marketing ☐
- Sales ☐
- Other (Please specify): _____ ☐

### 9. What is your age?

- Under 20 ☐
- 21-29 ☐
- 30-39 ☐
- 40-49 ☐
- 50-59 ☐
- 60-over ☐

### 10. Are you:

- Male ☐
- Female ☐

### 11. Which computer publications do you read regularly? (Please list)

_____
_____
_____
_____
_____
_____
_____
_____
_____
_____

**Comments**: _____
_____
_____

Fold here and scotch-tape to mail.